2001

# PETER GREENAWAY

## INTERVIEWS

CONVERSATIONS WITH FILMMAKERS SERIES
PETER BRUNETTE, GENERAL EDITOR

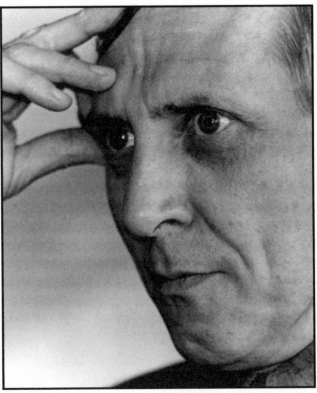

Photofest

# PETER
# GREENAWAY
## INTERVIEWS

EDITED BY VERNON GRAS AND
MARGUERITE GRAS

UNIVERSITY PRESS OF MISSISSIPPI / JACKSON

www.upress.state.ms.us

Copyright © 2000 by University Press of Mississippi
Manufactured in the United States of America

08  07  06  05  04  03  02  01  00        4  3  2  1

∞

Library of Congress Cataloging-in-Publication Data

Greenaway, Peter.
    Peter Greenaway : interviews / edited by Vernon Gras and Marguerite Gras.
        p.      cm. — (Conversations with filmmakers series)
    Includes index.
    ISBN 1-57806-254-3 (cloth : alk. paper) — ISBN 1-57806-255-1 (pbk. : alk.
paper)
    1. Greenaway, Peter—Interviews.   2. Motion picture producers and
directors—Great Britain—Interviews.   I. Gras, Vernon W., 1929–    .
II. Gras, Marguerite.   III. Title.   IV. Series.
    PN1998.3.G73 A5    2000
    791.43'0233'092—dc21                                            99-052478

British Library Cataloging-in-Publication data available

# CONTENTS

# INTRODUCTION

THE FILMS OF PETER GREENAWAY run unmistakably against the main current of present cinematic practice. They have done so from their very beginning. He is quite dismissive of the psychologically motivated plots that provide the standard fare of what he calls Hollywood cinema. Hollywood films tell stories; they translate literature with its linear narrative onto a medium that should be preeminently visual, claims Greenaway. Instead of foregrounding the image and the composition of visual elements such as we see in the long history of painting, Hollywood-style directors seem mesmerized by the "and then and then." They are masters of building up suspense, subordinating the physical background, the site, and human forms to the need of finding out what happens next. Images function as ephemeral background to action. Visuals are subordinated to storyline. If you wish to find out what happens in a story, says Greenaway, read a book. In terms of using the potential of cinema as an image based medium, he asserts most film directors seem maimed or semiblind. They do very little with the potentialities of the visual medium and produce uninteresting, even boring films. Greenaway, and he states this repeatedly in many of his interviews, wishes above all to bring the aesthetics of painting to filmmaking and to diminish the influence of narrative. Bringing the aesthetics of painting to cinema is not a highly emotional endeavor, he admits, and thus, he will never attract the huge audiences or achieve the gigantic financial successes Hollywood films do. But his films have brought him enough financial success so that he can continue making the kind of films he wants to make. Pursuing these same aesthetic principles, he is now (at the end of the nineties) entering a new phase of his work that mixes film with television and CD-ROM. He feels that the traditional cinema of the last hundred years is dead. Imagination, innovative technology, and financial resources are all going into television and the internet. The making of images will continue as it always has but, says Greenaway, it will be developed electronically in the future. Thus, his latest work *Tulse Luper's Suitcase* will be a multimedia extravaganza.

Early in his life, Greenaway knew that he wanted to be associated with painting. He elected to attend the Walthamstow Art School rather than enter university. But his interest in film crystalized when, still an art student, he viewed Ingmar Bergman's *Seventh Seal*. He remembers viewing the film for nearly two performances a day over a five day run. Instead of the psychodrama of American films, it dealt in metaphor and symbolism such as Death playing chess, a distancing medieval background, a forgotten mythology brought to life. In the next two years, he went through "a crash course in European cinema" focusing mostly on Antonioni, Pasolini, Godard, and Resnais. He managed to obtain a temporary job at the British Film Institute as a "third-assistant-editor-on-trial" which in time landed him a "proper job" at the Central Office of Information. This was a well paying job and he slowly rose up the ranks at COI from sweeping up the trims to becoming an editor and director. Greenaway often describes the COI as the propaganda arm of the British Foreign Office. On film, it documents aspects of British industrial, agricultural, and cultural life to show in classrooms all over the world. Harmless enough, this documentary propaganda informed viewers "how many sheepdogs there are in Wales" or "how many Japanese restaurants are in Ipswich." The making of statistical documentaries impressed on Greenaway how blurred was the line between fact and fiction. He experienced first hand the lack of fit between geographical terrain and activities on one side and the maps, lists, and classificatory schemes used to explain and control natural phenomena on the other.

From this lack of fit and the prevailing structuralist/semiological ideas prevalent in the sixties, Greenaway drew several consequences for his filmmaking. He came to repudiate the documentary realism still left over in England as a legacy from John Grierson. He could no longer take seriously the tradition that believed documentaries to be a transparent window to the world. When creating statistically "objective" documentaries, Greenaway personally experienced the elements of fiction and manipulation that went into creating them. As he declares to Michel Ciment, "the way I produced documentaries brought them close to fictional narration. The line between them is blurry. In and of itself, no subject matter is documentary."

Earlier he had remarked to Karen Jaehne that the first twenty films he made all concerned themselves with the "question of representation," with how we interpret the external world. He believed man's complicated relationship with the world should be expressed on the screen. Meaning-giving should be the focus of films because the only authentic insight that art can deliver is the fictionality or artificiality of itself. Good art in Greenaway's understanding of it has to be artificial and call attention to itself as a construct. It can't pose naively as a mirror or window to reality. Or even worse, art shouldn't feed human wishful thinking with sentimental, delusional happy endings or tragical, heroical closures so self-serving, consoling, and money producing as does the Hollywood cinema. As most stories need closure and such endings are propelled by human psychological needs, Greenaway avoids emotional psychodrama. He informs Stuart Morgan that history never has had an ending. Historical narrative doesn't exist; it's made up by historians. Instead of phony narrative, Greenaway wants cinema to shift away from content or story to spotlight the meaning-giving process which image, composition, and frame can structure and form. All of Greenaway's films foreground their aesthetic structural aspects because content is ephemeral while form endures. He cites Poussin to Marcia Pally as a good example: "Content always atrophies. Poussin's paintings, for instance, are rather recherche in their classical references and most people don't know what the hell they're about. Yet we still admire and enjoy a Poussin painting. The form exists long after the content fades."

The aim of postmodern art should be to show the *how* and not the *what*. It must be self-referential. If art is not revelatory of Truth, it should reveal the past vocabulary of how humans configured the world. Like Borges and Márquez, Greenaway wants his art to be encyclopedic in its cultural references to order. Cinema has its own vocabulary and syntax just as literature has its language. Why not display its idiosyncratic systems just as contemporary writers like Calvino, Borges, and Márquez display those of literature? It would be accurate to say that of all contemporary filmmakers, Greenaway comes closest in giving the filmic equivalence of the self-reflexive fiction of Calvino, Borges, and Barth. Like them, he puts the meaning-giving process on display. He has done so brilliantly, and for that reason he has already found his niche in the history of cinema.

The most reiterated statement in all the interviews is Greenaway's insistence that art be artificial. What he says to Gavin Smith, he repeats often to others: "My cinema is deliberately artificial, and it's always self-reflexive. Everytime you watch a Greenaway movie, you know you are definitely and absolutely *only watching a movie.* It's not a slice of life, not a window on the world. It's by no means an exemplum of anything 'natural' or 'real.' I do not think that naturalism or realism is even valid in the cinema." Furthermore, if all his feature films foreground their artificial status as constructed aesthetic objects, the heroes in his films are surrogates for himself, and their activities parallel his own activity as filmmaker. He admits this in varying degrees of detail in many interviews. The draughtsman, the architect, the cook, the scientists, the game players, Prospero the magus, Nagiko the calligrapher—all function as near or far displacements of himself and illustrate the ordering of chaos which motivates the human meaning-giving process and every artistic project. One of his fullest expressions of the self-reflexivity of his cinema is recorded by Marcia Pally: "That's what art is about isn't it—trying to find some order in the chaos? That's what civilization is about, some way to understand, contain this vast amount of data that's pushed at us all the time. . . . The French chef in *Cook Thief* . . . is also me. With each film, I invite people to my table and I make the meal. I take the cultural systems I admire and try to set them out in one place. I demand, as we all do, some sense of coherence, of order in the world. And we are always defeated. This is the human condition."

The result of always being defeated in our interpretive endeavors has two main consequences for Greenaway. One is deconstructive and ironic in which his films liberate viewers from their illusion of being at home in the world. Emancipation from illusion is done in a style Greenaway describes as "cosmic irony" and predominates in his early work. It suffuses early films like *Vertical Features Remake, The Falls,* and *Acts of God* but is present in all his work. Its purest expression in a feature film comes in *Drowning By Numbers.* Whether the viewer experiences the open-endedness of "cosmic irony" that Greenaway claims in many of the interviews may be doubted. What is foregrounded constantly in his films is the failure of the various classificatory schemes. The question comes up then whether art is worth doing if it is fated never to succeed. It is one of the questions Greenaway poses in *Belly of an Architect* and discusses with Marlene Rodgers.

Can man make himself immortal by reproducing himself in sculpture, paint, photography, or photocopies? No, because all these attempts fail, says Greenaway. *The Belly of an Architect* ends with the cry of a newborn child "at the selfsame moment as the artist . . . the architect throws himself out the window." Thus, biological reproduction seems the only way we can imagine a sense of immortality. *Belly*'s ending places "an enormous question on the significances not only of civilization but of all cultural pursuits. So it's still a question for me—am I doing something which is valuable, [or] is this a total waste of time I'm doing." But Greenaway wants no consoling solution to this tension between his desire for rational control of the world and man's vulnerability to chaos and decay. For him it remains an ongoing debate. The hero of Greenaway films is usually Greenaway himself.

The other consequence of the failure to jump the culture/nature gap is to downplay interest in the referent, the *what* and to focus on the *how,* i.e. to pursue a semiotic interest in cinema as language. Greenaway continually experiments with new technologies and at the moment seeks to combine the possibilities of television and CD-ROM with film. It puts him on the cutting edge of experimentation in how to manipulate visual language. Still feeling himself more of a painter who makes films, Greenaway reveals more loyalty to the rendering of images than to cinema. The making of images has a much longer history than cinema and will continue in the new electronic media, he affirms, while cinema will fade away. In both *Prospero's Books* and *The Pillow Book,* Greenaway mixes computer enhanced hi-definition TV images with 35 mm celluloid. In his most recent interviews with Lawrence Chua and Sabine Danek and Torsten Beyer, Greenaway enthuses over the electronic future and explains his departure from cinema into curating museum shows and setting up city-wide exhibitions like *The Stairs.*

*The Stairs,* he tells Danek and Beyer, exhibits aspects of cinema as medium and reveals his disenchantment with it. In Geneva, "we lit locations throughout the city—the cathedral, the fountain in the lake, the opera house, the art gallery, and other major buildings. We . . . erected 100 staircases, grand staircases, each of which has a viewing platform on the top that frames up some part of the city." Because framing is part of how humans discipline the world and plays a big role in cinema and television, *The Stairs* exhibit "takes the concept of the frame out of cinema and put[s] it into a more public situation." Instead of a two hour film, he now has an exhibition that lasts 100 days, at 100 sites, and provides "a 24-hour continual viewfinder." Its users can now produce their own narratives.

This opening up of the art work to the viewers is discussed more fully in the Chua interview. Greenaway describes *The Pillow Book* as dealing "with the fragmentation of the relationship between cinema and all the post-televisual medium(sic): the CD-ROM, the Internet...French intellectuals have criticized the film, saying *The Pillow Book* is not a film, it is a CD-ROM. I could think of no higher compliment." Both *The Pillow Book* and the earlier *Prospero's Books* experimented with the liberation from the single frame which repeats its format chronologically from a beginning to an end. Now framing allows escape into what Greenaway calls a "lateral way of thinking." The new technologies can expand the cinematic vocabulary because they allow the treatment "of past, present and future all in one plane" and they can place "the close up, the wide shot, the portrait, the still life, all in one frame." The new technology in terms of "multimedia" and "interactivity" allow Greenaway to reconceptualize the relation of image to text as well as work to audience.

In his last interview with Sabine Danek, Greenaway talks exuberantly about the potentialities of the new electronic future: "My dream is to make CD-ROMs for Omnimax located in large halls with excellent sound. From there one can tie into scores of large libraries and museums. Sitting before a giant screen, one has contact with the whole world. That is really fascinating." *Tulse Luper's Suitcase* is to launch him into this new endeavor.

Conforming to the policy of the University Press of Mississippi in regard to this interview series, the interviews collected in this book have not been edited in any significant way. Though this form imposed editorily by the series leads to a certain amount of repetition, Greenaway's articulateness and plenitude of ideas reveals itself in rich ongoing variations on selected themes. The variations almost always add another layer or perspective to previous statements. Nor is he afraid to repudiate an earlier opinion.

We would like to thank Uwe Hemmen and Bruno Bollaert for their considerable labor in setting up Greenaway websites. Uwe Hemmen was particularly helpful in locating recent interviews.

We owe special thanks to Peter Brunette, a longtime colleague and the general editor of this series, for asking us to undertake this book of interviews and to Anne Stascavage, editor at University Press of Mississippi, for providing helpful models and steady guidance throughout the project.

# CHRONOLOGY

1942   Born in Newport, Wales. Father was a builder's merchant; mother was a teacher.

1945   Moves to Essex and brought up mostly in Chingford.

1948   Attends Forest Public School—a high Anglican private school "that preserves the worst traditions—fagging, burning the pubic hair of new boys...." But he does learn literature and history.

1954   Decides to become a painter.

1961   (circa) Prefers to attend Walthamstow School of Art in east London than go to university. Studies there for three years.

1964   Exhibits for the first time at Lord's Gallery.

1965   Begins work editing documentaries for eleven years at the Central Office of Information. Gains practical knowledge of filmmaking by working his way up from cutting room to film editor.

1966   Starts making short films influenced by continental structuralist/poststructuralist philosophy

1975   *Windows*. Greenaway regards this film as the beginning of his public cinema. Presages everything that comes after.

1977   *Dear Phone*. Farce. Refuses to use cinema's normal enactment of written text.

1978    *A Walk Through H.* A soul's journey via 92 maps to heaven or hell. Tulse Luper (Greenaway's alter ego who continually reappears in his work) organizes maps. Wins Hugo Award at Chicago Film Festival.

1979    *Zandra Rhodes.* Documentary made for COI. Wins Chicago Hugo Award for documentaries at Chicago Film Festival, 1981.

1980    *The Falls.* The first British film to win the BFI award for Best Film in thirty years. "It's a catalogue movie, made with an enthusiasm for Tristram Shandy, Borges, and Thornton Wilder's *Bridge of San Luis Rey.*"

1981    *Act of God.* Documentary about 30 people struck by lightning. Absurd humour in dead pan style. Intent parallels *The Falls.*

1982    *The Draughtsman's Contract.* First feature film. Set in 1694 on an English country estate with very stylized costumes, wigs, and dialogue. Very successful in England; gets mixed reviews in U.S.

1983    *Four American Composers.* John Cage, Robert Ashley, Philip Glass, Meredith Monk. Begins television work to complement filmmaking, e.g. *Making a Splash* (1984), *Inside Rooms — 26 Bathrooms,* and *TV Dante: Canto 5* (1985).

1986    *A Zed & Two Noughts.* Looks at death and decay in explicit way without consolation. Finds Darwin's evolutionary stages as mythic as Genesis.

1987    *The Belly of An Architect.* The last nine months of a man dying of stomach cancer. Brian Dennehy wins Best Actor Award at Chicago Film Festival.

1988    *Drowning by Numbers.* Because based on script written years earlier, reverts back to structuralist concerns of earlier films. It is, perhaps, the purest expression of his cosmic irony. Cannes Film Festival: Best Artistic Contribution. A short film, *Fear of Drowning,* is made of Greenaway and crew filming *Drowning By Numbers.*

    *Death in the Seine.* Two things have universal interest: sex and death. Greenaway continues his TV work with images of death.

1989    *A TV Dante — Cantos 1–8.* Finishes collaboration with Tom Phillips in bringing part of Dante's *Inferno* to TV screen. Sir John Gielgud is Virgil and Bob Peck is Dante.

*The Cook, The Thief, His Wife, and Her Lover.* A revenge tragedy in which a wife does in her brutal husband with mythic and historic overtones using metaphoric and self-reflexive staging. Greenaway's greatest commercial success.

1991   *Prospero's Books.* Remake of Shakespeare's *The Tempest* with Sir John Gielgud as Prospero. Pictorially, the most stunning of his films and quite innovative in its use of computer enhanced technology. "Remarkable. . . . Nothing quite like it has been seen before."

*M Is For Man, Music, Mozart.* One of six television shorts commissioned by the BBC and other television companies.

*Rosa.* A dance film based on the music of Béla Bártok. Wins Dance Screen Prize: 1992.

*Darwin.* One in an educational series of 100 made for television funded by a conglomerate of television companies. Uses *tableaux vivants* and 18 scene changes in 52 minutes.

*The Physical Self.* Curated at the Boymans-van Beuningen Museum in Rotterdam. The first of his many museum and city wide exhibitions staged primarily on continental Europe.

1993   *The Baby of Macon.* The third film set in the seventeenth century to which Greenaway seems attracted. A tale of greed, opportunism, exploitation, religious manipulation and power in which the newborn infant's sister wants to profit by passing herself off as the miracle child's virgin mother.

1994   *The Stairs.* A film of Greenaway's city exhibition *The Stairs* held in Geneva that year featuring aspects of cinema. Here the focus is on "location." In Munich, the next year, *The Stairs* continues with a focus on "projection."

*Rosa, A Horse Drama.* Writes and helps stage an opera. Likes the pageantry of opera. Brings in filmic elements. Music by Louis Andriessen. Performed by Netherlands Opera Co.

1995   *The Pillow Book.* Based on the pillow book of Shei Shonogan from the tenth century. It pursues the metaphor that "the body is a book, the book is a body" by having the heroine do calligraphy on the naked bodies of her lovers. It also furthers the dominance of image over narrative by placing the close-up, the wide shot, the portrait, the still life, all in one frame and thereby coalescing narrative. French intellectuals claim the film is a CD-ROM, not cinema. So much the better says Greenaway.

1997    *100 Objects to Represent the World: A Prop Opera.* Begun as an exhibition in Vienna, turned into an opera for Salzburg, it receives invitations to play at many venues, e.g. Paris, Brazil, Copenhagen.

1998    *Christopher Columbus.* Restages and rewrites the Darius Milhaud/Paul Claudel opera for the Berlin Staatsoper.

1999    *Eight And A Half Women.* A hommage to Fellini's *Eight and a Half.* While Fellini's film was about filmmaking, this is "an elaboration on the subject of eight and a half archetypes of male sexual fantasy. Shot location shifts between Geneva and Kyoto.

2000    *Tulse Luper's Suitcase.* Tulse Luper returns to track down Raoul Wallenberg, the Swedish diplomat who saved many Jews during WWII and disappeared under mysterious circumstances in 1945. A multimedia extravaganza with five feature films, a TV series, several CD-ROMs, and a Website. Striking innovation is to allow audience to interact and help interpret/create story.

# FILMOGRAPHY

Films written and directed by **Peter Greenaway** except where noted.

1966
TRAIN
5 minutes

TREE
16 minutes

1967
REVOLUTION
8 minutes

POSTCARDS FROM CAPITAL CITIES
35 minutes

1969
INTERVALS
7 minutes

1971
EROSION
27 minutes

1973
H IS FOR HOUSE (reedited 1978)
Narrator: Colin Cantlie, **Peter Greenaway**, and family.
Music: Vivaldi, *Four Seasons*
10 minutes

1975
WINDOWS
Narrator: **Peter Greenaway**
Calligraphy: Kenneth Breese
Music: Rameau's "La Poule"
4 minutes

WATER
Music: Max Eastley
5 minutes

WATER WRACKETS
Narrator: Colin Cantlie
Music: Max Eastley
Calligraphy: Kenneth Breese
Sound: Tony Anscombe
12 minutes

1976
GOOLE BY NUMBERS
40 minutes

1977
DEAR PHONE
Narrator: **Peter Greenaway**
Calligraphy: Kenneth Breese
17 minutes

1978
1-100
Music: Michael Nyman
4 minutes

A WALK THROUGH H: THE REINCARNATION OF AN ORNITHOLOGIST
Production: BFI
Narrator: Colin Cantlie
Camera: Bert Walker, John Rosenberg
Calligraphy: Kenneth Breese
Sound: Tony Anscombe
Music: Michael Nyman
41 minutes

VERTICAL FEATURES REMAKE
Production: Arts Council of Great Britain
Narrator: Colin Cantlie
Camera: Bert Walker
Music: Michael Nyman; Theme music: Brian Eno
45 minutes

1979
ZANDRA RHODES
Documentary COI
15 minutes

1980
THE FALLS
Production: BFI
Producer: Peter Sainsbury
Camera: Mike Coles, John Rosenberg
Editor: **Peter Greenaway**
Music: Michael Nyman; also Brian Eno, John Hyde, Keith Pendlebury
Speakers: Colin Cantlie, Hilarie Thompson, Sheila Canfield, Adam Leys,
Serena Macbeth, Martin Burrow
185 minutes

1981
ACT OF GOD
Production: Thames TV, London
Producer: Udi Eicler
Camera: Peter George

Editor: Andy Watmore
25 minutes

1982
THE DRAUGHTSMAN'S CONTRACT
Production: BFI/Channel Four Television
Producer: David Payne, Peter Sainsbury
Camera: Curtis Clark
Editor: John Wilson
Production Design: Bob Ringwood
Music: Michael Nyman
Cast: Mr. Neville (Anthony Higgins), Mrs. Herbert (Janet Suzman), Mrs. Talmann (Anne Louise Lambert), Mr. Noyes (Neil Cunningham), Mr. Talmann (Hugh Fraser), Mr. Herbert (Dave Hill), Green Man (Michael Feast)
108 minutes

1983
FOUR AMERICAN COMPOSERS: JOHN CAGE, ROBERT ASHLEY, PHILIP GLASS, MEREDITH MONK
Production: Channel Four Television/Transatlantic Films
Producer: Revel Guest
Camera: Curtis Clark
Editor: John Wilson
55 minutes each

1984
MAKING A SPLASH
Production: Channel Four/Media Software
Producer: Pat Marshall
Music: Michael Nyman
25 minutes

1985
A TV DANTE—CANTO 5
Producer: Sophie Balhetchet
Screenplay: **Peter Greenaway** and Tom Phillips
Camera: Mike Coles, Simon Fone

Editor: John Wilson
Video Editor: Bill Saint
10 minutes

A ZED AND TWO NOUGHTS
Production: BFI/Allarts Enterprises BV Nederland/Artificial Eyes
Productions/Film Four International
Producer: Kees Kasander and Peter Sainsbury
Camera: Sacha Vierny
Editor: John Wilson
Music: Michael Nyman
Production Design: Ben van Os and Jan Roelfs
Sound: Garth Marshall
Costume: Patricia Lim
Cast: Oliver Deuce (Eric Deacon), Oswald Deuce (Brian Deacon), Alba
Berwick (Andréa Ferréol), Van Hoyten (Joss Ackland), Van Meegeren
(Gerard Thoolen), Beta Berwick (Agnes Brulet), Catherina Bolnes (Guusje
van Tilbrough), Venus de Milo (Frances Barber), Stephen Pipe (Ken
Campbell), Joshua Plate (Jim Davidson), Felipe Arc-en-Ciel (Wolf Kahler),
Fallast (Geoffrey Palmer)
115 minutes

INSIDE ROOMS — 26 BATHROOMS
Production: Channel Four/Artifax Productions (Video)
Producer: Sophie Balhetchet
Camera: Mike Coles
Editor: John Wilson
Music: Michael Nyman
25 minutes

1987
THE BELLY OF AN ARCHITECT
Production: Callendar Company/Film Four Internation/British Screen
Hemdale/Sacis
Producer: Colin Callender and Walter Donohue
Camera: Sacha Vierny
Editor: John Wilson

Production Design: Luciana Vedovelli
Music: Wim Mertens and Glen Branca
Sound: Peter Glossop, Matthew Whiteman
Cast: Stourley Kracklite (Brian Dennehy), Caspasian Speckler (Lambert Wilson), Louisa Kracklite (Chloe Webb), Flavia Speckler (Stefania Casini), Io Speckler (Serio Fantoni)
118 minutes

1988
FEAR OF DROWNING
Production: Allarts (for Channel Four)
Producer: Paul Trybits
Co-director: Vanni Corbellini
Cast: **Peter Greenaway** and the cast and crew of *Drowning By Numbers*
26 minutes

DROWNING BY NUMBERS
Production: Film Four International/Elsevier Vendex Film
Producer: Kees Kasander and Denis Wigman
Camera: Sacha Vierny
Editor: John Wilson
Production Design: Ben van Os and Jan Roelfs
Music: Michael Nyman
Sound: Garth Marshall
Cast: Cissie Colpitts I (Joan Plowright), Cissie Colpitts II (Juliet Stevenson), Cissie Colpitts III (Joely Richardson), Madgett (Bernard Hill), Smut (Jason Edwards), Jake (Brian Pringle), Hardy (Trevor Cooper), Bellamy (David Morrissey), Nancy (Jane Gurnett), The Skipping Girl (Natalie Morse) Gregory (John Rogan), Jonah Bognor (Kenny Ireland), Moses Bognor (Michael Perceival), Sid the Digger (Arthur Spreckley)
108 minutes

DEATH IN THE SEINE
Production: Erato Films/Allarts TV Productions/Mikros Image/La Sept
Cast: Jim van der Woude, Jean-Michel Dragory
40 minutes

1989
HUBERT BALS HANDSHAKE
Production: Allarts Enterprises (for Rotterdam Film Festival)
5 minutes

A TV DANTE—CANTOS 1–8
Production: KGP Production with Channel Four/Elevier Vendex/VPRO
Co-directed with Tom Phillips (a painter)
Cast: Virgil (John Gielgud), Dante (Bob Peck), Beatrice (Joanne Whalley-Kilmer), Ceberus (Laurie Booth), Lucia (Susan Wooldridge), Francesca (Suzan Crowley), Caronte (Robert Eddison)
10 minutes each 3 8 episodes

THE COOK, THE THIEF, HIS WIFE AND HER LOVER
Production: Allarts/Erato Films Inc.
Producer: Kees Kasander
Camera: Sacha Vierny
Editor: John Wilson
Production Design: Ben van Os and Jan Roelfs
Music: Michael Nyman
Sound: Nigel Heath
Cast: Albert Spica (Michael Gambon), Georgina (Helen Mirren), Michael (Alan Howard), The Cook (Richard Bohringer), Mitchell (Tim Roth)
120 minutes

1991
PROSPERO'S BOOKS
Production: Allarts/Cinea/Camera One/Penta coproduction in association with Elsevier Vendex Film/Film Four International/VPRO/Canal Plus & NHK
Producer: Kees Kasander and Denis Wigman
Camera: Sacha Vierny
Editor: Marina Bodijl
Music: Michael Nyman
Sound: Garth Marshall
Production Design: Ben van Os and Jan Roelfs

Cast: Prospero (John Gielgud), Miranda (Isabelle Pasco), Caliban (Michael Clark), Ferdinand (Mark Rylance), Alonso (Michel Blanc), Gonzalo (Erland Josephson), Antonio (Tom Bell), Sebastian (Kenneth Cranham), Ariel (Orpheo, Paul Russell, James Thiérrée, and Emil Wolk), Trinculo (Jim van de Woude), Stephano (Michael Romeyn), Book Narrator (Leonard Maguire), Iris (Marie Angel), Ceres (Ute Lemper), Juno (Deborah Conway)
124 minutes

M IS FOR MAN, MUSIC, MOZART
Production: BBC/AVRO TV/Artifax coproduction
One is a series of 6 made for television
Cast: Ben Craft
29 minutes

1992
ROSA
Production: La Monnaie de Munt/Rosas Production
Choreography: Anne Teresa de Keersmaeker and Jean-Luc Ducourt
Cast: Fumiyo Ikeda, Nordine Benchorf
Music: Béla Bártok
15 minutes

DARWIN
Production: Telemax Les Editions Audiovisuelles/Allarts coproduction with Antenne Deux/Channel Four/RAI Due, Telepool/Time Warner
One in a series of 100 made for television
52 minutes

1993
BABY OF MACON
Production: Allarts co-production with UGC-La Sept, in association with Cine Electra II/Channel Four/Filmstiftung Nordrhein Westfalen/Canal Plus
Producer: Kees Kasander and Denis Wigman
Camera: Sacha Vierny
Editor: Chris Wyatt
Production Design: Ben van Os and Jan Roelfs

Cast: Daughter (Julia Ormond), Bishop's Son (Ralph Fiennes), Bishop
(Philip Stone), Cosimo Medici (Jonathan Lacey), Father Confessor (Don
Henderson)
120 minutes

1994
THE STAIRS
Production: Apsara Production
Music: Patrick Mimran
Film of **Greenaway's** installation exhibition The Stairs, Geneva 1994
First in planned series of 10
100 minutes

1995
THE PILLOW BOOK
Production: A Kasander & Wigman, Woodline Films, and Alpha Films
Presentation made in association with Channel Four Films, Studio Canalı,
and Delux Productions
Producer: Kees Kasander
Camera: Sacha Vierny
Editor: Chris Wyatt
Sound: Garth Marshall
Calligraphy: Brody Neuenschwander, Yukki Yaura
Production Design: Wilbert van Dorp, Andrée Putman (Luxembourg),
Koichi Hamamura, Hiroto Oonogi (Japan)
Cast: Nagiko (Vivian Wu), The Publisher (Yoshi Oida), The Father (Ken
Ogata), The Aunt and Maid (Hideko Yoshida), Jerome (Ewan McGregor),
The Mother (Judy Ongg), The Husband (Ken Mitsuishi), Hoki (Yutaka
Honda), Jerome's Mother (Barbara Lott)
124 minutes

LUMIERE ET COMPAGNIE
52 seconds

1999
EIGHT AND A HALF WOMEN
Production: Movie Masters BV, Woodline Productions LTD, Delux
Productions s.a. Continent Films GmbH

Producer: Kees Kasander
Camera: Sacha Vierny
Editor: Elmer Leupen
Sound: Garth Marshall
Production Design: Wilbert van Dorp (Luxembourg), Emi Wada (Japan)
Cast: Philip Emmenthal (John Standing), Storey Emmenthal (Matthew Dela-mere), Kito (Vivian Wu), Simato (Shizuka Inoh), Clothilde (Barbara Sarafian), Mio (Kirina Mano), Griselda (Toni Collette), Beryl (Amanda Plummer), Giaconda (Natacha Amal), Giuletta/Half Woman (Manna Fujiwara), Pal-mira (Polly Walker), Celeste (Elizabeth Berrington), Marianne (Myriam Fuller), Simon (Don Warrington), Philip's Wife (Claire Johnston)
120 minutes

2000
TULSE LUPER'S SUITCASE
A multi-media project involving film, CD-rom, printed media, and the internet
Projected: Film: 8 hours
   TV: 16 episodes
   CD: 2 cds
   URL: extensive internet site
   Screenplay and books

## Exhibitions: Museums and Cities

1991
THE PHYSICAL SELF
Boymans-van Beuningen Museum, Rotterdam, Netherlands (November)

1992
100 OBJECTS TO REPRESENT THE WORLD (Hundert Objekte Zeigen die Welt)
Akademie der Bildenden Kunste, Hofburg Palace, and Semper Depot, Vienna, Austria (October)

FLYING OUT OF THIS WORLD (Le Bruit des Nuages)
The Louvre, Paris, France (November)

1993
WATCHING WATER
Palazzo Fortuni, Venice, Italy (June)

SOME ORGANIZING PRINCIPLES
Glynn Vivian Art Gallery, Swansea, UK (October)

THE AUDIENCE OF MACON
Foto Gallery, Wales Film Council, Cardiff, UK (October)

1994
THE STAIRS: GENEVA: LOCATION
Geneva, Switzerland (April)

1995
THE STAIRS: MUNICH: PROJECTION
Munich, Germany (October)

1996
IN THE DARK—SPELLBOUND: ART & FILM (Group show)
Hayward Gallery, London, UK (February)

COSMOLOGY AT THE PIAZZA DEL POPOLO
A history of the Piazza from Nero to Fellini using light and sound, Rome,
Italy (23–30 June)

1997
FLYING OVER WATER
Miro Foundation, Barcelona, Spain (March—May)

## Theater/Opera

1994
ROSA, A HORSE DRAMA
Production: De Nederlandse Opera, Amsterdam
Music: Louis Andriessen
Staging with Saskia Boddeke
Revival given in 1998 at Musiektheatre, Amsterdam

1997
100 OBJECTS TO REPRESENT THE WORLD: A PROP OPERA
Music: Jean Baptiste Barríere
Salzburg: Zeitfluss Festival Tour and Europe
Revival given in June 1999 in Copenhagen Summer Festival

1998
CHRISTOPHER COLUMBUS
Music: Darius Milhaud
Script: Paul Claudel
Re-staging in collaboration with Saskia Boddeke
Deutsche Staatsoper, Berlin
October/November — 5 performances

PETER GREENAWAY

**INTERVIEWS**

# A Walk through Greenaway

NIGEL ANDREWS/1979

THERE IS NO DOUBT who the British cinema's new folk hero is: Tulse Luper, ornithologist extraordinary, member of the IRR (Institute of Reclamation and Restoration) and apocryphal hero of British filmmaker Peter Greenaway's two most recent films. Greenaway's 40-minute surrealist fantasy featuring Luper, *A Walk Through H,* was shown at last year's London Film Festival and extravagantly praised by many of us; it also jumped straight into two London critics' Top Ten for 1978.

A glance at Greenaway's other films shows that *A Walk Through H* is no flash in the pan. The mixture of pedantry and poetry, of method and madness, that characterised that mythic journey through a series of brightly coloured maps pervades not only his earlier films (*Intervals, Windows, Dear Phone, H Is For House*) but also his newest work, *Vertical Features Remake.* The last named is another pastiche of bureaucratic delirium: this time an account of the IRR's attempt to collate research material left by Luper after his death and pertaining to the aesthetic-ecological significance of different vertical features (trees, posts, poles, etc.) in the English landscape.

An alumnus of the Walthamstow College of Art, Greenaway graduated first to a career at the Central Office of Information, where he worked directing and editing a series of documentaries designed to purvey the British way of life to foreign TV viewers. Eight years of making films in strict obeisance to propagandist formula took their toll—or possibly produced just the right climate of creative frustration. Certainly a love-hate

From *Sight and Sound,* Spring 1979. Reprinted by permission.

relationship with institutionalism seems to fuel all or most of Greenaway's work. "Maps and catalogues and systems fascinate me. They are all attempts to classify chaos. They try to demonstrate that there is an order and an objectivity in the world. What the IRR represents for me is the absurdity of this: it's an organisation that keeps revising the truth while each time pretending that the new version is definitive."

"My starting idea for *A Walk Through H* came when I found a collection of Ordnance Survey maps that had mistakes—roads going left instead of right, orchards painted blue instead of green. Here we are, it seemed, trying to define and circumscribe nature, and it's as if nature were sabotaging or satirising our attempts. In *A Walk Through H* 'real' shots of birds keep interrupting the maps—to break up the artifice. What amazes me in seeing all my recent films in one session"—which, in a preview theatre off Soho Square, we had just done—"is the overpowering presence of nature, especially the omnipresent, lush English landscape."

The English landscape is certainly present in his two best films prior to *A Walk Through H: Windows* (1973) and *H is For House* (1974). In the first, we glimpse through a series of windows belonging to a house in the rural parish of "W," gorgeous squares of spring countryside while a voice-off (Greenaway's own) solemnly and hilariously inventories recent deaths by defenestration. Energetic harpsichord music accompanies the film. "I took it from Rameau's "The Hen," which I thought had just the right exuberant, manic insistence."

In *H Is For House* shots of a country garden, and the green hills beyond, offer a visual focus while a voice—the unmistakably plummy tones of Colin Cantlie from *A Walk Through H*—pedagogically intones bits from a child's alphabet: "H is for Hollywood, H is for home movies . . ." etc.

The fascination with academic methodicality which pervades Greenaway's work, sometimes in comic battle with its opposite—nature, spontaneity, instinct—sometimes standing alone, reaches fetishistic dimensions in *Vertical Features Remake*. "I took the idea of a film made in protest by Tulse Luper about the deterioration of the English landscape. The premise is that Luper was himself working on a State Landscape Programme at the time of his death, and the IRR discovered this film and made various attempts to reshape it."

Each of these reshapings—Vertical Features Remake 1, VFR 2, VFR 3—is shown within Greenaway's larger film, and sandwiched between them are burlesque snippets (very funny) from the imaginary academic controversies that greeted each version. "When I showed the film at the Riverside Studios," Greenaway says, half with pleasure, half with surprise, "everyone was breaking up with laughter."

How much are his films made as absurdist impromptus, deliberately choosing minimal themes around which to spin a web of intellectual or bureaucratic complexity; and how much are they centered on subjects that Greenaway himself cares about? "I care about the English landscape and about its vulnerability to sloppy or short-sighted 'development.' My earliest films, which I wouldn't dream of showing you and which I myself now watch with varying degrees of embarrassment, were very simple, sensuous, pictures of landscape features—sand, snow, sea—set to music: different kinds of music, from a Bach chorale to Brian Eno."

"What I've tried to do in my films since is make them less simplified than that, less one-layered. Evoke nature by putting its opposite in the foreground—artifice. Also, my composer on *Vertical Features Remake* and *A Walk Through H* was Michael Nyman, and we've worked a lot together trying to evolve a system whereby the music and the visuals are created simultaneously and each has its own independent life. We've made up our own multi-media show—our 'circus,' we call it—and we've taken it to a lot of places in England and abroad: showing my paintings, playing his music, screening our films."

Greenaway's bewilderingly prolix array of forthcoming projects includes *Goole By Numbers,* a film about the converted water tower near Hull in which Tulse Luper's *Vertical Features* film was allegedly found; a music-based collaboration with Michael Nyman called *Start With the Sea, Finish with Her Ear Caeserea* for short); and a 3-hour, BFI-subsidised film called *The Falls,* featuring 92 biographies of 92 different people. Greenaway is also writing a complete biography of Tulse Luper in novel form, the mind boggles...

# Greenaway's Contract

## ROBERT BROWN/1981

EVEN BY PETER GREENAWAY'S eclectic standards, *The Draughtsman's Contract,* at first reading of the script, might appear to lie right outside the main concerns of his earlier work. Set in the last decade of the 17th century, the film deals with the relations of a topographical artist and his wealthy patroness. A plot of intrigue and murder, reminiscent of Restoration tragedy, provides a strong dramatic perspective to the artist's contemplation of the peculiarly English landscape of the country house. One might have thought that such a theatrical framework would have been anathema to a filmmaker whose previous eighteen films, the first made in 1966, at the age of 24, have all been constructed in the form of either documents about fictions or fictions about documents.

With Greenaway, however, nothing is quite what it seems, and a visit to Groombridge Place, a handsome Jacobean country house near Tunbridge Wells, helped to clarify the picture. There, in panoramic wide-shot for the 1:1.66 Super 16mm format, I watched Janet Suzman, Anthony Higgins, and Anne Louise Lambert as they strutted round the grounds, rivalling the resident peacocks in their resplendent but extraordinary costumes and wigs. And I listened as the first ever Greenaway performers to talk to each other declaimed their literate but artificial lines. It became apparent that the elaborate devices of the period film themselves instituted the formal conceits within which the filmmaker has always liked to place his own highly personal preoccupations.

---

From *Sight and Sound,* vol. 51/1, 1981–82. Reprinted by permission.

"I just think it is a logical progression from what I have done before," Greenaway said. "I've been given a sufficiently larger budget to expand some of the ideas I have been working through, and that suggests that we have come to a time when I begin to use 'actors.' The dialogue is deliberately artificial, somewhat declamatory and not particularly conversational. So, in that respect, it still has some of my earlier formalist-structuralist concerns."

All the same, Greenaway admits that there is probably a considerable jump between his last film, *The Falls,* and *The Draughtsman's Contract.* Although there are close visual parallels with *Vertical Features Remake, The Draughtsman's Contract* may finally be most remarkable for its detailed portrayal of an obsessively fastidious draughtsman at work. Watching Greenaway's gently precise direction of cast and crew, it was no surprise to learn that the main character, Mr. Neville, is intended, in the manner, if not the matter, of a self-portrait, as an English landscape artist torn between drawing what he sees or drawing what he knows. Indeed, the drama of Mr. Neville's enterprise accurately reflects the internal dynamic of all Greenaway's work, that tension between the Romantic inclination of the painter trained at art school and the Materialist discipline of the documentary film editor once employed by the Central Office of Information.

"It's my particular problem," Greenaway said, "especially exemplified in the film I remain most fond of, *Vertical Features Remake,* this balance between a rigid extra-frame consideration of filmmaking and a very English romantic concern with visual imagery. There is this romance and structure battling all the time." The deep attachment to domestic landscape, a literary turn of mind and the learnt procedures of structuring an often arbitrary selection of footage are the foundations of that ironic contradiction, central to Greenaway's work, between the Romantic author of a fiction and the Structuralist fiction of an author.

The plot of *The Draughtsman's Contract* hinges on the inclusion or exclusion of certain objects within the artist's drawings, an issue which comes to relate directly to the wider question of whose authority and desires really lie behind the draughtsman's contract. "The film is essentially about a draughtsman drawing a landscape," Greenaway said, "and the facets of the drawing and the landscape are compared on another level of representation, the film. I want those three ideas to be present in the whole structure of the movie, so that one is aware that we are making comparisons all the time between the real landscape, Mr. Neville's image of it and, ultimately, us as viewers seeing those ideas represented on film."

Underlying these words is a wry recognition of the essential arbitrariness of the relationship between the living author and the inanimate world of his creations, between the world of subjects and of objects. It is this largely intuitive recognition that chiefly prevents the internal collapse of Greenaway's dizzying Towers of Babel, and not his own professed interests and influences, whether the Romantic love of English landscape or the formalist fascination with Borgesian theorems.

"One difference about *The Draughtsman's Contract* is that all my previous movies, by and large, have not been overscripted. They have developed very much in the editing process. There's been Idea A. Wouldn't Idea A look good with Idea B? And then A and B produce C, and so on. Now, because of the money and structures involved, and the disciplines necessary with actors, this film had to be scripted closely, and that I have never done before. The text became a written object." No longer, perhaps, will the previous excesses of narrative content and methods of representation be used for the willfully obscurantist ends of building heretical systems of classification, only then to laugh in the face of their hopeless inadequacy. Rather they may serve to raise more directly that question of authorship which lies at the heart of all Greenaway's films and which places him within, not just an English tradition of landscape art, but the international center of avant-garde film.

In Greenaway's early shorts, either the images insist on the ghostlike presence of an author while the commentary ridicules the notion, or vice versa. Image and narration often seem arbitrarily related. In *Water Wrackets,* shots of water in all its liquid patterns and under every light are laid over a narrated fictional history which approximates a very Unseen translation of Caesar's Gallic Wars. *Dear Phone* effectively attempts a visual record or all the telephone boxes in England, at every time of day and in every shape of place, while the soundtrack relates a rare collection of eccentric phone calls. *Windows* also pretends to be a taxonomy of the world: windows are a visual leitmotif for a collation of fictional suicide statistics. *H Is For House* is a home movie (one domestic set-up is used) which has been overlaid with a haphazardly spiralling lexicon. The author's home, perhaps, represents the world: the scenes of his daily life must stand for an outside world which remains a mere concept, a language, a lexicon.

The feature-length *A Walk Through H* and *Vertical Features Remake,* both released in 1978, bear the more noticeable marks of a strangely haunting obsession with the passage of time and space. In *A Walk Through H,* fictional map drawings evaporate into a single meaningless symbol either just before or just after the narrator reaches their place-scale. In *Vertical Features,* one of the most beautiful films of the last decade and Greenaway's most considerable work, the interest in the film's time-scale is brilliantly matched to the director's own sense of place. Real places, not just artefacts, vanish before they can really be seen or, in Greenaway's terms, known. The "vertical features" are choreographed with Michael Nyman's pulsing chords in three separate dimensions of landscape. They are born with the light of dawn, live during the day, decay in the dusk, and are resurrected again in any and every order that they may ascend into eternity with the last frame of film. "None of these objects was ever manipulated," Greenaway has said. "Everything was found." In other words, the central question the film implicitly addresses is: How can an author reconcile his own time and space with those of his fictional representations?

Greenaway has approached this question not theoretically but through practice and intuition. And perhaps his work can best be "known" if it is compared to that of the avant-garde filmmaker Raul Ruiz for whom the matter of the relationship between the author and his subjects, both documentary and fictional, provides a basic conceptual premise. The apparent antithesis of Greenaway, Ruiz is a highly political and theoretical filmmaker. Like *A Walk Through H,* Ruiz's *Snakes and Ladders* is about a character named H (is this the answer to Greenaway's riddle about the real identity of H?) who travels through place-scales represented not by fictional maps but by real landscapes. *Of Great Events and Ordinary People* shares the same formal concerns as all Greenaway's films, particularly *The Falls,* but its context is a real place, a district of Paris, and a real time, the 1978 French elections. One of Greenaway's current projects, *The Bathroom Arrest,* has close analogies with the favorite short story, Kafka's "The Penal Colony," which Ruiz has himself filmed as a political metaphor for the Latin American situation. The Greenaway project, however, envisages a literary remake of *Vertical Features.* Thus, for Ruiz, what is real is that cerebral truth that cannot be represented transparently. While for Greenaway, what is real is precisely that physical truth which cannot be represented.

This is most clearly articulated in *Act of God,* Greenaway's documentary about people struck by lightning. Here the essential intrigue revolves round the practical problem of how to represent the incomprehensible nature of an act by the Supreme Unknowable Author Himself. Not only is a lightning strike an exact metaphor for the arbitrary relationship between subject and author, it also provides the ideal correlative for Greenaway's own fictional universe. The film's mixture of statistics and apocrypha at once shows up the absence of both the real Author and the real Act (of creation/death). The film is a real metaphor for a fictional universe, it is at once Romantic and Semantic.

The apogee of the author and his art/facts/artefacts from the real world is reached in *The Falls*. It's premise is a fictional version of *Act of God*: a Violent Unknown Event has struck the world leaving behind some nineteen million survivors; ninety-two case histories are catalogued. And Greenaway is similarly concerned with organising diverse forms, still, documentary, live-action, interview, reportage, within a coherent text. "I was just interested in all the different ways that you could put pictures together," he said. "In a sense it was a compendium of all the editing techniques I've learnt and also a few more I've found for myself. And also all the other forms of representation vis à vis the visual tradition of Europe."

With *The Falls* Greenaway's structuralist quest for coherence is seen to collapse into nothing more than a rather despairing mirror image of his own romanticism. Both look back to his own past as a film editor with the COI and to the forebears of that organisation, the GPO and EMB film units of the '30s and '40s. The marks of Griersonian aestheticism, however, are always undercut by the film's amusement at its own status as a cultural object. Greenaway's statement about *The Falls* might be interpreted as implying that the filmmaker had finally accepted that the splintering forms of the world were ultimately unclassifiable. And so the only truth left to represent was his confession that, as the spurious inventor of self-consistent artefacts, he himself was a fiction. Hence the film discourses with neither its subject matter nor its authorial style but its audience, ninety-two random people gathered to watch a white screen. Greenaway's most recently completed film, *Zandra Rhodes,* a COI documentary on the dress designer, secretively demolishes a character who sees herself as an author of world taste. "Zandra Rhodes," the label as personality, represents—to quote another Ruiz title—*The Scattered Body and the World Upside Down.*

*The Falls* was joint-winner of the 1980 BFI Special Award, and *Act of God* was judged best short film at the 1981 Melbourne Film Festival. Public recognition, however, might raise more problems, create more ironies and lead to more subversions than can possibly be contained within the past scope of Greenaway's work. This said, Greenaway, at thirty-nine, has long thought it time to make "a more public commitment." Mamoun Hassan, managing director of the NFFC, wished to ask him whether he was a private or a public filmmaker. "The gap between *The Falls* and *The Draughtsman's Contract* is an attempt to answer that question."

Greenaway's approach to the shooting of *The Draughtsman's Contract* was guided by *Last Year in Marienbad,* which he wanted to show to his cast and crew as an indication of his own aims. The wide framing of the main characters and the use of a fixed static camera are his chief devices for maintaining the requisite distance from the emotional foreground of a stuffily theatrical plot. But as Resnais recognised, even with an artificial narrative, the story does matter; and here much more so than in the "drama-docs" because players are "real people working for a living." And, it has to be admitted, Greenaway has never seemed particularly interested in the daily story of human frailty and vanity, except in so far as it concerns the relationship of an artist to either his patron or his subjects. "Your significance, Mr. Neville," a second patroness tells the draughtsman, "is attributable to both innocence and arrogance in equal parts."

Nowadays Greenaway rarely goes to the cinema, his expressed purpose being "to bring together the painting and the literature for which film is the ideal medium." His latest project, *Jonson and Jones,* is concerned with the stormy relationship between the writer (Ben) and the architect (Inigo). Meanwhile, *The Draughtsman's Contract* will test Greenaway's range and the scale of audience which the BFI's most costly production can attest. If it does make money, then it could prove doubly important. For, in a significant development in the field of independent filmmaking, the Fourth Channel has made a £280,000 subvention to the BFI Production Board. The board allocated £40,000 of this plus £80,000 of its own money to *The Draughtsman's Contract.* But even with a further £40,000 from unspecified sources, the film finished a week and a half over a seven week schedule and way over budget. On the strength of a show reel, however, various distributors are reported to be keen to make up the deficit, a hopeful sign for future cooperation between the British film and television industries.

In many ways, Peter Greenaway does represent the ideal artist for such patronage, combining in his work the authorless modes of television and the myth-based structures of cinema. Moreover, he himself sees his art as rooted in an English tradition. Here the provenance of *The Draughtsman's Contract* is revealing. "Summer of '76, beautiful summer, drawing the rather nondescript Victorian house near Hay-on-Wye belonging to a friend. I was interested in the ways that either the drawings reflected or did not reflect what was in front of me. The question of whether the draughtsman draws what he sees or what he knows. Thought what a nice idea, how could I use it in a larger scenario?" He later added, "The thing I enjoy doing most of all, and I don't want to sound too romantic, is just the experience of landscape. At its very best, the reality of landscape is much more profound than any attempt to try to change it, transform it into an art form. It makes me a very English filmmaker. It's been a concern for English literature, English painting for four, five, six hundred years."

# Breaking the Contract

## STUART MORGAN/1983

STUART MORGAN: *Is it true that the original version of your film* The Draughtsman's Contract, *1982 was over four hours long?*

PETER GREENAWAY: Yes, a mass of stuff was cut from the present version having to do with symbolism, allegory, the relationship of people upstairs and downstairs, and the continuation of the living-statue conceit. (The statue had a wife and dog.) All the minor characters played the game of aping their masters. Maria, Mrs. Herbert's servant, and Philip, Mr. Neville's assistant, had sexual liaisons after dark in the garden in the same places that the drawings were made. Also, the mechanical manipulation of the drawings was shown stage by stage, as well as a scene where Porringer attacks Mr. Neville in the garden, accusing him of various relations with his mistress.

SM: *So Philip knew. Maria knew...*

PG: Everybody was in on it. At one point Philip was going to be present, masked, at his master's death.

SM: *What happened after Neville died?*

PG: In the six years up to 1700 Mr. Noyes married Mrs. Herbert, of course, because that was preordained; the little boy died of scarlet fever; Mrs. Talmann had an heir who would ultimately take over, and Mr. Talmann, being impotent, acquiesced. Philip became the new draughtsman and

---

came back to redraw the house for van Hoyten after he had landscaped it in a Capability Brown, post-Repton manner.

s м : *So many possibilities exist.*
p g : Yes, it would be interesting to change things so that the elder, not the younger, woman conceived. With his mother-in-law conceiving, Mr. Talmann would not even become his illegitimate child's ward, and would lose any connection with the inheritance.

s м : The Falls, *1980, was both a summary of your work so far and a way of utilizing remnants—pieces discarded from other films, fragments left unfinished, even home movies. It seems unlikely that the discarded 150 minutes of* The Draughtsman's Contract *will be neglected for long.*
p g : Since all my projects link together I'm very reluctant to leave things. One plan to refashion the unseen footage is a film called *The Hedgecutters.* In it Mr. Porringer, the protagonist, is a 20th-century gardener to 12 country houses. He moves from estate to estate looking after pomegranates and cutting hedges. As a rainy summer wears on he is forced to take on extra help—a man called Clancy and another called Noyes. He dislikes both of them but sublimates this dislike into a time-slip, like the famous incident that transported two Victorian ladies back into the 17th century as they were walking through the grounds at Versailles. In the distance is a child on a swing, who becomes the child in *The Draughtsman's Contract.* Porringer sees a man drawing, who becomes Mr. Neville. When he goes to be paid he finds the lady of the house being...

s м : *Offering Mr. Neville unrestricted freedom of her most intimate hospitality?*
p g : Precisely. Ultimately Porringer is up a tall ladder, falls over and gets pushed into a pond. From time to time he visits the museum in Norwich and, in a shady corner where no one ever goes, finds 12 drawings of a country house, ascribed to somebody called Philip.

s м : *To get back to the original 12 drawings by Mr. Neville...*
p g : You'll find that there were only 11.

s м : *What happened to the 12th?*
p g : I got bored drawing it. Actually, 13 were planned. The 13th is the one he came back to do at night. Thirteen, an unlucky number, is responsible for his death. It's a baker's dozen.

s m :  *The "dozen" drawings seem an equivalent of the lists we find throughout your work; for example, the official report in your film* Windows, *1975, or the directory in* The Falls. *In the process of working through these the viewer recognizes patterns and coincidences, and eventually the list is buried by a surplus of interpretation. By then the systematic nature of the original structure has been lost, "plot" has evaporated or been overwhelmed, a degree of maximum ambiguity has been reached, but something is on the point of emerging. It isn't enacted or incorporated or even described. Just adumbrated. Maybe it's an event or an idea. Or both, since normal rules of cause and effect have been suspended.*

p g :  People have certainly been upset by the lack of so-called resolution in the plot of *The Draughtsman's Contract.* They seem so accustomed to Agatha Christie. Where does the point you describe occur?

s m :  *With Neville's death.*

p g :  Right. One new project for TV is called *Fear of Drowning.*

s m :  *So what emerges is a set of coordinates for a new work. Lack of closure is a means of appropriating and revising your oeuvre, permitting other structures to develop, which determine other events. From these a pattern will arise and be overwhelmed in its turn. You're attracted to closed systems with rules which alter in time. The structural principle is one of geometric progression, lists that creak under their weight of cross-references.*

p g :  I'm working on a novel called *Three Artificial Histories,* a reconstruction of three centuries—one in the past, one in the present, and one in the future—very loosely based on the 14th, 20th, and 26th centuries. This provides an excuse to examine the whole problem of lists, indices, and catalogues, and thereby consider what the making of history and fiction is all about.

s m :  *What is the problem?*

p g :  The novel form is comparatively recent; it has only existed from (shall we say) about 1600. But authors have been making lists for very much longer. Take *The Pillow Book of Sei Sh;amonagon* or Rabelais. Later Sterne and Diderot do it a lot, and J.K. Huysmans, in *Against Nature.* As one way of reconsidering narrative—to make a savage paraphrase of the idea that everything exists in order to be put into a book—I suggest that everything exists to be put into a list, that if you wait long enough everything will find itself in a list somewhere or other and that if you are genius enough everything will appear in every list. Examining lists means playing with the re-creation of history. History doesn't exist; it's only made by historians.

S M :  *So in your film* Vertical Features Remake, *1978, the debates between the characters Castonager, Gang Lion, and the others about editing and re-editing* Tulse *Luper's Vertical Features will never be settled.*

P G :  Put it this way. In *Three Artificial Histories* the second chapter is concerned with maps, as was *A Walk Through H,* 1978. Yet another plan is for a film called *The Cartographers,* about 20 different mapmakers who all approach one specific bit of landscape and map it in their own fashions. Map 1 will be the merest outline indicating mountains, marsh, and a plain through which a river runs. In Map 2 other, quite idiosyncratic features like passages of deadly nightshade and areas of peacock are much more significant than towns. So each cartographer perceives the landscape in a different way according to his particular interests. You go through the preoccupations of a baker, a weaver, a pederast, a man who's never seen the sea but wants to, another who's mining diamonds, and so on. The same piece of land can be refashioned, reorganized, recolored. Like history. *Three Artificial Histories* has an apocryphal apologia suggesting that it exists to find a use for the indices. In other words, you create indexes first, then write a novel based on them. There are lots of types: an index of place-names, of people, of birds, of ephemeral events. . . . Though it sounds like a device it's essential for me, because there are so many characters, so many bits of action, that I keep getting lost.

S M :  *This brings up the question of mistakes, deliberate or accidental. One of the delights of your early work was the habit of linking an arbitrary visual level to a more deliberate soundtrack. Now and again an accident on one level would be explained away on the other level. In* The Falls, *for example, when a character suddenly disappears from view the commentary excuses this as a symptom of the mysterious ailment that afflicts everyone in the film. A more disturbing characteristic is your blatant use of red herrings.*

P G :  For example?

S M :  *All the women in* Dear Phone, *1977, were called Zelda, they were all driving their husbands mad, and thrown in for good measure was a cleaner whose favorite novel was* Tender is the Night. *None of that serves any purpose whatsoever in the film.*

P G :  It serves the purpose of not serving a purpose, surely quite a valid one. Life is full of a thousand red herrings, and it takes the history of a civilization to work out which are the red herrings and which aren't. The actual red herring conceit turns up in the scenario for another planned film called *Zed and Two Noughts* (which spells "Zoo"). There's a little girl who is taken to the aquarium and, bluffed by adults, keeps asking the keeper where she can see a red herring. You could say that the two unexplained corpses in *The Maltese Falcon* are red herrings because nothing is really resolved at the end anyway, as in *The Draughtsman's Contract*. You could say that the ghost in *Hamlet* is a red herring, too. It depends on your viewpoint.

S M :  *Come come. Your examples are too strategic. Not even the men who wrote it understood the plot of* The Maltese Falcon. *Next you'll wheel out* Last Year at Marienbad, *which Alain Resnais and Alain Robbe-Grillet disagreed about.*
P G :  One wouldn't in any way suggest that this particular phenomenon makes them less interesting works of art.

S M :  *The trouble is that you're suggesting that it makes them* more *interesting.*
P G :  Indeed I am.

S M :  *One possible red herring in* The Draughtsman's Contract *is van Hoyten, Keeper of Owls at the Amsterdam Zoo. In previous films he is the sworn enemy of Tulse Luper, the polymath artist, ornithologist, filmmaker, and author of* Migratory Birds of the Northern Hemisphere. *Here van Hoyten is introduced, speaks a couple of sentences in Dutch, then walks away flapping his arms as if he's trying to fly. Why is he there at all?*
P G :  Playfulness. He's the new man, a shadow of Mr. Talmann, one of the Northern Europeans appearing for the first time in English politics and life. He turns up all in black, looking like a Puritan.

S M :  *What's happened to Tulse Luper?*
P G :  He's quietly gone to sleep for a few years but will doubtless be resurrected. Cissie Colpitts, his lover/wife/mistress, is the subject of a project planned for next spring called *Drowning by Numbers*.

S M :  *She split into three as a result of the Violent Unknown Event in* The Falls, *didn't she? And had difficulty getting back together.*
P G :  She's also three in this movie. One woman three times.

s m :  *One Cissie Colpitts married a bicycle manufacturer from Leeds, we're told in* The Falls. *Another ran an avant-garde film society with its headquarters in a disused water tower in Goole.*

p g :  The third was her coheir, who took over. In *Drowning by Numbers* the eldest woman is 64; the middle Cissie is 36; and the youngest is 19. And all three murder their husbands.

s m :  *Why?*

p g :  Oh, various reasons—most of them nonviolent. The first finishes hers off in a bathtub in front of the kitchen fire. He's drunk and has been unfaithful. Wishing to make it look accidental she enlists the aid of a local coroner called Madget. He and his son Smut succeed in concealing the crime. Seeing Cissie Colpitts I evade detection, Cissie Colpitts II bumps her husband off in the sea. He's obese, and her excuse is that he's eaten too much. Again Madget and Smut are involved. Cissie Colpitts III, who wants to be rid of her husband of three days, lets him drift away while teaching him to swim in a local pool.

s m :  *Where is it set?*

p g :  On the north banks of the river Humber, not a particularly photogenic area. It's extremely flat; the only things that stick up are church steeples, distant derricks, docks, and water towers.

s m :  *Obviously it's about that conspiracy of women against men already explored in* Dear Phone *and* The Draughtsman's Contract. *What else is it about?*

p g :  Games. There are three games in the film. The first is cathartic, to help Cissie Colpitts I recover from her grief. It's an alternative form of cricket invented by Madget, using two wickets, two umpires, three balls, and a mad dog. It's called Grace. The second takes place on a wide foreshore of the tidal Humber and involves any number of people. Like lacrosse. You can play lacrosse all over the world provided you know where the goalposts are. This game, though, has a series of allegorical figures with capital letters to identify them, as in Hogarth: The Hangman, The Judge, The Ghost, The Fat Man, The Harlequin . . . As many as you can invent. This one is played at the wedding of Cissie Colpitts III. The last game, which concerns Noah's Ark, is again played on the beach. It happens when all the husbands have been killed and is to celebrate the conception of a child. All the animals are collected and put into arks when a storm breaks, the women go off on a boat on the river to escape it, and the last you see of them is that they're floating out to sea. Madget and Smut commit suicide because they realize that the women have gone out of their lives. There is talk of Cissie Colpitts the elder dying in a cinema in Philadelphia, hemorrhaging so the blood that wells up in her lap is the same color as the plush seats she's sitting on.

S M :  *Another form of drowning.*
P G :  She's watching Jean Renoir's *Boudu sauvé des eaux* (Boudu saved from drowning), about a tramp who fell into the Seine, pretended to be drowning, and was rescued by a family without wanting to be. In the end he went back into the water.

S M :  *There seems to be a connection between water and games.*
P G :  Certainly there is for Cissie Colpitts. *Fear of Drowning* is a plan for an eight-hour TV serial tracing the life of Cissie Colpitts from the womb to the age of 18, which was also the date that the Lumière brothers patented the first cine camera; her life is also the history of the cinema. It shows that she inherited both her gameplaying and her terror of drowning from her father, a man called Cribb. Every episode will contain a different game. The first, learned from a shipwrecked Italian sailor, Cribb plays on a beach to determine his daughter's future. It involves drawing squares, each of which is your destiny. You play hopscotch and throw rocks. Where they land indicates certain patterns of behavior. Another, the Lobster Quadrille, is an obstacle race relating to all the fears sailors have of the sea: deep chasms in the China Sea, the aurora borealis, the Sargasso Sea, the Strait of Magellan, all represented in miniaturized, allegorical form as obstacles on the beach. The games become grander, first involving a man and his child; then a man, his wife, and child; then maybe twenty people; then finally about five hundred players. The last game is cataclysmic; Cribb dies just as Cissie reaches the age of 18.

S M :  *But she will continue to play games until she dies.*
P G :  And at the age of 36 will meet Tulse Luper, the arch game-player.

S M :  *It's worth adding that drowning isn't the only violent event in your work. Act of God, 1981, a short TV documentary, is a series of interviews with and facts about people struck by lightning;* Windows *is an illustrated list of defenestration casualties.*

P G :   Like me, Madget, the coroner in *Fear of Drowning,* is obsessed with deaths, and keeps a card index of ways of dying. We know for a fact that the composer Charles Alkan reached for the Talmud on a top shelf of his library, the entire bookcase fell on him, and he was asphyxiated. The composer Jean Lully was beating time with a cane, struck his own foot, it went gangrenous, and he died. Those two real-life composers have been written into an opera, *The Death of Webern.* It's about the deaths of ten composers, starting with Anton von Webern and ending with John Lennon. All of them were shot. Each time the same ten clues were present. They were all smoking, all wearing hats, all left grieving widows, all wore glasses, the deaths were all perpetrated by three bullets, their assailants all carried United States passports, and so on. The idea is of a conspiracy against composers set up by St. Cecilia, the patron saint of music, jealous of the success of her protégés. There's a reference to this in *The Falls,* and Geoffrey Fallthuis and Contorpia Folixchange, who appeared then, will reappear.

S M :   *It's time to stop. Just for a second it's possible to imagine that moment when everything appears on every list.*

# The Draughtsman's Contract:
# An Interview with Peter Greenaway

## KAREN JAEHNE/1984

CINEASTE: *Many of the new British filmmakers are focusing on chapters in history that appear to be "turning points"—Ghandi's India, England between two wars in* Chariots of Fire. The Draughtsman's Contract *is also a historical recreation—in fact, so deliberately so that you appear to be making or, rather, overstating a point. What is the context?*

PETER GREENAWAY: The narrative structure of the movie covers a number of themes. It's set in 1694, a crucial time for English history— a moving out of the old Catholic Stuart dynasty and a moving in of a Protestant-inspired, basically mercantile nouveau-riche aristocracy coming in from northern Europe. This time of changing values gave me an opportunity to fictionalize and invent characters and attitudes, which are not perhaps totally historically correct but do have some basis in historical fact.

CINEASTE: *Who is the draughtsman?*

GREENAWAY: There were toward the end of the 17th century a whole mass of painters, draughtsmen, and architects, who earned their living by going around the country—basically in southern England where all the wealth had accumulated—and drawing the houses of rich men. It was a form of status seeking. A rich man would have his property drawn, then prints made and engravings passed around among his friends and neighbors as a prestigious gift, in the way, for example, today—but a much more

From *Cineaste*, vol. 13, no. 2, 1984. Reprinted by permission.

humdrum level—one might send postcards of one's house. These men existed much further down the social scale than I have made the draughts-man. There is evidence that such people had much greater status in northern France and part of Germany, but in England it could be said that they were not much more important, shall we say, than the head of the stables? I do believe that I have taken a reasonable license, however, because we are not talking about London, not about Bristol, but rather about stretches of rural England of a very parochial nature and isolated from the culture coming over from France.

CINEASTE: *There is an obvious attempt at perfectionism in the film, so much so that many people have compared your work with that of Stanley Kubrick, who works on a much greater budget. But there is also a self-consciousness about the perfection your draughtsman seeks. Is fastidiousness a flaw here?*

GREENAWAY: Of course there have been those comparisons, particularly in respect to *Barry Lyndon,* but the general nature of the recreation appeals to people who look for that in a film. There were also many comparisons to the movie *Tom Jones,* quite another matter! For me, the temperament is derived much more from French cinema—for example, *Last Year at Marienbad* by Alain Resnais or Eric Rohmer's *The Marquise von O,* and to a certain extent, even Fellini's *Casanova.* These were all films that related back to the, if you will, genre of the film—so much so that a cinema in Bristol put on a season of films called "The Draughtsman's Con*text,"* which included all those films that by accident or design, unconsciously or quite consciously influenced the film.

The deliberate, thoughtful visual quality of the film can be traced back to late 17th century painting—Carravagio, de La Tour, even late Raphael and so on and the famous interiors of the Dutch painters. Some of the compositions have been taken over and moved consciously into the film, sometimes with a rather blasphemous result, because the original paint-ings have an ecclesiastical feel about them. For example, two compositions are absolutely integral to the film and center around the signing of the sexual contract. They are based on a painting by Georges de La Tour which, in fact, includes the Virgin Mary and Mary Magdalene, so that the visual metamorphosis is one in which women have been changed from their reli-gious counterparts to completely "lay" (if you will) equivalents.

CINEASTE: *The painterly manner of the film is also a result of the stationary camera: In this age of frenetic camera work, weren't you afraid of a static and possibly boring image?*

GREENAWAY: One of the essential conceits of the film is that the camera does not move. Of course, there are a few occasions when it slides slightly from side to side—at mealtimes—but that is the only time and it is extremely inorganic. It is a mechanical movement.

Now there are three reasons for this. First, the facetious reason: paintings don't move. Secondly, with a still camera you throw the emphasis on the dialogue and soundtrack. It is extremely important that all the words are heard—not just heard, but listened to, because of the puns, conundrums, word plays, red herrings, and so on. It is necessary to keep your ears tuned or you'll lose something. Thirdly, it is a sheer reaction to the St. Vitus dance of filmmaking over the last years. It seems to me that most camera work is done for no good structural reason, or even good emotional or mood reason. The desire to keep the camera on the move is an unnecessary pursuit by international filmmakers.

CINEASTE: *This film has been called the first entertaining structuralist film. How could you be sure it would entertain?*

GREENAWAY: Well, it was meant that way, in spite of all its intellectual pretensions. I sometimes go into the cinema to eavesdrop on the audiences. If they're sitting there, hand-to-brow looking very serious, it's a great disappointment to me. I want people to enjoy its visual splendors. I want people to get caught up in its intellectual games.

CINEASTE: *The major intellectual game is a murder, and the clues are built in to the scenes the draughtsman is agonizing about—for the wrong reasons, it turns out. How did you develop this elaborate method or art of framing not only the image but also the artist within it?*

GREENAWAY: Well, I have also made over twenty films, all of them concerned with questions of representation, which applies as much to language as it does to visual phenomena. Do words say what we mean them to say? When we phrase an idea, are we using the right words to phrase it? What words don't mean, or appear not to mean, has always been of interest from my very first films—some three and a half minutes long. That has been a continuing concern that gets me into certain kinds of trouble, because a lot of these films don't travel well. If those who understand English have trouble, what on earth do the French, Italians and Belgians make of this?

*The Draughtsman's Contract* has taken a period of history when so-called conversational style was very formal. But there again, if you examine the dialogue, you'll find it is based on the contemporary playwrights of the period, Sheridan, Congreve, but you will also find a considerable difference. Because I don't think there is much point in reproducing a period for its own sake.

CINEASTE: *To that extent, you differ from Kubrick's attitude toward the recreation for* Barry Lyndon?
GREENAWAY: Yes, perhaps. *The Draughtsman's Contract* takes cognizance of the 300 years of history that have passed since 1694 and has developed a language based also on received opinions of that particular era, preconceived ideas of what that period sounded like. It's also very much aware of 20th century idioms. I'm reluctant to call it a period movie. I like to think it has great resonances in the 20th century.

CINEASTE: *The word usually used for a film like this is "talky," and that immediately establishes it as intellectual and limits its audience. Have you sensed that reaction, or does the visual elegance simply overwhelm the critics?*
GREENAWAY: I am in no way apologetic for having made a "talkie." I would like to stand up and say this very loudly, clearly! Words have become integral to certain sorts of filmmaking. It's not a particularly American tradition, not even an English one, but it's certainly a French, Italian, and German tradition. Many people find this an aberration for British cinema and call *The Draughtsman's Contract* a "continental" film. The film is prepared to trade ideas, to put up arguments, red herrings and cul-de-sacs and to play with the whole business of conversation. I would like to think that's what it does: it plays with ideas through words. The fact that it is also beautiful to look at, if I may be so modest, in no way detracts from this phenomenon, because I think there is a useful symbiosis between the look and the sound of a film.

CINEASTE: *I was struck by the ability of the music to express so much about the story and the period. Is it contemporary? How did you go about coordinating so many stylized, or stylish, and arch elements?*

GREENAWAY: It is an important binding—cement, if you like—between the sound and the images. It was composed by a friend of mine, Michael Nyman. We have collaborated on the last five or six films, and he is also interested in the whole business of organizing material. He is what might loosely be called a systemic composer, owing a lot to the American composers like Steve Wright and so on. We are both concerned to find some equitable balance between music and the visual image. Traditionally in the filmmaking process, the visual image is decided on and the composer is brought along at a much later stage, which puts music in a secondary, even tertiary position, which I find unsatisfactory. So we had to find a working method whereby we both collaborated at a quite early stage to ensure that the music lent the film some structural significance.

CINEASTE: *There seems to be a tendency to think the score is derived from 17th century music. Where did the modern application affect it?*

GREENAWAY: The music is based on the English composer Henry Purcell. What has happened is that Michael has taken certain phrases, certain note structures, and incidentally, the music of that period had a great deal in common with modern systemic music. It's based on layers, repetitions, cyclic movement within the use of notes. Any ear that knows the music of Händel or Purcell will immediately recognize that the history of music in the 300 years since the time have been utilized in the structure of the score.

CINEASTE: *Considering the abundant symbols and careful layering of clues within the tableaux, isn't there a danger of making a recondite film? What can you tell us to help us understand where to look and what to look for in the first viewing? It's a film that will require a second, third, and, I'd guess, a still delighted fourth viewing.*

GREENAWAY: I would like to think that the film worked on many different levels, and the kind of criticism that has been generated over its puzzles leads me to believe it means many things to many people—both intended and un-. For example, one English newspaper interpreted the whole game of the film as a description of the problems in English football. There are references to lost shirts and hidden football boots, and the players all change their colors at half-time. This is a wonderfully amusing approach to the film which I take no great pains to deny. I'm so glad people can find such references. It's also been regarded as an anti-Thatcher allegory, too, about outsiders trying to become part of the establishment and ultimately being repulsed. It's been regarded as a pro-feminist film and, likewise, an anti-feminist film. Someone wrote that it was an allegory of neo-colonialism with a reference to Britain's rather unfortunate past in Africa. All these things I take under advisement. Precisely because it's not a mindless entertainment, it intrigues people looking for some further significance and allows them to project into it what they will. I made the film to entertain, not to instruct, so if I knew what it "meant," I'd be the last to tell.

CINEASTE: *One London observer opined that the reason your box office in England has been right up there with E.T. is that the eroticism brings in the crowds. Do you think they find a solution to their problem?*
GREENAWAY:  It's my belief—one certainly shared with a lot of other people—that the greater sense of eroticism can be gained by suggestion rather than shall we say a catalog of gynecological details? I believe the eroticism is much more implied than seen, and that is a much more satisfactory state of affairs.

CINEASTE: *What are we to make of the naked sprite in the garden? Is he a witness? The culprit? The victim? A shadow of the ni....?*
GREENAWAY:  I've come to the point that I have serious doubts about that figure. If so many people ask, I may have slightly miscalculated in this thing. I sometimes wonder if I should have elucidated the mystery more. But, at any rate, that particular statue is informed by two conceits. In northern Europe, and particularly in England at that time, it was fashionable to have in your garden hollow statues made of lead and hooked up to the local water supply. The idea was the your unsuspecting guest would walk by the statue and a gardener would turn a hidden tap, and the water would spurt out and spray the guest. It was considered very humorous. Great ingenuity was applied to this particular trick, and it obviously amused them.

The second conceit is that England, after a long period of turmoil and strife, was at last settling down to a period of prosperity, and the sons of landed gentry were being sent abroad to complete their education. They took off on what was known as the Grand Tour and ended up in either Rome or Greece. It was terribly current then to bring back mementos of their tour, since neo-Classicism was quite the thing, and a statue did nicely. (It's all beginning again with Melina Mercouri complaining about the Elgin Marbles in the British Museum!) Another way of seeing that figure is that the landowner was either too mean or too uninformed to bring back one of these statues, so he gets one of his minions or servants to dress up and pose in parts of the garden in order to impress his neighbors. Now this particular character, being a bit simple in the head, will perform this task enthusiastically, so that any time anyone is in the garden, he will pop up from the herbage and pose in some approximation to Hermes or Herma-phrodite, or whatever.

But he is also relevant to a tradition in literature of the fool, who is allowed to behave in a way which any more self-respecting mortal would shun. Thereby he can become a silent witness to all sorts of behavior which the other characters do not even take cognizance of. So here the fool steps in, where everybody else is afraid to tread. Because he is the last figure seen, there is an insinuation that he is somehow responsible for what has happened throughout the film.

CINEASTE: *So who did kill the master of the house?*
GREENAWAY: I could be enigmatic and throw the question back, but for me, everybody was responsible, because everybody had reason to gain from the death of Mr. Herbert. So, like the murder on the Orient Express, everybody is guilty.

# Interview with Peter Greenaway:
# *Zed and Two Noughts (Z.O.O.)*

## MICHEL CIMENT/1985

c: *Given the critical and commercial success of* The Draughtsman's Contract, *it is astonishing that you waited several years before making a new film.*
g: It is always difficult to find money, however good a reception you've gotten. After the modest but real success of *The Draughtsman's Contract* in international art and writing circles, I thought I would be able to obtain financing without much difficulty. Because I didn't lack for either ideas or enthusiasm: I had circulated to the studios three or four screenplays that were in a more or less advanced stage of preparation. *The Draughtsman's Contract* had allowed me to start some new things, to contemplate new ways of making movies. I was very eager to get to work immediately. But nothing came through. Despite all the praises bestowed upon me by the financiers, they didn't match their actions (that is, their money) to their words. A well-known attitude.... Another consequence of my success with *Draughtsman* was that Hollywood became interested in me. Through the intermediary of my agent there, they began to send me screenplays, but it was clear that they were more confident in my ability to make their movies than my own. They saw that I knew how to work, that I had a good visual and narrative sense, and they wanted to use my services. They sent me 60 or 70 screenplays, but given my lack of responsiveness, they've now pretty much ceased contacting me.

From *Positif,* April 1986. Reprinted by permission of *Positif* and the author. Translated from the French by Judy Schroeter-Deegan.

During this time, I did a great deal of work for television, creating about six hours of programming for Channel 4 on a variety of different topics. In addition, I wrote a half-dozen screenplays—I virtually never had an idle moment. In fact, between *The Draughtsman's Contract* and *Z.O.O.,* two films could have been made: *Drowning by Numbers* and *The Suitcase of Tulse Luper.* The first one interested several potential silent partners (hence Channel 4) and will be made one day or another. The second was inspired by a plan for an exhibition I had. The series of programs that I made for television kept me busy for around 18 months. They included four one-hour shows titled *Four American Composers* dedicated to John Cage, Philip Glass, Robert Ashley, and Meredith Monk. Then I made *Making a Splash,* a fairly extravagant film, about 25 minutes long, which celebrated the human body in water. I attempted to tie the images with the music of Michael Nyman without using words. We filmed the movie in the middle of winter. England really doesn't have a swimming culture and we would have been better off filming it in California during the summer, but we didn't have the resources for that. I also began another series, *Inside Rooms,* which, from the perspective of post-modernist architecture and decorative art, was intended to take an ironic look at the contemporary English way of life. There were supposed to be six episodes: the bath room, the living room, the bedrooms, etc., each a half-hour in length. So far, only one episode has been completed. It was another way for me to resolve certain formal issues.

c :  *What was the original idea that inspired* Z.O.O.*?*
g :  As you probably know from having seen the films I made before *The Draughtsman's Contract,* I have always had a keen interest in ecological issues. No doubt this interest comes from the fact that my father was a naturalist who specialized in ornithology. From childhood on, I was literally brainwashed into sharing this interest. I resisted but it still stayed with me. Films like *The Falls* and *A Walk Through H* have nature as a background—countryside and also birds. Like many Europeans, I'm interested in and troubled by the destruction of animal and plant species. I'm also fascinated by the zoo as a metaphor, the Ark as a storehouse of animal life, as a catalog of all the species united in one place. As you know, I love catalogs and lists.

For a long time I thought about shooting a film around a zoo. As I was traveling the world promoting *The Draughtsman's Contract,* I told myself

I would visit the zoo in every city I passed through. I must have seen a dozen in Europe, several in the U.S. and one or two in Australia. The two that made the strongest impression on me were in Berlin and Rotterdam because they were located inside the city. You could see a hippopotamus standing in front of a tramway. It was this relationship between man, animal and object that appealed to me. In this respect, Berlin is an especially powerful symbol, because one might consider the city itself a zoo. For financial reasons, we finally did the filming in Rotterdam. One of the first images that struck me when I visited this zoo was the one-legged gorilla abandoned by its parents in childhood. This moved me and seemed to me to be very significant. I then sought a parallel between human and animal activity, nevertheless recognizing that the Western world tends to take a very anthropomorphic view of animals—which this movie also testifies to. Two other images made an impression on me: one, of a secretary bird, a black bird of African origin that I saw in a zoo in Sydney, that had swallowed broken glass from a Coca Cola bottle some visitor had dropped; the other image was, again, something I saw in Rotterdam—some enormous tigers pacing ceaselessly back and forth in a tiny, tiny cage. This appeared to me to be a very powerful image of imprisonment, and the human equivalent is represented by the film's two protagonists pacing the zoo.

These, then, are the images that stimulated my imagination. I should add the image I saw of a decomposing mouse on a documentary on the BBC. The space suddenly changed scale. The worms that were methodically devouring the corpse of the rodent looked like small white elephants. What struck me is that the decomposition itself appeared arranged, composed. At the end of the show, the man responsible for the program announced that his secret hope was one day to record the death and decay of an elephant. This seemed to me an absurd idea which no doubt will never materialize but which nevertheless seized my imagination.

Another source of inspiration was the idea of twins. I already had twins in *The Falls,* the Quaij brothers, who were very thin and very strange. There were also twins in *The Draughtsman's Contract.* It's related to the idea of one half seeking the other, of encountering oneself in a mirror. Once more, Borges's territory...

The film is structured around the eight evolutionary stages identified by Darwin. The idea that, for life to flourish, we need death, is not original, but it still deserves attention. The stages [of my film] were developed along three axes: the decomposition of dead animals, the liberation of animals, and extracts from scientific documentaries on the BBC. These are the parameters that shaped the ideas behind the script.

c : *How did these ideas give birth to a fictional narrative? Because, though the film is not as close to a police investigation as* The Draughtsman's Contract, *it contains the same large quantity of unfortunate mishaps, the first of which is a fatal accident. One of the Oswald brothers seeks the truth about the death of his wife.*
g : Because of my background, my fictional films contain documentary elements. In some ways one might describe *The Draughtsman's Contract* as a documentary account of the seven-day heatwave during the summer of 1694. And *Z.O.O.* a documentary about zoos and animals. After identifying the issues that preoccupied me and finding a structure [for them], the narrative flowed naturally. Among the characters, I had to have twins, I had to have a central character with one limb amputated. These three characters suggested an eternal triangle and before long they had to enter into a relationship with one another.

With the zoo as an ark, it is natural for animals and humans to have more intimate relations — hence the sexual activities that produce such extraordinary hybrids. This led me to refer to classical mythology, which envisioned the most somber of these hybrids: the sphinx, the centaur. The zoo thus begins to resemble a Greek pantheon. At the center is Juno (Andréa Ferréol), the goddess of the hearth and of fertility. The twins, obviously, are Castor and Pollux. And slowly but surely the pantheon fills up: Jupiter, the director of the zoo, the master of both animals and humans; Venus de Milo, who is a prostitute but also Eve, which ties her to Genesis; Diane the chaste hunter, under the guise of Caterina Bolnes; Mercury who is both a pimp and a messenger with his wings of silver; Neptune whom we see only twice and who feeds the fish. Some of these characters were invented in *A Walk Through H.* One of the characters in the latter film, Van Hoyten, who reappears in *Z.O.O.,* had a map archived in the Amsterdam zoo. This was already a reference to Holland. People have asked me why I chose this country as the location for my film. A bit like Kafka, who had never gone to America yet used it as the basis for his novel from reading travel brochures, I had an imaginary knowledge of Holland: a country where children put their finger in the dam to hold back the floods, where people speak "double dutch" talk. On a more elevated plane, I have always been interested in

Dutch painting of the 17th century and been impressed by the fact that the Low Countries were one of the first European republics. Furthermore, I am very fond of Vermeer and all that connects him with the development of optical instruments—a notion we toyed with in *The Draughtsman's Contract*. Vermeer worked in Delft around 1640, a time of intense interest in certain lenses that had just been discovered. With microscopes and telescopes, people could look at the world differently. The "camera obscura" became all the rage and it is almost certain that Vermeer used one. His paintings have a photographic quality yet at the same time there is something mysterious about the figures in them that goes beyond the purely objective.

Not long ago I read a text by Godard in which he described Vermeer as a master of light whose interests and concerns matched the true goals of cinema. He also spoke about Vermeer's ability to capture almost instantaneous motion, as demonstrated in the painting *The Milkmaid*. Thus, in a certain sense, Dutch painting is an early forerunner of cinema. I've since thought that the visual quality of film has something in common with Vermeer. We know very little about him. He painted between 26 and 28 paintings and, as the years went by, the list of his works grows smaller and smaller. We've discovered fakes and this idea of fakery is what led me to introduce the great forger Van Meegeren, who, at the end of WWII, sold so-called Vermeers that he'd painted himself to Goering, Goebbels and others. He had managed to convince the European art world that these were authentic works, which, today, seems unbelievable, since they seem very dissimilar to the real Vermeer: all the figures have a Greta Garbo look, with big eyes and long faces. He succeeded in fooling the establishment, which delights me because I love the interplay between reality and illusion, journalism and fiction. I admire people who know how to deceive their fellows. The other evening, someone asked me: "Greenaway, are you a forger?" It's up to him to answer. But, in a certain sense, all filmmakers are forgers since they are constantly manipulating fantasies, fabricating images to create a sense of illusion among the public.

c : *All artistic creation is made up of borrowed ideas or images. The difficulty is to know where ["borrowing" ends and] plagiarism begins.*
g : Precisely. I am currently in the process of putting together a major project on Dante, and it is astonishing to see how far the influences both on and from Dante's work extend. The cantos of Pound are clearly related to

Dante, just as Dante refers back to Virgil and Virgil refers back to Homer. Cinema is only 90 years old and I would like to relate it back to its prede-cessors, which, in my view, are the visual arts. I know that others see cinema as more closely related to theater and literature. But that's not how I see it. It is quite possible that in the coming decades cinema will either transform itself completely or disappear. A century of cinema, this is almost nothing in comparison with the history of iconography. But I, personally, would like to synthesize all of my artistic interests. I'm aware that I've been sav-agely criticized for this, that I've been reproached for referring [too closely] to literature and painting. There are clearly differences with *The Draughts-man's Contract.* For example, it was not, perhaps, without a bit of arrogance that I replaced my own drawings in *The Draughtsman's Contract* with Ver-meer's work. He was the film's organizer.

c : *Vermeer takes on more and more importance as the story progresses. The interiors evoke those of his canvases.*

G : One of the themes is death, or, if you will, the stagnation of the species and the mortal nature of the individual. The belief in Europe is that art is a way for humankind to attain immortality. We know, objectively, that this isn't true, but we are nevertheless driven to create. It is also true that the nameless people who populate Vermeer's canvases were all immortalized by him. I recall that with my chief camera-man, Sacha Vierny, I searched for a visual style, and we adopted the lighting in Vermeer that consists of light going from left to right, about a meter from the ground. That's where we decided pretty much systematically to place the lights. This may seem silly but it gave us a clear line of conduct and permitted us to achieve a fluid coherence.

c : *The association of the rhinoceros with Vermeer comes from Dali and* The Lace-Maker?

G : Actually I was thinking more of Longhi and his painting of the rhinoc-eros in Venice. The horn of the rhinoceros is an aphrodisiac and the animal in the film is connected with the scene in which the two men make love in the bed with Bewick.

c : *Isn't the best way to avoid plagiarizing to play openly with the references?*

G : In one scene we deliberately reproduced one of Vermeer's most famous canvases, *The Art of Painting.* In the beginning, the camera frames the back of the painter who is wearing a piece of clothing with black and white stripes, thus evoking the stripes of a zebra. Then the camera reveals the set which, in cinematographic terms, is an exact reproduction of the 17th century painting. If you look closely, you'll see the initials of Sacha Vierny on the wall, just as you can see those of Vermeer on his canvases. Another reference is [to] the *Woman in the Red Hat,* a small painting in Washington, D.C.'s National Gallery and which many experts consider to be a fake.

On the subject of imitation—this practice was most widespread during the baroque period when art contemplated itself and exaggerated this style to an extreme. I am reclaiming this tradition, although I place myself more in the camp of Poussin than that of the more flamboyant manifestations of the baroque, such as in Bavaria. Yet, in spite of its baroque concerns, the film has a classical structure: every action is pushed to its conclusion.

c :  *You open the film with the scene of a little girl with a dog. How did you get the idea for such an opening?*
g :  The characters in *The Draughtsman's Contract* were almost all unpleasant, with the exception of the child. This may not be very original, but there was a belief there in the goodness and innocence of children. We find the same thing in *Z.O.O.* The children in the first scene are walking a dog, which, even more so than the horse, is the most stunning conquest of man. From the very beginning of the film, I show a female dog with black and white fur who is in intimate relationship with the child and who refuses to enter the zoo. It's a warning that the place is dangerous.

c :  *Why is it a swan that provokes the accident?*
g :  I had already employed the symbol of the swan in *A Walk Through H.* The swan is often seen as an exterminating angel. In classical mythology, that is the disguise that Jupiter assumed when he came to Earth to seduce Leda and father Castor and Pollux. I should also point out that the name of Alba is Bewick; the Bewick swan is the most widely known in England. The license plates for her car reads N.I.D. [(which means nest in French)] and the accident takes place on Swan's Way, which is an allusion to Proust.

c :  *Other filmmakers—one thinks of Buñuel in* The Golden Age, *of Makavejev in several of his films, of Resnais in* Hiroshima Mon Amour*—have toyed with mixing journalism and fiction as you have done.*

G: As you know, my initial filmmaking experiences were at C.O.I., the Central Office of Information, where I made a series of propaganda films that showed the rest of the world how the British lived. During the eight years that I spent there, I was always fascinated by the interplay between fact and fiction. Even though I was obliged to make documentary films, the way in which I produced them brought them close to fictional narration. In any case, I believe that the line between the two realms is blurry. It is all a question of point of view, of how cinema is conceived, because in and of itself no subject matter is documentary. *The Falls,* my mammoth film of three and a half hours, poses this problem: it consists of fictional material presented in a documentary manner. According to the English school of filmmakers, documentary reality *is* reality. But we know that the pursuit of reality is a waste of time. Jane Austen today reads like science fiction.

C: *Obviously, fiction would tend to impose an order that opposes the anarchy of real life. Culture would be the bearer of an order that contrasts with the disorder found in nature. In fact, there is in nature itself a hidden symmetry.*

G: It is, in effect, a paradox. As I was filming *The Falls,* I was also putting together a documentary for television, *Act of God,* about people who have been struck by lightning. In this film, every fact was true, but seemed so bizarre, so unbelievable, that the viewers were led to believe that everything was made up. Similarly, certain events reported in the newspapers would provoke incredulous laughter if they were depicted in fiction.

C: *With the eight documentary extracts, you have evoked the different stages of Darwin's theory of evolution.*

G: Yes, I begin with the dawning of life and suggest that because of the introduction of oxygen in the atmosphere, life miraculously changed over a period of 250,000 years, which is one stage on the evolutionary scale. This rendered life unstoppable. Bacteria oxygenated the atmosphere and ultimately made possible the appearance of man; they also produced ozone layers that prevented ultra-violet rays from destroying organic matter. It appears that at the end of the 20th century, we are at a fundamental turning point a la 2001. Because of pollution, in a sort of about-face, we have reached a point in the cycle where the air, the ozone layer, are disturbed. The destruction of the Amazon rain forest, the lungs of the planet, is one of the most striking proofs. The off-stage voice of David Attenborough in the film poses the problem in these terms.

c : *At the beginning, the twins are separated, then the fiction [part of the story] brings them back together.*
g : I have always been fascinated by literature on twins. They are very competitive with one another, they battle for their own space, for other people's affection. They experience a profound attraction yet just as profound a repulsion for one another. I've encountered cases in which the twins didn't want to be known as such. The film contains three absurd propositions that aren't impossible but are highly improbable: 1) Siamese twins who don't want to be reunited; 2) a woman fascinated by zebras who dreams of being raped by them; and 3) a crippled woman who gives birth to twins, whose fathers are also twins. These are deliberately bizarre notions that we'll be trying to render believable using all the artifices of cinema.

c : *As in* The Draughtsman's Contract, *the architecture is very symmetrical and presents an interplay of correspondences.*
g : Everything is based on the number two and the lateral divide. We all have lateral divides, each of us is divided in two, even while walking. We have two cerebral hemispheres, etc. . . . In order to marry form and content, it is pointless to select arbitrary images created by the imagination. Therefore Vierny and I played with mirrors and all else that allowed us to suggest echoes and reflections.

c : *On the other hand, unlike in* The Draughtsman's Contract, *here there are lyrical, romantic traveling shots, such as of a botanical garden at night or on a river in a boat.*
g : It was about time that I started to move the camera, even if just to make some progress in my vision of the world! In fact, every time there is a slow traveling shot, it is at a moment of transition in the plot. Once again, there are eight significant movements of the camera, which are related to the eight stages in the development of the species.

c : *The character of Felipe Arc-en-ciel [i.e., Rainbow] is parallel to that of Alba Bewick. He is a legless cripple, etc. . . . *
g : If the two brothers hadn't been the fathers of the child, it would have been necessary to invent an adoptive father. Arc-en-ceil/Rainbow refers to that which God threw into the sky after the flood. The beginning of the

movie is saturated with water and rain. As soon as Arc-en-ciel/Rainbow arrives, Alba cries: "The rain has stopped, I've found my rainbow!" Later, the water is kept in check, it comes only through pipes.

The first time we see Venus de Milo, she is dressed in black with white piping, as she will be throughout the film, because her opposite, Alba, is dressed in white with black piping. Thus, when the women are united, they form a zebra. In one scene, Arc-en-ciel/Rainbow, who is standing near the zebra cage, proposes to Venus de Milo that they create together the perfect animal, a zebra-centaur. He is in white, like the angel Gabriel; she is in black and, once again, the zebra is present in the background.

c :   *The two twins are also complementary. One twin focuses on death, he studies the process of decomposition, while the other, a lover of life, frees the animals at night.*

g :   Absolutely correct. And we also tried to keep one always on the left side of the screen, the other on the right side. When they visit Alba, they always sit in the same seat and never cross the room. And when they're in bed with Alba, one of them says: "I always feel more comfortable on the left side." Oliver is a "hot" character, Oswald is "cold." That's why Sacha and I wanted to divide the space into two sections separated by a diagonal line. When Oliver is seated to the left, there is a warm and diffuse light around his face. I'm not sure we always managed to convey this but it was our goal. In any case, the further along one gets into the movie, the paler the cool colors become. The two brothers represent in a symbolic manner the human condition: the mind and the heart.

c :   *The two brothers' activities connect them to their dead wives. Oswald is fascinated by what happens to his wife's body after she dies and Oliver carries out his wife's wish to free the animals.*

g :   The entire movie is crammed with mirror images and parallels. Certain were elaborated during the filming itself and therefore gave us a better opportunity to make adjustments so that all the various parts would function. At the same time, we played with Jungian symbols such as keys. Venus de Milo never gets the key that would allow her to open all the locks, while Alba has hundreds of keys but no locks.

c :   *How did you choose which animals would represent the letters of the alphabet?*

g :   I looked at French, English, and Dutch children's books and tried to find animals that would be symbolic of these different cultures. For Z, the zebra was a natural choice. For other letters, the animal is different depending on the language. There were also constraints inherent in the Rotterdam zoo. For example, that zoo does not house a camel. Thus, we needed a different animal for the letter C.

c : *Several times during the film the image of the countryside where Alba lived is shown.*
g : That's to evoke the Garden of Eden, where, at some hypothetical time, man and the animals were in a state of innocence. It is also, perhaps, the place where they will die, to achieve symmetry, a balance.

c : *The film has an even more complex texture than* The Draughtsman's Contract. *It reminds one of the preceding film, but also of your documentaries and your experimental films.*
g : There are many parallels with *Draughtsman*. Once again, there is a conspiracy between two women, and, in a certain sense, they manipulate men. The conclusion is similar [in both films]: it rejects the hope of finding the meaning of life through "exoticism" or, as is the case in the present film, through evolution. In *Draughtsman,* there is a scene in which two men stroll down a very dark path. There's the same sort of scene here—in the laboratory. The same structure, too: a prologue, three acts, and an epilogue. But the film is less "easy" because *Draughtsman* flattered the British nostalgia for ancient dwellings and nature. Here I could have called upon their love of animals but I refused.

c : *There is also the same erotic component.*
g : Venus models her future erotic writings on the three key works of Anaïs Nin, Pauline Reage, and Aubrey Beardsley, *Venus Erotica, The Story of O,* and *Under the Hill*—which suggests that maybe the film itself could have been written by Venus de Milo. She is also given a text, *The Obscene Animal Enclosure,* that I published three years ago in *Time Out.* The story takes place during a period of time that I find fascinating, when people like Richard Burton were seeking the origins of the Nile and continually sending stuffed exotic animals back to London.

c : *You worked with a new set designer?*
g : For production reasons, I collaborated with a Dutchman, Ben van Os (which means "beef" in Dutch!), who had worked on only three films

before (one of which, *Naughty Boys,* was with Henry Alekan as chief cameraman). I plan to work with him again on my next film, which will be shot in Rome in April, because he has great feeling for baroque interiors. Half of the movie was shot in real settings and the other half with constructed sets, such as the hotel room.

c :  *Of course, you hooked back up with Michael Nyman for the music.*
g :  We also worked together on the number eight. Once the music was recorded, I'm not sure I always used it the way Michael Nyman intended. In general, the music in movies (even the fruits of my collaboration with Michael) is a mere adjunct, and I think this should be remedied. We are currently working on an opera project, *The Case of Webern and Others,* which is to be staged in the Hague in two years. Our producer, Kees Kasander, has already rented the opera. We wanted to reveal a relationship between living music and dead film, as cinema since 1929 has always been the prisoner of its own optical resources. We wanted to create a dialogue between the characters on the stage and the characters on the screen — a notion with which René Clair, I believe, had already experimented in the 1920's. Woody Allen, too, played with this idea in the *Purple Rose of the Cairo. The Case of Webern and Others* is, once again, the story of a conspiracy, this time, against musicians — a conspiracy that began with the murder of Webern in 1945 and concluded with John Lennon's murder in 1980.

c :  *The music in Z.O.O. is very somber.*
g :  I particularly admire the simultaneously slow and solemn funeral march in *The Draughtsman's Contract.* I asked [Michael] to use it as a starting point [for the music for this film] since it too deals with death and mourning and I didn't want the music to be too romantic or sentimental. I needed a very strong musical structure. Michael spent a month writing the music and then played it on the piano. Then he came to the Netherlands to present all his themes and we applied them throughout the entire film. But we were still a long way from using all the music he gave us.

c :  *How did your collaboration with Sacha Vierny go?*
g :  I found Sacha delicate and reserved, very conscientious and in perfect control of his craft. Of course, he has a great deal of experience and I was astonished by his infallible choice of lens [through which to shoot various scenes]. He is also patient and decisive.

c :  *How long did the filming take and what was the budget?*

G :  Seven and a half weeks and 650,000 pounds. But it was a movie—like others of this type—made more for love than for money. Many people worked on the pre-production portion of the film for almost nothing. Ben van Os, the set designer, had friends who were costume designers, painters, carpenters, etc. who helped us primarily out of the goodness of their hearts.

c :  *How did you come to choose Andréa Ferréol?*

G :  I wanted [to create] a human zoo as much as [I did] a zoo of animals. I therefore needed to gather together people of different cultures. For the character of Alba Bewick, I didn't want a British actress. In addition to Andréa Ferréol, I thought of Isabelle Huppert and Hannah Schygulla. For the twins, I wanted Ian Charleston who played in *Chariots of Fire* and Christopher Lambert, who, interestingly, looks like Ian. Andréa Ferréol is in synch with the quality of amorality in the film. I didn't want too much emotion in the characters and my primary directive was: "quicker and cooler." I wanted the dialogue to have a rhythm that would not necessarily be tied to a psychological state.

c :  *How was the selection of tunes on the record player made?*

G :  They're connected to my childhood. There was a television program, *Children's Hour,* that I used to watch. *The Teddy Bear's Picnic* and *An Elephant Never Forgets* I find very evocative, very strange, also, in the sexual metaphor they express—if you listen carefully to the words, that is. They are also the opposite of Vermeer who represents Great Art, the ultimate in the European attitude toward culture. But this popular music is no less splendid in my view. And it is the child who provides this music, whereas it is the adults who provide Vermeer.

c :  *And the snail comes to die on top of the record.*

G :  Yes, it never stops reappearing. It is a hermaphrodite that can satisfy its own sexual desires. I once raised snails and own a large collection of shells. I hunted snails at Norfolk, and at the age of 18 I read every book on the subject. There are hundreds of snail species but what distinguishes them is infinitesimal and recognized only by zoologists. I might add that if I eat them I get sick!

c : *Some people reproach you for cutting yourself off from the main public.*

G : I heard the same criticism for *The Draughtsman's Contract* which, today, appears simple. I suppose that it is a question of time. I also think that everyone has an elitist approach to his own art, a complex knowledge of it, whether he is a clockmaker or an engineer. And I think it's perfectly legitimate to make use of this knowledge because it enriches the overall texture of life. Vermeer had an extraordinary knowledge of the painting of his time, he collected Italian paintings, and his own canvases were filled with symbols and metaphors. Man has a complicated relationship with the world and I don't see why we shouldn't express that in movies. What is accepted in theater, in literature, in music, seems to be rejected [when it is expressed] on the screen.

c : *Are you expecting then to continue along the same path?*

G : Certainly. My next film, *The Belly of an Architect,* will be made in Rome with a budget of one million dollars and will focus on an architect, Kracklite, who lives in Chicago, the center of modern architecture. He goes to Rome to organize an exhibition of Etienne-Louis Boullee's work, the architect of the French Revolution whom some see as the source of the 20th century totalitarian period architecture in Germany (with Speer) and in Italy under Mussolini. What I like about Boullee is that nothing of his materialized: his work consisted of dreams on paper. The film will allow me to evoke the responsibility of architecture. But it also has a story line. During his trip to Rome, the architect [Kracklite] will conceive a child with his wife at the same time as he is dying of stomach cancer. Rome itself is the belly of Western culture. The ensemble may seem lugubrious but that's not the tone I want to give the film. Rome is a city which is continually reborn and which thumbs its nose at individuals. The whole time that the architect suffers and his child is born, Rome couldn't care less.

c : *In the newspaper that appears in Z.O.O. and which announces the car accident and the death of the two women, there is also an article about the death of an architect.*

G : Yes, that's my next film.

# Belly of An Architect: Peter Greenaway Interviewed

## DON RANVAUD/1987

PETER GREENAWAY'S NEW FILM, which opens in London in the autumn, relates the confrontation in Rome of two architects, one of whom is a historical figure, the other a fictional character. The historical figure is Etienne-Louis Boullée (1728–99), a visionary French architect whose latent influence can be detected in the neo-classical monumentality of the twentieth century Fascist style; and the fictional character is Stourley Kracklite (Brian Dennehy), a middle-aged American who, like Boullée, has received few commissions and who has come to Rome to organise a large-scale exhibition of his predecessor's work. As the film unfolds, Kracklite finds even this project slipping away from him, in part because of the machinations of his ruthlessly ambitious Italian collaborator Caspasian Speckler (Lambert Wilson), whom he suspects of having seduced his wife (Chloe Webb), in part because of an increasingly neurotic obsession with his physical condition and his fear that he might have been poisoned.

DON RANVAUD: *In a timely development for you, a new sense of the status of architects has developed in Britain since you started working on* The Belly of an Architect, *with debates in the press, lavish exhibitions at the Royal Academy on Foster, Rogers, and Stirling. Why did you choose this subject?*

From *Sight and Sound*, Summer 1987. Reprinted by permission.

PETER GREENAWAY:  It is a truism of this century that it's easily possible to avoid looking at painting or even reading literature, but it is extremely difficult to avoid dealing in some way with architecture. I like to think, if I may be so arrogant, that it's possible to compare the work of a filmmaker with that of an architect. We both have to be accountable to our backers and to the man in the street, but we also need to satisfy ourselves and our idea of culture. It would be too close to the bone, obviously, to make a film about a filmmaker, so at the back of my mind I have been searching for some time to find an appropriate parallel.

It was said about *The Draughtsman's Contract* that the filmmaker must have been trained as an architect. Completely untrue, but I *was* very interested in all that country house architectural side, which of course involves a certain amount of snobbism in the English approach to the country. I was fascinated with the business of photographing architecture, with the logistical problems of parallax, verticals, and horizontals; and given that all my filmmaking is based on grids, there had to be a connection somewhere.

*A mixture of personal and aesthetic considerations, then. Which is more important?*
They have equal status, although there is a lot that is very personal about this film, more so than the others, I think. But these two main reasons—a semiautobiographical comment on the relation between the architect/artist and the audience; the wish to use architecture and continue to play with what it's all about—lead me to the third key reason. I have long been attracted to that period between the end of the baroque and what may be described as the modern cultural revivalism of the nineteenth century: that transient period between the end of the Counter Reformation and the beginning of the French Revolution. Our contemporary world seems to reproduce those basic conflicts. Leonardo, Raphael, Michelangelo; then the second period around the French Revolution in the paintings of Poussin, and the third which is the shadow of Picasso on the one hand and Le Corbusier on the other. This is the groundwork, as it were, and one figure in this context—Boullée, hardly known outside architectural circles—seems to straddle them all.

I was particularly fascinated by the fact that Boullée drew and designed a lot, but got nothing built. That seemed to be so symptomatic of filmmaking. So many films exist only on paper. I have 15–20 scripts in various stages of development and have no doubt that most of them will not be made; if you multiply that by all the active filmmakers around the world, you would probably end with an enormous Tower of Babel or words of babble. I cannot help thinking that if Boullée's extraordinary drawings had been realised—the size and bulk of his conceptions would fit perfectly well in the twentieth century metropolis—they would have had a great impact on the history of architecture. What would have been phenomenally expensive to build at the time would have generated an atmosphere of daring and enterprise. Of course, the French Revolution produced great turmoil politically and socially but very few cultural artifacts. David's *Marat* is perhaps the only really strong cultural artifact from the period that everybody remembers.

*Boullée's times may represent upheavals in Europe, but Britain was relatively stable then, and although you are making films abroad now, you have been defined as the quintessentially English (not British) filmmaker.*
At the same time that Boullée is designing buildings, Jane Austen is writing novels: one is looking backward while the other is looking forward. I don't put the two together, for it wouldn't work, but I was sufficiently intrigued by this to write a short essay as though written by Jane Austen on the occasion of a visit to an exhibition of Boullée's work, describing it in her own language to try to define it for her contemporaries. There is a sense in which the past is reconsidered in all my movies. *The Draughtsman's Contract* is a prime example. I am interested in discovering how we approach history, both in terms of how we think people lived at a particular moment in time, and what were the cultural and aesthetic imperatives in the textures of society. Also, more simply, what is and what isn't true. What happens next, where is culture being pushed toward at any moment, and what are the consequences. I suppose this is more of an eighteenth century attitude than anything else.

*Boullée is very much the kind of character you might have invented had he not existed in reality. I must confess I thought at first you had invented him, until I remembered a passing tribute to him in the building of the disco hall at the end of Bertolucci's* Tragedy of a Ridiculous Man.
He is indeed the ideal man for Kracklite to invent.

*Are* you *not Kracklite, then?*
I'm sure a thesis could be organized to demonstrate a correlation. It might
fall down on closer examination, but the frustrations of a man dedicated
to setting up an enormous project and those of a filmmaker cannot be
entirely separated. Neither can the idea of the mafia circles around the art
world taking it over be completely foreign to movies . . . there is always a
fear that the film or the exhibition might be taken away from you, be used
by other people for other ends, leaving you only a footnote in a catalogue.
There are also all the domestic problems that accumulate while these situations are being played out.

*But the excuse, at least in the film, is that Kracklite is sick.*
That, I am happy to say, is not my problem as of this moment. But, well,
I don't know how personal I ought to be about it . . . both my parents died
from stomach cancer, my mother recently, my father some time ago. All
my films are about loss in some way—*A Zed & Two Noughts* about a very
serious loss, obviously—and although I do not feel extraordinarily emotional about it, somewhere in the back of my mind I want to explore the
consideration society gives to cancer as a disease; what we do about it,
what it means in our lives. The theme of loss goes right back to *A Walk
Through H,* a film made just after the death of my father. So much information gets lost when somebody dies. Whether that information is valuable
or not is another matter; it was valuable to me because I learned a lot from
my father's phenomenal knowledge of ornithology and ecology. A personal
aspect, if you will, lies deep within the film somewhere.

*The character of Boullée, as interpreted by Kracklite, gradually recedes in the
film. That has a curious and maybe slightly disturbing relation to what you just
said. Is Boullée ultimately only a McGuffin?*
As always, the man that was conceived in the script isn't perhaps quite
the same man that ended up in the film. I think that to begin with it was
much more of an ensemble piece, where the other characters like Kracklite's wife and her lover—the Italian side of the exhibition—were much
more vigorous. Brian Dennehy turned in such an extraordinary performance that the film has become more like a true biography. He is in almost
every frame. The other factor which helped to shape it in this way was
having to cut the film down to a reasonable length.

Boullée made some very foolish mistakes and his judgment was generally poor; his obsessions destroyed his common sense, and you feel he is
a victim of his own stupidity/obsession. While we seem to allow people
obsessions, I suppose we don't allow them stupidity; but there is a correlation there somewhere. He turns out to be a sad fall guy, in both his private
and his public life. I am still very close to the film and it's difficult to be
completely lucid about this. Boullée and Kracklite are riddled with the same
contradictions: both are aiming for perfection, and like Boullée, Kracklite
is unable to realise his projects. It's important that Kracklite should have
chosen someone like Boullée to celebrate in the manner he has envisaged.

Boullée did extraordinary drawings, but if the buildings don't exist,
have not suffered from the effects of weather or changes in fashion, are
not subject to criticism for being well or badly constructed, then a final
judgment cannot be made. There is nothing finite to criticise, which is
a useful position for someone who doesn't want to commit himself too
much. Basing one's life on visionary drawings rather than on actual buildings could perhaps be seen as a flaw in character, a fear of laying ideas
open to public inspection. This, again, might contain an autobiographical
element somewhere . . .

*I was struck by your use of the buildings in Rome, especially the fascist architec-*
*ture of Piazza Venezia.*
The seven buildings, the seven stages of Roman architecture I chose for
the film, are all tombs—memorials to the dead, reminders to the bereaved
of what went on before. Slam bang in the middle of Rome is this enormous
building for which I have always had great affection and which the Romans
variously call the "Wedding Cake" or the "Typewriter." It's a rather vulgar
building, more typical of French high *beaux arts* than Italian: gleaming
white marble that doesn't seem to fit in at all with its surroundings. It's
really extraordinarily ostentatious and grotesque when you think that
during the First World War it was adapted as a memorial to the unknown
soldier and widows were encouraged to take their gold wedding rings there
as donations to the war effort. Behind it, shadowing it almost, we find the
cradle of western civilisation: the Roman Forum.

Frankly, when I wrote the script, I never thought we would be allowed to
shoot inside the "Typewriter," an emblem of architecture at its worst and

most curious. But through the good offices of the architect Constantino Dardi and our art director, we managed to get in there. Then, as always happens, some remarkable associations came right out of the blue. For instance, the man who built it, Zucconi (we used his bust in lead in the film, incidentally), was a rather sad man who got into a lot of trouble for importing the marble from his home town. He was a typical local boy who "makes good in Rome," but like Kracklite, he committed suicide. I think someone was playing me along, but they said he did it by jumping off that very building.

*And Piazza della Liberta? No Italian would dare shoot there after Fellini's* Roma, *and few would take their cameras into the tourist trap of the Pantheon.*
You can put that down to the naive Englishman. I mean, can you imagine the reverse—a European director coming to London to set his scenes in Carnaby Street, Trafalgar Square, and the Tower of London? It makes you shudder, doesn't it?

*More so in that your previous style of filming seems to owe not a little to an almost Pasolinian concept of frontality. Characters are often flattened against the shapes that threaten constantly to devour them. Yet here, thanks to Boullée, and the rotund shape of Kracklite and his obsessions, the conceptual framework of the film is well and truly "rounded."*
Just as *The Draughtsman's Contract* was based on twelve drawings, and *A Zed & Two Noughts* on the eight Darwinian stages of evolution, *The Belly of an Architect* is based on the figure seven. The seven hills of Rome, of course, but also . . . I reckon there were seven clear influences that emanated out of Rome and affected the whole of western civilisation. The film is neverthe-less quite seamless now: it's difficult to find the joins, but there are still seven intended correlations being brought into the narrative. That rigidity helped me to structure the script, with Kracklite's emotional and psycho-logical deterioration acting as counterpoint to these ideas. Everything gets gradually tighter and tighter, so that when we come to "celebrate" Musso-linian architecture, we do so in a montage sequence that exists almost entirely on its own. Kracklite goes to the window, and there, triumphant, is this extraordinary Italian fascist apology of a building, reprised by a sec-ond section which mobilizes the same music in the Foro Italico, thus merging them, reappraising them together.

*Do you feel that architecture and philosophy are particularly close to each other?*
Yes, the architect needs to have knowledge and a strong awareness of
everything around him. One character says as much in the film: he needs
to know about literature, art and the price of bread, but on top of all that
he must, like Le Corbusier, be aware of the consequences of summing all
the ciphers together. Boullée was prone to making grand philosophical
statements, and some of these have happily found their way into the film.

*Brian Dennehy has the emotional power to sustain a character as the old
Hollywood actors used to, and this is something that is perhaps missing in your
other, colder films.*
You are right, and it's something I have to acknowledge. My concerns reit-
erate a wish to bring the aesthetics of painting to cinema, and this is not a
highly emotional endeavour. I am also a product of the post-Brechtian
alienation of the late '60s, not of *Kramer vs Kramer.* I like to approach the
cinema as much through the mind as through any emotional involvement, and that has been the colouring for films like *The Draughtsman's
Contract* and *A Zed & Two Noughts,* where all the actors were essentially
signposts to ideas. This is a new departure, and I can see now how I could
make it work for me. Since a lot of the ideas I dabble with concern a metaphorical use of cinema—which I still want to use as a language—I know
it can be difficult for people to grasp, and this is obviously a device which
could turn into a very useful tool.

   Having said that, I was very surprised by the performance that Brian
Dennehy gave, and I am grateful: if he helps to encourage people to engage
with the other parts of the film, then that is great. That sounds manipulative, but I don't mean it to be, and would certainly like to work with
Dennehy again. When he was presented with the script he didn't know
me from Adam, and why should he, small-time eccentric, esoteric Englishman that I am? He identified with so many aspects of the character that
he felt he simply had to take it on. With his tough guy image, many people will find his presence in an art film strange. But he comes over, I think,
as a guy who forces his personality intellectually as well as physically. Certainly his love for Boullée and all the anxieties he has are intellectual as
well as physical. Some of my obsessions are ludic and ephemeral, like the
photocopying obsession, and he has made them work.

*Why the obsession with photocopying?*

I could produce a long thesis, but . . . a lot of my films have been concerned with reproduction, and I mean both human and artistic. *The Belly of an Architect,* for those who want to look, has tried to explore all the different means by which art has reproduced the human form. So we have paintings, sculpture, photographs, and ultimately the current cloning idea of reproducing art on a treadmill. But it's all in quotes, as it were. There is a photocopier in every office, like sellotape, a kind of shorthand. Most people photocopy texts, here it's works of art. It's a way of being inquisitive, just running the whole gamut of art on a photocopier.

*What about new projects?*

A French critic referred to me as a gay pessimist, with gay used in its older sense, and talked of Cocteau in the same breath. Perhaps I am a pessimist, but there is a certain hedonism about it as well. It is not nihilistic. It's through the pessimism that one might get filled with desire to carry on and try to comprehend things. I'm afraid the scripts that are coming up are full of death and decay as well . . .

The one I have just been officially commissioned to do, by Tangram in Italy—though the script is virtually finished—is called *The Stairs* (*La Scala*), a working title that seems quite useful. Again it's about baroque, showmanship and the theatrical nature of art, which I want to associate with a general consideration of *trompe l'oeil* in the cinema, in painting, and also in human relations: how we play games with one another. The main character is an English painter of great ability who goes to Rome to paint a vast baroque ceiling. He gets involved with a production company preparing to make a film about an old Monteverdi opera called *The Marriage of Aeneas,* and becomes their art director. By the time the movie is shot, you discover that a conspiracy has been going on in usual Greenaway fashion. I want to use the story as a vehicle to explore tricks of culture, tricks of the cinema, tricks of painting.

# Two Things That Count: Sex and Death

## HARTMUT BUCHHOLZ AND
## UWE KUENZEL/1988

*Peter Greenaway, in recent years, British cinema has experienced an amazing revival. What do you think has caused this?*

GREENAWAY: In my view, during the seventies, there was an attempt everywhere to create something new in cinema. In western Germany, directors like Fassbinder and Schloendorf attempted it, whose films also made a political statement. In England, it was different—we didn't have that common aim. The revival of British cinema has its origin due more to financial grounds. Two people were responsible for this more than any others. One is Daniel Putman, who, quite obviously, had the Hollywood or American film as model. The other was Jeremy Isaacs who operated the private television station, Channel Four. Although they are two quite different individuals who followed completely different intentions, they share in common the thanks due for at least the first five years of the so-called "renaissance of British film."

But the films that came into existence during this time differed from each other completely. There was my *The Draughtsman's Contract* as well as Hugh Hudson's *Chariots of Fire* or Neil Jordan's *Mona Lisa* and *My Beautiful Launderette* by Stephen Frears—these films were totally different from each other. Thus, it appears that a very good requisition system came into being. While we don't have a great amount of money at our disposal—none of these films cost more than a million pounds (roughly, three and a half mil-

From *Zoom*, 16 November 1988. © 1988 by *Zoom*. Reprinted by permission. Translated from the German by Vernon Gras.

lion German marks)—yet this sum was fairly regularly put at our disposal by the moneylenders.

A notable difference between the present day British films and those created in the sixties is that they no longer have any relations to literature or theater. Perhaps this expresses an unfulfilled desire. Actually, we had lacked an independent cinema in Great Britain for a whole decade.

*How would you describe your own position in the contemporary film landscape of your country?*
Well, I find it a bit difficult to speak about or for British cinema in general. I certainly don't belong to the mainstream, that is to being one of its main representatives. I am more a footnote in the margins. I believe that British cinema has always looked toward America. In contrast, I have always preferred to look toward continental Europe: I like a cinema of ideas and my heroes were always the great French and Italian directors like Resnais, Godard, Antonioni, or Pasolini.

*Which of your colleagues in England are turning out "mainstream" movies? Stephen Frears, for example, or David Leland?*
Those two, certainly. They operate in the tradition of "realistic" or naturalistic British filming. Television has something to do with that and also John Grierson, the great pioneer in film documentaries who worked during and after the Second World War. It's a tradition still very much alive: films like *Letters to Brezhnev* or *My Beautiful Launderette* come out of it. My cinema, in contrast, brings with it a consciousness of a specific aesthetic that has been used by artists like Alain Resnais or Jean-Luc Godard. In England, that makes me an outsider from the start.

*Does that give you problems in financing your films?*
Basically, there are always problems in acquiring money for a film. But as long as we hold down our budgets, relatively speaking (measured against the immense sums that American films cost), I believe we will be able to continue making our films. Notwithstanding, conflicts will naturally arise. I wish to create very personal films which simultaneously means that they then can't become big box-office hits. So we have to be certain from the beginning that we can also distribute the films worldwide. Accordingly, advance sales have to be negotiated—television contracts, video contracts.

When the films do play in the movie houses later and make some money—
so much the better, but that is more often the exception. Even though
Greenaway films have over time developed a substantial viewing public
and the number of people that wish to see my films has continually
increased, I won't ever have gigantic successes.

*In an interview, you said that cinema is too important to hand over to the story-
tellers.*
That statement has brought me grief, especially in England. It appears
that English and, even more so, American films are perfect in recounting
a straight line narrative. They achieve it through the use of suspense and
asking the viewers to identify with the main characters. That accounts for
all those psychological dramas.

I think that the greatest art works—and I exclude those found in film—
have had far greater means at their disposal. Only cinema narrows its
concern down to its content, that is to its story. It should, instead, concern
itself with its form, its structure. Artistically, film is a very rich medium;
it has so many indescribable possibilities, and hardly anyone uses them.
It seems to me that the majority of directors make their films with only
one eye open and their arms tied behind them. The capability of film to
become an extraordinary and astonishing medium is completely ignored.
One should not tell stories as straight line narratives. There are so many
other possibilities, and film would only enrich them. Most of the time, I
am utterly bored in the cinema; I think that most films are poorly made.

*But your films also tell stories.*
That's true. But for me the stories are only the hook on which to hang
one's hat. After a very short time, one understands the plot of my films;
it isn't that important to me what happens, only how it happens. Most
films insult the viewers whereas I believe the public is far smarter and receptive than many producers and directors give them credit for.

*Could one describe your kind of filmmaking as essayistic?*
Yes, one could say that for certain. My films are certainly theoretical deliberations: *The Draughtsman's Contract* considers a draughtsman and his
contract giver, but also English country living and landscape architecture.

*A Zed and Two Noughts* attempts a theoretical observation on the relation between humans and animals—in the concrete example of the zoo, but beyond that in mythology, literature, the erotic, etc., etc. The setting is a whole field of possible aspects to engender contemplation. *The Belly of an Architect* is an essay on the responsibility of contemporary architects to history and their relations with it. My recent film, *Drowning By Numbers,* is ultimately a bit more difficult to describe. Probably two more years will have to go by before I can explain in simple words what theoretical deliberations lurked behind it . . .

But I must add that all these concerns shouldn't be taken as dry or academic and tangential discussions. They have to be entertaining above all. If my films didn't entertain, they would have failed right from the beginning. I make the greatest effort to be entertaining in every area: in the discovery of images, in the composition of the picture, in fleshing out the characters in form and content, in the utilizing of music, in the work on the sound track. And I take great pains with wordplay, with a certain kind of humour. Very important to me is a certain kind of irony, for which the Americans have a noticeable lack of appreciation . . .

*Does that mean that the Americans don't understand you?*
Well, *The Draughtsman's Contract* did very well on the east coast of the U.S. It did less well on the westcoast. But after being shown in certain venues—in film clubs and the Museum of Modern Art in New York—it has become part of the repertoire. I believe right now as we speak that it's gleaming out somewhere on American television.

What few people know: I had made about thirty films before I created *The Draughtsman's Contract* in 1982 as major evening entertainment. Those films were in all formats and forms—narrative films, experimental films, very short ones of only three minutes, but also quite long ones. For example, *The Falls,* my favorite, which lasts three and a half hours.

*How do you feel about your main producer, Channel Four, constantly interrupting the transmission of your films on television with advertisements?*
They aren't interrupted that often. There are only two commercials, one after the first twenty minutes and then one again twenty minutes before the end. That's just how things are and ultimately that is where the money

comes from. I can't change that. Besides, they don't do that bad a job: in *The Draughtsman's Contract,* for example, the advertising slots were for fruit and for English country houses.

*In your films, numbers or alphabetical letters reoccur frequently as structuring principles of the whole work.*
There are many reasons for that. When I started to make films, there was a tendency everywhere—especially in Europe but also in some parts of the U.S.—a sort of agreement among the experimental directors to create films without any action. And somehow that seemed to me to be a self contradiction. It seemed very important that every artistic form occurring temporally has a beginning, middle, and end—no matter how reduced these might be. Despite this, all these experiments implemented this repudiation. But if you have no story to tell, you need to come up with another method by which to organize the material. Many sought to do it with music—but that seemed to me to borrow the structure of a different medium.

So I searched as it were for universal structures—like the alphabet. Or mathematical equations or perhaps number series. It wasn't meant to be taken seriously, it was more like pleasurable play or a crossword puzzle. But I soon realized that the outcome was a dry, static kind of cinema so I started to tell stories again. Stories, thus, found their way back into the structures. And this is still my basic position—I seek an abstract foundation for the whole film. For example, in *Drowning By Numbers,* one counts from one to a hundred. But there are also inner structures. I use two skeletons—one builds the core and the other creates the outer form. If from one point of view all this sounds trivial—well, it most certainly is. But naturally I incorporate another idea: I believe that we have very narrow margins to express our "free will." Ostensibly, we are capable of making decisions, but these decisions are really very limited. The film should exhibit this by having its story as inner skeleton embed itself in an outer one which reveals this limitation—something like fate, though I don't like the word. Our lives, after all, are circumscribed by conditions over which we have no control—our surroundings, the climate, our personal contingent relationships. For me, the mathematical structures signify those boundaries that constrain us.

*Do you mean that your films are scientific constructions? And how important are other disciplines or art forms to you? You, yourself, did begin as a painter.*
That's true. And I still believe that painting is the most essential of the visual arts. I still prize the direct relationship that the painter has to his tools. He can ignore the pressure to have to cooperate with hordes of others that making films of necessity mandates. Two areas of filmmaking please me the most: Nurturing the original idea and writing out the script and then the time spent in the cutting room when the film once more becomes my possession and I don't have to share it with several hundred other people.

But back to your question. Let's take architecture as an example. I really don't know much about architecture and, though I once studied painting, I also don't know that much about painting. But to film *The Belly of an Architect* I thought it important to understand what an architect does and what technical and psychological problems arise in his profession. And in *A Zed and Two Noughts* I had to mull over the connection between the theories of Darwin and the traditional creation story. It became a general treatment of the everyday creation story and evolution. And the suspicion the film transmits is simply that the Genesis story is untrue and has no plausible answers to those questions which concern us: Why are we here? Where do humans come from? But natural science, quite obviously, has also not provided us with right answers. The fact that Darwin simply relegated Adam and Eve to the realm of mythology did little to answer our fundamental questions. From the beginning of the nineteenth century until the end of World War II people were convinced that science would answer all our questions and solve all our problems. And now, at the end of the twentieth century, we clearly know that that's not the case.

*At the end of* The Belly of an Architect, *the main character, Stourly Kracklite, dies of cancer. Does this kind of disease signify a similar disease in modern arts and sciences?*
Before AIDS made its appearance, cancer was simply the worst disease. That has changed; a moral sickness has been added to the physical. In *Belly of an Architect,* sickness has a very real as well as symbolic function. Somebody said that Rome had been the oldest civilisation in the world,

and now comes a man from America, from Chicago (the equivalent to Rome in the modern world), and he dies in this ancient city from a modern disease. Surrounding him are all these statues showing their age by their stage of decay. All these ideas fuse together into only one possible end for Kracklite.

*Most of your heroes die at the end of your films — for example, the draughtsman, Neville, in* The Draughtsman's Contract *and the twins in* A Zed and Two Noughts.

Many people say that my films deal only with death. I think they are correct. But there are only two things which really count: one is sex and the other is death. What else is important? One can disguise sex as romance or love but it's always about sexual desire. And death is the phenomenon that none of us can escape. All of western literature deals with nothing else, as does painting and also film. Naturally, cinema often embellishes these themes into unreality. Death in American films only has to do with tomato ketchup most of the time. It becomes something conventional. But everyone of us has been touched by death in some form already — perhaps we have lost a relative or friend. Or we became sick and had to deal with it directly. Personally, I have not experienced a great tragedy yet in my life — and so I use these themes in my films as a kind of catharsis to prepare myself for the inevitable.

But there are still other reasons: All great western drama ends as a rule either in death or in marriage. Tolstoy's *War and Peace* ends with a marriage; there are people that actually affirm that marriage is a small death. Or take Shakespeare: All of his dramas end with the death of the hero. In general, my approach to cinema is very classical: my films often base themselves on the structures of grand opera: Prologue, three acts, and an epilogue. Or on the nineteenth century idea that drama needs three acts. *The Belly of an Architect* has an extremely classical design, above all in its temporal dimensions. In addition, the film was made in Rome and everything in Rome is ultimately classic. . . . Just think of twentieth century painting that has been erected on these foundations.

In *Belly of an Architect* one could even claim that the cameraman worked like an architect. He saw only two dimensional planes or facades in front of him as if they were drawings. Only at the end with Kracklite's death does all this break down. The settings then suddenly take on corners and edges; the picture compositions take on diagonals.

*There are very complex camera movements in this film. For example, the take that ends on Kracklite as he sits in front of the Pantheon. Is that very difficult to arrange?*
It took us one half-day to prepare that shot. The actual take took only five minutes. But it's these preparations that give me the most pleasure.

*In general, how do you prepare your sets? Do you start with sketches, are the pictures already on paper before you begin to shoot?*
Sometimes, I make sketches, sometimes not. There are reasons why I don't always do so. Such drawings restrict me, at least in those cases where the cameraman and set designers have taken them as the basis for how a scene should look. When we then start to shoot, there's little possibility left to improvise. Sometimes, however, such preparations can be very beneficial—above all when they can be used to explain to participants what specifically I want. But I never use a regular filmscript. Of course, I do use a book which holds the dialogue and sometimes the script goes so far as to describe the smell of the flowers which are just then on view—even though this can't be substantiated on film. But that may suggest to the actors a bit of how I imagine the scene. Still, in my filmscript there are never specific directions like where exactly the camera should be placed. That decision is made on location, on the actual, concrete site, and I usually need a half hour to deliberate how I want to structure the scene depending on what the situation calls for. In that, I differ from someone like Hitchcock, who had sketched out in minute detail each set ahead of time. It was claimed of Hitchcock that he had already finished the film once he completed his sketches and someone else could have directed his films as well as he. That would bore me because any spontaneity or charm of the ephemeral which can excite, disappears completely.

*What do you do with your material in the cutting room? In contrast to Hitchcock, you should still be able to influence the outcome a great deal.*
That I do. My first experience in the film industry was as an editor. I spent eight years at COI (Britain's Central Office of Information). It's a kind of

propaganda bureau for the British Foreign Office; it sends out documentary films over the whole world. Hearing the word, propaganda, one shouldn't think of Goebbels—what the COI made was rather harmless. Its films inform you how many sheepdogs are in South Wales or how many Japanese restaurants exist in Ipwich. I had a well paying job there while simultaneously it was a kind of initiation into filmmaking, especially into how through montage alone one can manipulate pictures. That was very important to me. My first films focused more than anything else on what could be done by assembling images differently. All this made me happy and even *The Draughtsman's Contract* still focuses on what one can achieve through editing, with how image and music, for example, can relate to each other.

*In* Zed and Two Noughts *there is a shot of a newspaper in which the reader learns that Stourley Kracklite, the protagonist of* Belly of an Architect, *has died. Did you have that film in preparation already? And, in general, do inner relationships exist between your films?*
I can answer that in a variety of ways. Each of these films should be able to stand alone; each has its own unity. Naturally, there is always a point, and that too is a European tradition, even in literature—just think back to Balzac and his *Comedie humaines*—where all these works meet. Minor characters appear in one book who become main characters in another. And this has also something to do with Jean Renoir's idea, when he said that artists basically have only one idea which they spend the rest of their lives trying to forget. To which he added deprecatingly, that one idea was more than enough for just one life. And so it is with me—my idea naturally continues from film to film. My total work should then also be viewed as an overall unity.

*Could you tell us something about future projects?*
At the moment I'm working on a television series for Channel Four that is based on Dante's "Inferno" from *The Divine Comedy*. Overall, that should take about three years. Probably in November, I will begin a new film with the title *The Cook, the Thief, His Wife, and Her Lover*. That is going to be a very dark story about restaurants, sex, revenge, and death. It will be a kind of Jacobin comedy, a revenge-tragedy really. It will have four main roles but also another 26 speaking roles, which comes to quite a big cast. And

for the first time, I shall try to shoot the whole film in studio — so from the beginning to end it's going to be completely artificial. And its central point of departure is food coupled to the idea that everything is eatable. Absolutely everything! That, of course, has a long tradition: Think back on *La grande bouffe*. The structure this time will be having ten menus over ten days.

# I Am the Cook:
# A Conversation with Peter Greenaway

ANDREAS KILB/1989

THE SCENE: A SUBURB in west London, a grey public main street, then a rear courtyard; inside, a short distance, cosy and grotesque, a red door that leads into a long building, half barracks, half sorcerer's habitation: Greenaway's production office. Greenaway shows up in a colorful quilted coat by Jean Paul Gaultier in which he looks like a noble clochard. Inside there is no heating unit, only an antique hot air blower giving off more noise than heat; the room, in keeping with the coat, is an illustrious chaos, a spiritual lumber room. In the room adjacent, Greenaway says, he edited and spliced some of his short films. I imagine him at his cutting table dressed in coat and scarf with motto underneath: Artist with Headcold. Outside, the storm rages, a rainy November afternoon in which the wind moans, the answering machine beeps, and Greenaway, the Oracle, speaks.

DIE ZEIT: *If one compares the five major films you have produced since 1982 with the usual films of the eighties, your films stand apart. They fit into no category, neither auteur nor genre film. Many critics, especially the English, it seems to me, have a difficult time with your art of speculating with images, with your masks and intellectual games.*

---

From *Die Zeit*, 24 November 1989. Reprinted by permission of *Die Zeit* and the author. Translated from the German by Vernon Gras.

GREENAWAY:  That comes from most people having an American film model in their heads which is nothing but a total illusionary masturbatory massage. I am simply not interested in that. I never wanted to become a mainstream director like, say, Stephen Frears, that hypocrite and opportunist, who airs out his political orientation for a few films and then dismisses it in order to film something as trashy as *Dangerous Liaison.*

*Oh. Actually, I thought...*
... Trash, terrible trash. I am only interested in works of art that are self aware of their artificiality. It's impossible for cinema to be a window to the world, a slice of life. Everything that I do is self-reflexive in this sense, filled with signs which emphasize the artificiality of the action, like the curtains in *The Cook, the Thief, His Wife, and Her Lover* which are drawn apart at the beginning of the film and closed again at film's end. My working methods and my cultural background are more Apollonian, rational—and have little to do with conventional narrative cinema. My stories are very classic and simply constructed; first, a prologue, then three acts, and an epilogue. For I truly believe that what matters is not *what* happens, but *how* it happens. In that I feel myself contemporary with the South American novelists, and also Calvino, Kundera, etc. The constellation is quite simple: the cook, the thief, his wife, and her lover. The eternal triangle, and the fourth who keeps it in motion.

*And the classical Greenaway themes: sex, violence, and death. The film begins with a rather shocking scene, in which a man is forced to eat shit...*
... and not just shit, but dog shit, which if you read Dante and the Old Testament is one of the deepest humiliations possible for humans. That all my films circle around the theme of death has over time become a cliché in film criticism. Basically, the entire European culture treats only two subjects, sexuality and death. Since the sixties, one can talk quite openly about sex, and it's being widely discussed, but death is still the true challenge, the deepest tabu, the worst obscenity. And there is a great need to talk about this tabued theme. Cannibalism, murder, rape, necrophilia, a need for provocation. One of my heroes is Pasolini, a provocateur par excellence. If we wish to have a living cinema, a cinema that deals with really important things rather than being some popcorn entertainment or ivory tower observation then we must have the courage to articulate and

show these things. Unfortunately, that doesn't happen very often. The last film of this kind that I have seen was David Lynch's *Blue Velvet,* and before that Bertolucci's *Last Tango in Paris.* If one says a film is about death that's equivalent to saying that it's about life. The positive and the negative go hand in hand.

*Just like the order and chaos in your films.* The Cook, The Thief, His Wife And Her Lover *shows disintegration, decay, devouring, and being devoured, the setting of the film is a kind of hell, but in this hell there are many secret arrangements, underground structures.*
If you have viewed my earlier films, then you know that I always seek out visual arrangements, classifications that lie on the surface of things. The alphabet in *A Zed and Two Noughts.* Newton's law of gravity in *The Belly of an Architect,* the number order in *Drowning By Numbers.* Telling a story is something completely arbitrary and to escape this arbitrariness, I invent systems, universal structures that organize this contingency. In *The Cook, the Thief . . .* the organizing principle is color. That owes something to my beginnings as a painter. Painting in the twentieth century has succeeded in divorcing colors from their objects. Because of that, both colors and objects become freely useable and open to choice. One can't regress to get behind this event. That's why I attempt to make colors into a constitutive part of the structure rather than using it as a decorative afterthought. When the characters in the film change color, it relates to the fact that in some sense we are all chameleons. We adapt to our changing surroundings; we converse with different people in different ways just as I speak differently with you than I do with my children . . .

*. . . only the cook doesn't change color, he remains white, he doesn't eat, he doesn't kill, he stays outside the action.*
Obviously, I am the cook. The cook is the director. He arranges the menu, the seating order of the guests; he gives refuge to the lovers; he prepares the repast of the lover's body. The cook is a perfectionist and rationalist, a portrait of myself. I'm surprised that you didn't come to that conclusion yourself.

*But that's why I'm asking. When I try to bring together all the many levels, citations and allusions in your films, I get dizzy. Shakespeare, Brecht, Buñuel,*

*Surrealism, "the Theater of Cruelty," "the Theater of Blood," the English Baroque Drama, the metaphor of the digestive tract, color theory, Dante, Boccaccio, the Old and New Testaments . . . don't you have to prepare yourself with a tremendous amount of research for each film?*

No, absolutely not. I make almost no preparations at all. Only sometimes, when it's necessary, do I research a few facts. I have a fairly wide academic background concerning European culture, especially painting. But in many areas, I'm self-taught: I'm certain that the great artists, for example Rembrandt, were not especially knowledgeable. In a sense, one must stay limited in order to create a great work of art. *The Draughtsman's Contract* revolves precisely around this question: One can't make a drawing if one knows too much. After *The Belly of an Architect,* everyone thought I was a great authority in the field of architecture. I was invited to America to lecture on fascistic architecture, whereas I had very little knowledge to contribute on that topic.

*Back to Shakespeare. As your next project, I have read that you wish to film* The Tempest.

It's more a variation on that play, to which I have given the working title *Prospero's Books.* Do you remember the books placed in the boat to accompany Prospero in exile from the mainland? The film revolves around these books, who wrote them, what they are about. It's a kind of detective work. I imagine that Prospero builds up an enormous library out of his books, books that generate new books on this magic island. And Prospero will be the magus of all these books. The film takes place in 1611, at a time when medieval knowledge, alchemy and cabbala, began to mix with modern empiricism. All that I will stuff into the film. But the special interest that many people have about the film derives from Sir John Gielgud playing the main role, and not just that one but all the others, too. *The Tempest* is Shakespeare's last play, and as Gielgud is 84, it will probably be his last film. Thus, another play concerning old age, immortality, and death.

*Isn't it becoming more difficult to produce such films in Europe?*

Not for me. *The Cook, the Thief, His Wife, and Her Lover* has been a big box office hit in England and France. Even the English critics seem finally to have noticed what I'm about. But even if the film had disappeared immediately from the movie houses, I would have had the next one already

financed. I don't want to become wealthy or world renowned; I just want
to continue to work as a craftsman and artist. I really can't hope for more
than that and for the next three years this hope is fulfilled. What happens
after that, I don't know.

*Last year, you stated that the cinema would be disappearing shortly, that after
a hundred years its life span would be over. We are coming ever closer to this
moment. Do you wish perhaps to change your mind?*
I believe that the end has already arrived. Cinema is dying, in a social as
well as in a technical sense. All the power, imagination, and scientific
interest of the epoch has turned away from cinema. Into television, for
example. For me, this is not especially upsetting because I consider television a far more resourceful and intelligent medium than cinema. *The Cook,
the Thief, His Wife, and Her Lover* is still a purely cinematic film which is
why I chose the wide-screen format. But I won't weep any tears over the
demise of cinema. The 2000 years of western painting interest me more
than the last hundred years of film. The TV picture is not only cheaper
to create, it can carry many more levels of meaning than the expensive,
unwieldy cinema picture. There will always be images, regardless how
they're created. If all the cinema houses closed tomorrow, many many
people would lose their jobs, you, for example...

*If you can make TV films, I can become a TV critic. Perhaps in the extravagant,
encyclopedic lust for images found in your films hides a cathartic effect, the last
climax of an exhausted form of representation, the last banquet, the last orgy
before the end, before death. At the end of* The Cook, The Thief... *the crime
boss has the body of his intellectual rival set before him as a meal. Is that a political allegory, a social comment on Margaret Thatcher's England?*
On one hand, the situation in England during the last years did anger
me a great deal—this vulgar, unimaginative, anti-intellectual Thatcher
government and its social pendant, the new Yuppie middle-class that dec-
orates itself with art works and cultural achievements—so that some of
my fury did surface again in the film. On the other hand, I view the whole
matter from a cosmic perspective. I don't take a position. I believe that
there are no more positions to take, no certainties, no facts. Many people
find this confusing about my films; they say I am hiding out behind irony.
But from a cosmic viewpoint, it is eternally unimportant whether one lives

or not. That is Shakespeare's "to be or not to be." I came to the decision not to commit suicide; I decided to live, so I have to draw consequences from that, have an opinion . . . but when observed from the perspective of cosmic irony, it makes shit little difference. Now I've forgotten your question. Why don't you begin again.

# Greenaway by the Numbers

## JOEL SIEGEL/1990

The number seven is responsible for the colours of the rainbow and the seven primary metals, the seven primary planets and the seven dwarfs. It is also responsible for the seven days of the week, the seven seas, the seven sleepers, the seven ages of man, the seven wonders of the world, the seven hills of Rome and the seven orifices of the body. An important number.
—Peter Greenaway, *Fear of Drowning by Numbers*

NOTHING BEATS A TOUCH of scandal to draw overdue attention to an artist's work. Without the controversies fueled by *Lolita, Last Tango in Paris,* and the Corcoran Gallery's maladroit censors, would the public have ever been aware of Vladimir Nabokov's novels, Bernardo Bertolucci's films, or Robert Mapplethorpe's photographs? A moment of notoriety is often all that's needed to transform a cult figure into a household name.

This week, British filmmaker Peter Greenaway's moment has come with the release of *The Cook, the Thief, His Wife & Her Lover,* an astonishing movie that violates several taboos. Last Labor Day weekend, at the picture's Telluride Film Festival American premiere, some audience members walked out after the shocking opening scene. National Public Radio's *Weekend Edition* viewed the film and canceled its appointment to interview the 47-year-old writer-director.

In February, the Motion Picture Association of America (MPAA) honored the film with an X rating, not for any particular sequence but because of

From *City Paper,* 6 April 1990. Reprinted by permission.

its "overall tone." Appeal testimonies by prominent artists, critics, and cultural figures failed to persuade the MPAA to reverse its rating. In addition to stigmatizing a film with pornographic connotations, the X rating severely diminishes its commercial potential. Many theater chains, cable networks, and videostores refuse to offer X movies; most newspapers and television and radio stations reject advertising for such pictures. After the movie lost its bid for an R rating, Miramax Films, Greenaway's U.S. distributor, decided to release the picture uncut and unrated.

*CTW&L,* which opens Friday at the Cineplex Odeon Avalon and Dupont Circle theaters, is a film destined to be hotly debated for years to come. Initially, its sensational elements—coprophilia and cannibalism—will attract morbidly curious viewers, but its stunning visual style, dark irony, and corrosive moral vision will be remembered long after the controversies dim.

*CTW&L* establishes Greenaway as the first great filmmaker of the '90s, and will surely draw retrospective attention to his accomplished, rarely shown works of the past decade. In the next seven weeks, all of Greenaway's theatrical features will be screened in Washington: *Drowning by Numbers, The Belly of an Architect, A Zed & Two Noughts,* and *The Draughtsman's Contract.* In addition, two new Greenaway videos, *TV Dante* (co-directed by Tom Phillips) and *Les Drowned in the Seine,* will be presented as part of FilmFest DC.

Peter Greenaway has arrived.

A soft-spoken, courteous, rather donnish Englishman, Greenaway is an unlikely figure to inspire such controversy. At first glance, one might take him to be a college librarian or an art historian. Unostentatiously clad in dark blue pants and a subtly patterned blue shirt with matching pullover, this slim, voluble man doesn't look like the instigator of flamboyant, trailblazing cinematic visions. Greenaway's sedate clothing and composed manner camouflage swirling undercurrents of artistic audacity.

Having seen his early experimental feature *The Falls, The Draughtsman's Contract,* and *A Zed & Two Noughts,* and read several of his screenplays and articles, I snapped at the opportunity to interview Greenaway when he visited Washington in late February to promote *CTW&L.* His densely layered movies and writings reflect perhaps the most learned, wide-ranging intelligence that has yet expressed itself on film. Several days before our scheduled meeting, I learned that, preoccupied by plans for the imminent shoot of a new film, Greenaway had asked to bow out of the D.C. leg of his American visit. Cineplex Odeon's local publicity department and Miramax Films prevailed upon him to keep the commitment, but his reported reluctance left me apprehensive.

The moment we are introduced, in a sunny corner of the Park Hyatt's Melrose restaurant, Greenaway sets me at ease. Although he had awakened in New York at 5:30 a.m. to keep our 9:30 appointment, he seems rested and enthusiastic. For the next two hours, his conversation—or monologue, to be more precise, broken only by pauses to check that his sometimes over-whelmed auditor is keeping pace—will touch on politics, sex, literature, science, history, theater, aesthetic theory, ancient through contemporary painting, and, of course, filmmaking. Greenaway's thought processes are remarkable; his perspective is, at once, minutely specific and sweepingly synthetic, moving with quicksilver logic from a minuscule detail of an individual painting to the symbolic connotations of colors in various cultures.

Very quickly, I begin pondering whether he constructs organizational grids to serve the narratives of his movies or uses narrative as a pretext to explore and integrate an assortment of topics and ideas. The alphabet, the Greek gods, and an evolutionary bestiary are motifs that shape *A Zed & Two Noughts*. The story of *Drowning by Numbers* is framed by the chronological encoding of the numerals 1 to 100.

I begin by asking him to identify the germ from which *CTW&L* evolved. His reply reveals that he has sneakily contrived a structure for our conversation. "I can identify several areas of interest which were whirling around in my imagination for three or four years, maybe even longer," he announces, whereupon he proceeds to outline the seven principal concerns that, collectively, fused to create *CTW&L*.

At times, he strays from his list to inquire about the cultural climate of Washington or ask if the spread of AIDS is as pervasive here as in New York. But he always manages to return to the seven pillars of *CTW&L*.

## Jacobean Revenge Tragedy

"I've always been fascinated with the Jacobeans; I suppose they were the postmodernists of their time. Essentially, they came after Shakespeare and had a sense that the great days of drama, as they saw them, were over, behind them. They obviously took tremendous risks. At that time, roughly between 1590 and 1630, the Roman poet and dramatist Seneca was just being translated all over northern Europe. The plays of Seneca took things to extreme limits. The cutting off of limbs before the public—quite sensational stuff.

"I think there was a sort of *fin de siecle* sensibility in Jacobean theater. For me, these plays contain this peculiar mixture of violence and melancholia. You know the famous Durer painting of *Melancholia* which Ben Jonson apparently used to keep an engraving of on his wall? I am excited by this particular period because these people were approaching considerably sensitive, taboo areas.

"I suppose the main template for *CTW&L* would be John Ford's *'Tis Pity She's a Whore*. It deals with the difficult subject of incest, admittedly between consenting adults—brother and sister. It examines the phenomenon as the church, the state, and probably as the man in the street would see it. It's interesting that ultimately what's perhaps most shocking about that play isn't so much the sexual union but Ford's ideas about patrimony and birthright, because all of these things in a patriarchal society were dangerous and upset the status quo very much with regard to inheritance.

"Towards the end of *'Tis Pity,* when most of the drama has been completed, the brother, having stabbed his sister and ripped out her heart, comes down the stairwell holding this bloodied heart on a dagger. A lot of people have believed the play to be unproducible because of this melodramatic event. But what I like about it is that the idea of the bleeding heart on the dagger is a deeply religious, deeply Christian symbol—the Sacred Heart. It figures very much in all that Rosicrucian activity that was happening in the 17th century, and ultimately it's become a sort of Masonic symbol. So you have a very, very strong symbolic image, but here is the playwright trying to make it real, an actuality.

"Jacobean theater is such a strong and exciting area which has been with me ever since I initially studied it at school, and I find it has some very contemporary applications. This might sound a bit manipulative, but we are now in Great Britain at the end of the last years of the second Elizabethan age. The Jacobeans were working in the final years of the first Elizabethan age. Then, as now, there was a very rapidly growing new middle-class which ultimately ends in the factionism of the civil wars. You could say that their sexual scourge was syphilis; our new sexual scourge, of course, is AIDS. There's a way in which they were looking over their shoulders at the great Elizabethan age—the age of Drake and the new navigation to the West and so on. There's a way now that in Britain we're still looking back at the ideals of the old colonial empire. These are cultural and historical connections that one can make—maybe a little fanciful, maybe a little pushed—but it gives me an area I can play with.

"As for the Jacobeans' peculiar mixture of violence and melancholia, there's a way in which you can now open newspapers anywhere in the Western world, certainly in England, and they seem to be full of domestic violence, worthy of *Timon of Athens* and *The Winter's Tale*, worthy of Lady Macbeth. It has this grand, almost dynastic quality. *CTW&L* is, after all, the most typical soap-opera drama on one level—a sexual quarrel, arranging of trysting places, adultery starting very much as lust but obviously developing into something better. The quarrel between Mr. and Mrs. Macbeth would be the same in some senses, but Shakespeare endows it with general views of the human condition and makes the characters very heroic. I wanted to try to do something extravagant like that."

*The Cook, the Thief, His Wife & Her Lover* opens with one of the most unnerving sequences in screen history, a stomach-turning yet weirdly compassionate scene rooted in Jacobean theater. A curtain draws back to disclose the rear parking lot of an elegant French restaurant—delivery trucks, garbage, and foraging dogs. In strides the thief—gangster Albert Spica (Michael Gambon, the psoriasis-tormented novelist of Dennis Potter's BBC miniseries *The Singing Detective*)—and his seven henchmen. Spica assaults a hapless neighborhood restaurateur who has failed to pay protection money, and exacts a vomitous punishment. He and his cronies strip their victim, force-feed him dog turds, smear him with canine excrement, and urinate on him. Then Spica, followed by his goons, goes off to dine.

A Park Hyatt waiter takes Greenaway's order—an archetypal English breakfast of toast, marmalade, and Earl Grey tea. I ask about the composition of the dog shit, hoping to exhaust the topic before his meal arrives.

"It was chocolate pudding. The actor found it very tasty. What was strange is that the dogs in the scene loved it too, so there was this image of dogs eating their own shit all the time. Occasionally, a dog would actually shit, so we had to work out very carefully which turds were real and which were fake. It was quite cold, and they were all steaming slightly."

Our waiter returns with a steaming pot of tea, and we retreat to more savory topics. Seventy percent of *CTW&L* unfolds during nine consecutive evening meals at "Le Hollandais," the lavish restaurant run by Richard, a perfectionist French cook (Richard Bohringer). Each night, the bullying, profane Spica, his gang, and his passive wife Georgina (Helen Mirren) dine there, in front of Frans Hals' mural painting *Banquet of the Officers of the St. George Civic Guard Company* (1614). Spica and his dishonor guard are dwarfed and ironically counterpointed by this famous canvas.

At the first dinner, Georgina is drawn to Michael (Alan Howard), a silent, unassuming diner—the antithesis of her vociferous husband—sitting alone at a nearby table, reading a book and eating. The attraction is mutual, and between courses, they meet and make love in the restaurant lavatory. This impulsive, clandestine encounter develops into a series of evening assignations, conducted, under the cook's watchful protection, in various niches of the restaurant's enormous kitchen where provisions are stored. So confident is Spica of his control over Georgina that he's oblivious to her nightly infidelity.

When the truth finally crashes in on Spica, he threatens to kill Michael and destroy the restaurant. The lovers, naked and shivering in the meat locker where Richard has hidden them for protection, overhear these threats and seek sanctuary. The cook arranges to transport them to a hideaway, a vast book depository. Spica finds them and avenges himself, but Georgina, driven mad by grief, persuades the cook to assist her in a grisly retaliation—the film's last supper and final scene.

Spica, who regards dining out as a sign of social respectability, is a swine's banquet of vileness—vulgar, insensitive, abusive, obscene, sadistic, and murderous. If audiences consider him the most reprehensible character they have ever witnessed, Greenaway will have achieved the second of his purposes.

### Evil

"Another area is this desire, almost as a technical exercise, to invent a character who is wholly evil. We can think of hundreds of characters who are manifestations of evil in some ways. Laurence Olivier playing Richard III, for example, or J.R. Ewing in *Dallas*. Richard III has a way with evil that makes it somehow attractive. Milton in *Paradise Lost* creates a Satan who is so fascinating that you can't take your eyes off him.

"What I wanted to do was to take it a step further and make evil so thorough that there was no way you could love to hate this man, Albert Spica, there was nothing amusing, nothing affectionate, nothing redemptive, no way that you could forgive him. To do that I had to invent not a Machiavellian creature, but a thoroughly mediocre man. Television, before Christmas when *CTW&L* opened all over Europe, was full of images of Noriega and Ceausescu. A lot of people, especially the Germans, very quickly made cross-references to my character, Spica.

"So a manifestation of evil—not a particularly original idea—was something I've been wanting to do for some time. Spica does have some sense of wit; there's a way that he sometimes grabs hold of some peculiar statistic, like the fact that a cow drinks its weight twice a week in water, but then he immediately goes off on some horrible scatological trip. He covers everything around him with his slime and his excrement in the most appalling, horrible way. He's an anti-Semite, fascist, sexist, racist pig who bullies women and tortures children. He has no redeeming features whatsoever.

"I don't know whether you know it or not, but in England we have a gutter press. On the front page, it castigates unusual sexual activity of public figures, but then on Page 3 you have a photograph of a four-breasted 14-year-old girl—a horrible double standard. This personifies for me the character of Spica—scatological, slurring over everything, prying into people's affairs, a fascistic, totalitarian bully."

Evil in Greenaway's cinema is especially unsettling because it is presented in a context of intense visual beauty. In all of his work, richly colored, meticulously composed, painterly images are juxtaposed with merciless content—cancer, self mutilation, decay. He began shooting short, experimental films in the mid-'60s; between 1966 and 1979, he made 16 movies ranging in length from four to 45 minutes. These shorts received limited distribution, mostly in Europe, at film festivals and museums. In 1980, he made what remains his favorite picture, *The Falls,* a three-hour extravaganza, backed by the British Film Institute's Production Board, with a highly eccentric premise. On the assumption that some readers won't believe my summary, I will reproduce a synopsis from the BFI's *Monthly Film Bulletin:*

> 92 surnames, all with the prefix "Fall," from Falla to Fallwaste, have been picked out of the latest edition of the Standard Dictionary of the Violent Unknown Event (VUE) and the case histories of these randomly chosen subjects, "a cross-section of people with very varied biographies," offer an

admittedly partial history of the world but the only practicable history there is. *The Falls* gives an alphabetical account (in English, though there are 92 versions) of each of these subjects. Some of them belong to the same family; others cannot be discussed because their "case" is *sub pudice*; a few are in fact "fictional" characters and therefore inadmissible. These short biographies (hardly longer than five minutes at most and sometimes much shorter) vary in their detail, narrative style and content; some use voice-over exclusively, others include interviews, still others are enacted, but most impart information as to the subject's language (no two subjects speak the same language), the effect of the VUE on the subject, and the subject's view on the question of the responsibility of birds.

A work of mind-boggling intricacy and wit, *The Falls* has not been widely exhibited—it was screened here at the Washington Project for the Arts and the American Film Institute—but it demonstrated Greenaway's film-making ability so boldly that he was able to obtain backing from the BFI and British television's adventurous Channel 4 for a somewhat more conventional feature, *The Draughtsman's Contract* (1982). Set in Wiltshire in 1694, it's about an opportunistic young draughtsman hired by Mrs. Herbert, the wife of a well-landed gentleman, to produce 12 drawings of her absent husband's estate. In exchange for his work, he is to receive the hospitality of his hostess' home and table, as well as her sexual favors. Each drawing contains an item of the missing husband's clothing. When the landowner's corpse is found floating in the estate's moat, the draughtsman, afraid that he will be accused of the murder, blackmails his hostess and departs. He makes the mistake of returning to Wiltshire to draw a 13th view of the estate, only to face a gruesome comeuppance. *The Draughtsman's Contract* was shown in American art theaters, and though it received a mixed critical reception, it was Greenaway's first (and, until *CTW&L*, his last) wide exposure to American moviegoers.

U.S. distributors deemed his next feature, *A Zed & Two Noughts* (1985), too arcane for U.S. audiences. But Washington moviegoers were quite receptive when the picture was shown at the Hirshhorn, and it has subsequently enjoyed several successful revivals at the Biograph. *Zed* is about twin zoologists who are devastated when a swan crashes through the windshield of the car driven by their wives, killing both women. The twins, overcome by grief, embark upon a study of animal evolution and decay. Laced with allusions to Darwin, Vermeer, Nin, Muybridge, and Disney, *Zed*

blends the linear narrative of the director's previous feature with the taxo-
nomical obsessions of *The Falls*. It's a movie that bewilders some viewers
and mesmerizes others. A man I met while we were exercising our dogs
told me it was the greatest film he had ever seen, and one of my editors
claims it's the closest any movie has ever come to photographing the
inside of his mind. Greenaway is more modest in his evaluation. "It's a
very ambitious film, but very deeply flawed in some ways, especially in
the acting. It's a film I have great affection for. There were such big issues
I was trying to grapple with there, and so it remains one of my favorites."

Greenaway's next two features, *The Belly of an Architect* (1986) and
*Drowning by Numbers* (1988), have not been released in the U.S. because of
distributor snafus. "My distribution has been so bad over here, I'm almost
led to believe it's my fault. My films are often about conspiracy theory, and
sometimes I believe there's a terrifying conspiracy going on against my
work. I can only hope that maybe, if *CTW&L* takes off, that might oil
some wheels and open some doors so that those two films will be seen."
Hemdale ("that wretched company") purchased the American rights to
*Belly,* then decided it was "too obscure and too difficult for American tastes."
*Drowning* was sold to another company, which went bankrupt after making the first of three scheduled payments, leaving the picture in limbo.

I've recently seen a video of *Belly* and find it to be the least effective of
Greenaway's features. Brian Dennehy stars as Stourley Kracklite, a corpu-
lent, middle-aged Chicago architect who travels with his young wife to
Rome for the planning and opening of an exhibition devoted to the work
of Etienne-Louis Boullee, a visionary 18th-century French architect. The
trip proves to be a disaster—his neglected, pregnant wife leaves him for a
younger lover; his double-dealing backers wrest control of the exhibition
from him; his obsession with Boullee prevents him from acknowledging
and treating symptoms of stomach cancer. Although filled with handsome
views of Rome, the film is excruciatingly attenuated. Greenaway's screenplay keeps restating its themes with such relentlessness that, after two
hours, one's patience is exhausted. *Belly* lacks the subtexts and subordinate
structures that give the filmmaker's other films such engrossing resonance.

*Drowning,* though, is one of his finest efforts, as layered with intriguing
conceits and patterns as *Zed*. Three women, all named Cissie Colpitts (a
name introduced in *The Falls*), decide, for various reasons, to drown their
husbands. They persuade Madgett, the local coroner, to record the deaths

as accidents, an appeal he accepts in hope of receiving sexual favors from the Cissies. The women, however, have other plans for Madgett. Although the subject is grim, Greenaway's tone is playful, fleshed out with an anatomy of English games, bawdy Ortonesque repartee, and elaborate numerological devices. *CTW&L* is probably a better introduction to Greenaway—its dramatic narrative, characters, and meanings are more direct—but people who respond to it will want to take on the greater challenge posed by *Drowning,* which also premieres this week and will be repeated later in the month.

*Drowning's* plot and style are determined by mathematics. Not only are the numbers 1 through 100 encoded into the images—sometimes prominently, sometimes very obliquely—but other counts are interwoven. The film begins with a little girl jumping rope and counting 100 stars, speaking so rapidly that very few can be identified. Her names for these heavenly bodies comprise a catechism of Greenaway enthusiasms—painters, composers, cartoonists, movies (Kesnais' *Muriel*), and characters from his own past and forthcoming films (Kracklite and Spica). (This litany corresponds to *Lolita's* list of students in the nymphet's Ramsdale home room class, an opportunity for Nabokov to engage in homages, puns, literary allusions, and other name games.) Greenaway confides to me that the bedroom inhabited by coroner Madgett is furnished with 100 objects starting with the letter "M." Madgett's compulsive, lovestruck 13-year-old son, Smut, has 100 objects beginning with "S" in *his* room. The filmmaker admits that the only people who will spot these alphabetical puns are himself and his art department, but clearly he relishes them. He has written a book, *Fear of Drowning by Numbers*—printed with facing pages in English and French—which contains a staggering 100-part exegesis of the thematic and formal grids of *Drowning.* The longer one watches this eccentric black comedy, the more one risks being sucked down into a vortex of letters and numbers.

## Color-Coding

"I've always had a peculiar distrust for narrative. If you look at *The Draughtsman's Contract,* it's full of little narratives, people telling stories to one another. I always felt that narrative came a bit too easy for me. I've always wanted to have other structures to help propel the film along—the alphabet count in *Zed* and the numbers in *Drowning.*

"In *CTW&L,* I wanted to do something different, so I used color-coding. I had previously expressed my enthusiasm for Isaac Newton in *Belly.* He's mainly known for developing theories of gravity—the apple on the head—but what people don't always remember is that, long before Paul Klee, he evolved lots of interesting color theories. He was the first person, supposedly, in modern history to split down the colors of the rainbow, the spectrum. I was looking for a universal system, like the alphabet or the decimal count, and decided to use the seven colors of the spectrum to organize and structure the material of the movie.

"If you think about the spectrum, there's violet/indigo in there, which is a bit too subtle to spend a lot of time building a set around. I almost hate to admit to this concession, because, as a filmmaker who started out in minimalism, there's a way in which once you take a subject, you'd better stick with it—no compromises allowed. Philip Glass, Steve Reich, Rauschenberg, Stella—you name it. But I tried to work in a way that would still validate my interest in this color problem.

"Also, in 20th-century painting, color has become disassociated from content. A young man goes up to Picasso and asks, 'Why are you painting the sky green?' and Picasso says, 'Because I've run out of blue paint.' A facetious reply, but you can already see that somehow the divorce between color and content has been legitimized. Which means that color has been liberated and can be used for all sorts of exciting purposes. But on the other hand, it can become merely an embellishment, something cute, the decorator's art. In France they have a profession called 'coloriste' and that's all they do; they just select the colors for any particular circumstances—interiors, flats, whatever.

"I wanted to work out a system that would allow color to come back dominantly and somehow organize the material. So we have this six-part color system. Blue for the car park; green for the kitchen; red for the restaurant; white for the toilet; yellow for the hospital; and a golden hue for the book depository. Of course, we have certain, fairly fixed ideas about color symbolism. Blue obviously means cold; green, in the West, means safety. I believe the color for safety in China is supposed to be white, not green—green means danger.

"There are obvious reasons why the cold exterior car park is blue-coded—it's the nether region, furthest away from the center of the whirlpool of action. The greens of the kitchen, apart from indicating safety, suggest the color of nature—therefore it's healing and embracing, the color of chlorophyll. Green represents the mythological jungle where all the food comes from. Red means violence, carnivorousness, blood—the dining room where the center of violence happens.

"The uses of white in the toilet are a bit different. It's the place where the lovers fuck for the first time—it's heaven. Also, all colors combine to make white, so it's the focal point. A strange retinal activity happens in the lavatory scenes which I hadn't counted on. I deliberately wanted to use almost overexposed white. When the white comes on-screen, the audience is lit up—the light reflects back into the theater. You can see who's sitting beside you, so it's self-reflexive. This is sort of a crib from *Last Year at Marienbad,* which, although it was shot in black and white, had an extraordinary effect on the retina. Resnais and his cinematographer, Sacha Vierny, who has worked with me on three features, made some of the shots incredibly dark, and then cut to images that were extremely white, so there was this sensation of blinking. When you come out of the restaurant corridor and go into the lavatory, something like that happens which is quite interesting. I want to explore that in the future.

"Color-coding helps to achieve something that I want my cinema to do all the time—to tell people that they are only watching a film. This is an artifice, a construct. Let's not get completely taken away by manipulative involvement. Use your mind as well as your emotional reactions. The artificiality of the color schemes reminds audiences of this, which is taken even further when Georgina walks from the restaurant to the lavatory and her costume changes color from red to white."

It feels strange to be talking about *CTW&L*'s crimson, shadowy, and ornate Le Hollandais while seated in a corner of the Park Hyatt's understated Melrose restaurant—neutral beige/pink marble walls, massive light-flooded windows, and austere decor.

The contrast reminds me of one of the many charges often laid against Greenaway by his detractors. (He is hardly a critics' darling. Gary Arnold's *Washington Post* review of *Draughtsman's* is a classic of hostile incomprehension, and the *New York Times*' Vincent Canby wrote that he would rather watch 24 hours of weather reports than sit through *Zed.*) Some reviewers, especially those with political agendas, dismiss Greenaway as a disengaged aesthete, only interested in exploring hermetically personal worlds while ignoring our own. He's considered an elitist, whose works are overly weighted with learned references to classical art.

In self-defense, Greenaway argues that his cultural allusions are not affectations. They serve an important function, he feels, in the development of an introspective approach to filmmaking.

"I want to try and create a cinema which obviously is real in the sense that it reproduces the world, but does have, I hope, this very sophisticated multilayering of metaphorical meaning. It's dangerous, of course, because you don't know quite how much you are managing to pass over to the audience. As you probably know, I'm often accused of intellectual exhibitionism and all forms of elitism. Although I can understand this point of view, it's a rather wasted argument because, if we regard areas of information as being elite and therefore somehow not usable, it means our center-ground of activity becomes very, very impoverished. It grows less and less and less and less until there are almost taboo subjects which we aren't even allowed to consider because somebody puts his hand up and says, 'I'm sorry but you can't use that—it's too elite.' I think we should use all sorts of information of every description.

"I suspect also that people tend to regard me as an elitist because my information has very much to do with European culture and history. If I knew a lot about racing cars, for example, it would be all right. If I knew a lot about the sexual habits of the king penguin, that would probably be all right, too. My films are based in an area where a lot of people feel social and educational inferiority, but I want to use this material. It enriches the environment, it enriches the fabric of the film, and it enriches our enjoyment of everything. This knowledge is there to be shared, and that's why my films are very much based on 2,000 years of European culture. Mainly pictorial culture but also, in the case of Jacobean theater, on literary culture, too."

Moviegoers who know something about art history *do* have a special advantage in viewing Greenaway's pictures. His academic interests and accomplishments as a graphic artist—recently, he has had exhibitions of his work in America, Canada, France, and Japan—are reflected in every ravishing frame of his movies. In *CTW&L*'s lushly pictorial restaurant scenes, he recreates and elaborates upon a rather specialized but fascinating painting tradition.

## Table Painting

"This might strike people as being very academic, but for a long time I've been interested in what could be described as a genre of table painting.

*CTW&L* offers an amazing opportunity for me to play games with table paintings. Apart from a few kinetic paintings, paintings don't really move. Because I can move both the actors and the camera, I wanted to add some of my ideas to this genre.

"It's been going on for 2,000 years, ever since the House of Mysteries in Pompeii, 60 A.D.—there's a table painting in that. I suppose the biggest set of table paintings have to do with the Last Supper. There's a way in which even there you can see the problems. When people sit at a table— even a round table—they are usually seated on all four sides. The painter has to find a viewpoint where you can satisfactorily position everybody without masking anyone. There are certain solutions and devices like staggering figures. Of course, Leonardo Da Vinci completely avoided the issue by putting people on three sides of the table and leaving one side empty.

"It's interesting to see the different ways painters have coped with this problem. Tintoretto uses very dramatic diagonals, spacing the characters out carefully. It's also interesting in terms of religious iconography how Christ always has to be in the middle, Judas Iscariot has to be as far away as possible, St. Peter has to sit on the left-hand side—there's a series of conventions. In the late Renaissance, there were magnificent table paintings by Veronese, great wall screeds like *The Marriage Feast at Cana,* magnificent opulent pieces, all very exhibitionist.

"After that come all the Dutch painters, and I have to digress somewhat because this is a particular enthusiasm of mine that relates to *CTW&L.* The golden age of Dutch painting is contemporary with Jacobean revenge tragedy and is also distinguished by the same mixture of the received and real worlds. Take a Vermeer painting of a woman pouring milk. It's real milk, it's a real woman, and she stands in a real space—this is all recognizable—but the painting also carries a very heavy overload of metaphorical meaning. For me this particular period of painting was very satisfactory because I suspect that painters were probably closest to their audience then, much more than they were before or have ever been afterwards. Most painting prior to that time had been supported by the elitist aristocracy or the church, and afterwards the artist or painter as an individual created his own gap between himself and his audience. Dutch painting is very bourgeois. It celebrates domesticity, rich accouterments and all of that. When you see a painting of a lady with a lute and two strings are missing, it means that she has had two miscarriages. If there are three pomegranates on a table and two are open, it means she's got two children. Today we've lost those connections, but there's a lot of evidence to support that the Dutch audience grasped all of this, just as the Jacobeans understood Ford's stabbed heart in *'Tis Pity.*

"Table painting touches on the genre of still life. The French always call it *nature morte*—dead nature, but in Anglo-Saxon culture it's still life. Still life dead nature—interesting cultural exchange there. Table paintings became virtuoso pieces, so that a young apprentice painter, in order to prove his worth, could show his ability to handle a group of portraits and also handle still life. Frans Hals' painting, which hangs on the restaurant wall in *CTW&L,* is also part of this genre, but it's there for other reasons, too. Van Gogh's *Potato Eaters,* even David Hockney, have played with this genre and I wanted to play with it, too.

"I mentioned my interest in table painting to Thames and Hudson in London and there's some possibility that I might be able to make a book about it sometime, copiously illustrated—setting up the problems and examining how people found solutions to them. It's not an original thesis on my part. There have been confined studies about Netherlandish paint-ing—a subgenre about people sitting at tables counting money—and then there are people like Caravaggio and Georges de la Tour who have people sitting at table gambling. You have to display the cards so there's a conspiracy between the viewer and certain people in the painting, and certain other people who don't know what's going on. If you could turn a tabletop up, it would almost be the aspect ratio of wide-screen cinema."

Greenaway's painterly preoccupations—his notion of the film frame as animated canvas—clearly distinguish his movies from those of other highly regarded younger British directors. Though competent stylists, Stephen Frears (*My Beautiful Laundrette, Sammy and Rosie Get Laid*), Mike Leigh (*High Hopes*), and Richard Eyre (*The Ploughman's Lunch*) are less con-cerned with form than content—specifically, the political, economic, and social climate of present-day England. Their films confront these issues head-on, exploiting neo-realist devices—location shooting, fragmented plots—to involve viewers in "real-life" situations.

The extreme formalism of Greenaway's movies tends to distract audi-ences from perceiving his sometimes oblique but nevertheless demonstrable populist sympathies. More than any of his previous pictures, *CTW&L* man-ifests the director's hitherto unstressed political and social convictions.

Although these beliefs are still not bluntly enunciated, Greenaway's latest movie reflects his loathing for contemporary British materialistic values. In *CTW&L*, the current state of his homeland is very much on the filmmaker's mind.

## Margaret Thatcher's England

"*CTW&L* is a passionate and angry dissertation for me on the rich, vulgarian, Philistine, anti-intellectual stance of the present cultural situation in Great Britain, supported by that wretched woman who is raping the country, destroying the welfare state, the health system, mucking up the educational system, and creating havoc everywhere. But still she remains in there. There's a lull in the film where Spica says to the lover who is reading, 'Does this book make money?' That line really sums up this theme. In England now there seems to be only one currency, as indeed one might say about the whole capitalist world.

"So that's the third area—this concern for making, I hope, not just a parochial drama which is relative only to our little country in world events. That's what Stephen Frears does. I wanted to say something that would have much more *largess* about it, that could be appreciated and understood by someone in Sydney or Tierra del Fuego or Addis Ababa."

An hour of conversation with Greenaway, leapfrogging from Jacobean theater to art history to contemporary politics, leaves me dazed. I suddenly recall a sentence from my review of *Zed*: "Greenaway's film really made me feel dumb, a virtually unprecedented response to moviegoing in this dim decade." He seems to sense that his dissertations have overwhelmed me, and downshifts to focus on a more conventional movie-director topic—acting.

"In the past, I've had an aversion not only to using actors but to the general concern for psychodrama. Most of dominant cinema is sort of illustrated novels. Distributors and producers find themselves a novel and convert it. The practice continues. You might say that 70 percent of films, maybe more, begin their lives in a totally different art form. If a work is conceived in words, in literary terms, then why try to transform it? It's the old business of putting brick wallpaper up in plastic caravans [house trailers]—we just can't let go of it, can we?

"My early roots in non-narrative cinema led me to regard actors with great suspicion—the whole ethical dissatisfaction of one man playing

another man's part. A lot of filmmakers in Europe and certainly in North
America attempting to make non-narrative cinema have not only thrown
out the star system, but with it the concept of the actor as actor, so you
have experiments like Robert Bresson using only amateurs and so on.

"In the final stages of the rewrite of *CTW&L,* I finally had to give the
characters names—Albert, Georgina, Michael, and Richard—which I
selected to correspond to the actors I had in mind for those roles. Richard
Bohringer right down the line was the man I wanted for the cook and he
accepted it. He's appeared in *Diva* and *Subway,* a very still and quiet actor,
very Gallic. Obviously, I needed a French cook; I wasn't going to go for
some English actor with a cod accent. Albert was supposed to be Albert
Finney, but he turned it down flat. Michael, the lover, was meant to be
Michael Gambon, and Georgina was going to be Georgina Hale, whom
you might remember from Ken Russell's films. When I asked Michael
Gambon to read the script, he became fascinated by Albert instead, and
asked to play him."

Georgina Hale was unavailable, so Greenaway signed Vanessa Redgrave
to play the wife, but later she had to withdraw because of theatrical com-
mitments and her son's automobile accident in Rome. He then approached
Helen Mirren, whom he calls "the high priestess of stage and screen erotica." Mirren had been invited to play Isabella Rossellini's role in *Blue
Velvet*—Greenaway's favorite American film of the past few years—but
she had turned it down. She eagerly accepted Greenaway's offer to redeem
herself for "chickening out" of David Lynch's picture. Greenaway says,
"Looking back, I can't imagine anyone else in the part, but that's always
the way, isn't it?"

Appearing in a Greenaway movie poses great risks for performers. He
works almost entirely in long and medium shots; actors and actresses are
denied the indulgence of carefully lighted, star-making close-ups so common in the Hollywood system. Greenaway's cast, like models in a
life-drawing class, are forced to offer up their bodies along with their artistic souls. Nude scenes are usually included, but not the flatteringly erotic
nudity typical of most commercial filmmaking. To Greenaway's cool,
zoologist eye, human beings are merely another species of mammal; his
performers are naked rather than nude, not revealed but exposed. He
shows us the vulnerability and imminent decay of flesh. He emphasizes
the puckered ripeness of female bodies, and takes perverse pleasure in cast-

ing, stripping, and even mocking pudgy actors. (In *Drowning,* one of the Cissies observes her portly son-in-law sprawled naked on a bed and casually inquires, "Do all fat men have little penises?") No filmmaker has ever displayed his performers so clinically.

## Corporeality

"Most cinema deals with characters as personalities. I want to do that, of course, but I also want to stress the physical bodily functions—that the characters exist in the physical world. When they walk across a room, the floorboards creak under their feet. They throw heavy shadows; they create voids and solids in space in a very sculptural sense.

"I wanted to choreograph the people. This derives from my experience of using Brian Dennehy in *Belly,* this rather fat, somewhat white-fleshed, maggoty figure, moving in fixed and very beautiful architectural spaces— the relationship of the soft body to the hard core. The sets in *CTW&L* were all built so that we could organize space to our architectural satisfaction. Apart from the concern with bodies in space, those bodies bleed, copulate, fart, shit, pee—the bodily functions are very much emphasized, which relates back to Jacobean drama. Apart from Sergio Leone having Clint Eastwood spit in a bucket, and Resnais showing John Gielgud on the toilet in *Providence,* you don't see that kind of physicality on-screen very often. Can you imagine Paul Newman shitting in a movie?"

Greenaway's question is clearly rhetorical. Even if Newman, Streep, Redford, or Streisand were willing to have their excretory functions immortalized, who would finance such a production? Who, in fact, puts up the money for Greenaway's movies, which, in content and style, defy all the conventions of commercial cinema?

"I have this amazing producer, a man called Kees Kasander, the protege of the director of the Rotterdam Film Festival. I had *The Falls* and *The Draughtsman's Contract* in that festival, where I met this character. We've done three films together so far, and he's offered me a contract to make three more. He's a whiz at finding money from all sorts of strange places. This time, Channel 4, which partially funded four of my previous features, looked at the script and said, 'No—we can't be seen to be supporting *this.*' Ironically, Channel 4 has accepted *CTW&L* for theatrical distribution in England, and is engaged in haggling and bidding against the BBC for the television rights. But there was no British production money involved. A pretty healthy chunk of the money came from French and Dutch production companies. *CTW&L* only cost about £1 million. Everybody involved made a living wage, but everything, as they say so rightly, is right up there on the screen—no stretch limousines and fat cigars. We prepared extremely carefully, so we needed only eight weeks' shooting. By keeping the prices down, we hold on to everything; there's nobody dictating what costumes we can use or forbidding us to use four-letter words."

Three or four American companies expressed interest in the film when it was shown at the Telluride and Venice festivals. Eventually, Miramax purchased the American rights and, after a long silence, began making plans to release it. The picture was doing extremely well in Europe, breaking box-office records in France and Germany. Concerned about the film's content and two-hour running time, Miramax suggested that the director consider making cuts. Greenaway was grateful for the chance to trim several minutes he had been unable to excise in the rush to complete *CTW&L* in time for Venice. But he was not eager to do any additional cutting.

"Miramax somehow thought the film was too long for American attention spans, and were worried about receiving an X rating. We negotiated. I was certainly pressured by the Dutch backers, who put up most of the money and desperately wanted us to get into America, and to whom we are beholden for financing our next films. So, swallowing all sorts of objections, I said I'd consider it. We made some cuts, and assembled a new version in videotape. Miramax came over and wanted additional cuts. I was getting more and more unhappy about it.

"Suddenly the whole thing blew up when the *Village Voice* ran an article warning that Miramax was going to cut my version for the American market. That was fantastically well-timed for me. Miramax asked, 'If we make these cuts, what are you going to say to the American press?' I said I was going to tell the truth to anybody who would listen to me. I wasn't going to lie and say that this was the same version that was being shown in Europe. They got very upset by this, but then called the following evening and asked what I was going to do about America. I wasn't sure whether they were referring to the nation or the film. I told them I was preparing a new project and was too busy to be bothered with editing, and that I wanted *CTW&L* to be seen in America exactly as it was in Europe. They agreed. They have promised me they will not make any cuts and will accept the consequences of an X rating."

## Cannibalism

"Ever since the first custard pie was thrown in a movie, even before, people sitting eating has become an icon of filmic experience. Recently, there seem to have been a lot of food films — *Tampopo, Babette's Feast, Eating Raoul, La Grande Bouffe.* I wanted to use eating to make some comment about consumer society, to take it to its limits. To suggest that when you've finally devoured everything there is to be eaten, you end up eating one another — the whole cannibalistic theory.

"And I wanted actually to film food. Do you know how difficult that is? Directors of commercials tell you that shooting food is extremely demanding. It's a big thing — has developed its own genre almost. In England, over the last two decades, the British people have finally decided that eating out is a good thing. Therefore they use dining out, Mrs. Thatcher's yuppies again, as a new sort of expression — not just to eat but to dress up, show off their wealth and all that. Very obviously, the dining room in that context is a microcosm of human behavior.

"I don't take any marks of originality for that idea; it's an old, old theme that's still worth working on. And it's a rich subject that extends in every direction. A lot of compositions in *CTW&L* are based on Arcimboldo and relate to painterly concerns with food. Those great bloody still lives that indicate the rape of the world in a sense. This has certain moral implications; we don't need to eat exotic swans and precious fish out of the China Sea. My own feeding habits are very modest; I'd rather spend my time and money doing something else.

"Most of the food in the film is wasted, thrown away, destroyed, abandoned. You don't have to see the starving Ethiopians in this movie. They're there simply by the excess that's going in the other direction. 'What do I care what the bookseller ate?' Albert says. 'Everything ends up as shit in the end.' So the film is about the alimentary canal, mouth to anus, mouth to anus. This idea very vigorously starts the film, with that awful scene where the man is forced to eat not human excrement, but dog excrement, which in the Old Testament and Dante's *Inferno* is the worst thing that anybody can be forced to eat because a dog is a man-made, scavenging animal. The shit of a dog is therefore even worse than the shit of the man who made the dog.

"The catalyst for *CTW&L* probably occurred when I was making *Belly* in Rome. The architect comes from Chicago, Upton Sinclair's city of blood, meat, and money. One night I got stuck in a traffic jam, of which there are so many in Rome, in front of a butcher shop on the way to a late-night shoot. There was this cow's gut in the window, which I was forced to contemplate in the lurid glow of those blue lights which are supposed to keep the flies down. Obviously, that cow gut was destined for a human gut — gut meets gut — in a city of closed churches with these masochistic, sadistic images of the bloodied body of Christ hanging erotically absolutely everywhere.

"Ideas about cannibalism began then, and I started to think of others. There's Goya's Satan eating his own offspring — an extraordinary thing. Then there are the news stories that are marginal to our experience. A small plane goes down in what's left of the Amazon rain forest. The pilot eats the passengers, or the passengers eat the pilot. Everybody reacts with shock/horror. Three days later, everybody's forgotten about it; everybody's saying, 'You'd do the same, wouldn't you, under the circumstances?' What I wanted to do was take cannibalism out of the margins and put it right in the center of the table and garnish it with the most expensive French sauces and surround it with beautiful sauteed vegetables and see what would happen — to try and understand the implications of that.

"Cannibalism can be easily used as a metaphor for the end of consumer society. After we've eaten everything else, we shall eat up one another. Two hundred years ago, Jonathan Swift encouraged us to take that step, albeit very satirically. In *CTW&L*, I am only being ironic. The whole preposterous notion of this film is one of extraordinary irony. I have to try and convince an entire audience whose experience of cannibalism is either literary or extremely marginal that this proposition could take place, exist in a 20th-century restaurant in a sophisticated, cosmopolitan society in the 1990s.

"In a sense the whole film is moving towards cannibalism from the very beginning. There's a big mouth behind that screen. You know how children explore the world through their mouths — put every damn thing into their mouths? Albert Spica, with his infantile sexuality, is much more interested in the lavatory than the bedroom, much more interested in the anus than in the vagina. Indeed, his wife confirms this. When the little kitchen boy is being tortured, he's forced to eat buttons. We've already discussed the man eating dog shit in the opening scene. Even when the wife and the cook talk about sex, in their duologue just before the closing scene, it seems that the ultimate aim of sexuality is fellatio—cocksucking, putting the genitals into the mouth. It's the image of the 20th century; stuffing things in one end and shitting them out the other—the cycle going around and around and around."

Having finished his list of concerns with this excremental vision, Greenaway falls silent. I feel as though I have completed a college course—but I am not ready for a final exam.

Greenaway asks me whether I spotted any of the religious allusions he had included in *CTW&L*. What did I think of Michael Nyman's musical score? Could I identify the mystery movie referred to in a restaurant scene—a film in which the main character doesn't speak for the first 20 minutes? (I couldn't, though it turned out to be one I had seen—Wim Wenders' *Paris, Texas*.) It can hardly be said that Greenaway is unaware of his demoniac cleverness, but he unearths the nuggets buried in his work in a spirit of generosity. They are not so much possessions to be admired as gifts to be shared.

Having tested me, Greenaway proceeds to evaluate himself. "Was it Woody Allen who said that at best he can realize 30 percent of his intentions in his films? How close have I come in *CTW&L*—50 percent maybe? The ideal length for the film was two hours and 20 minutes, which we reached on our second cut. But my movies tend to be too long, and so in reducing *CTW&L* to two hours, some things had to be sacrificed. I think there are certain weaknesses in the relationship between the wife and the lover. I wanted to explain a lot more about how they were attracted to each other, what the attractions were. How men like the cook and the lover—the perfectionist culinary expert and the man who's obsessed with books—have a center of interest, a focus that makes them whole, and to put that in opposition to the thief who has no center, who is totally spineless. But that went—it had to be removed."

*CTW&L* is the first in what Greenaway conceives as a trilogy of transgressive movies. But these projects will have to wait until he finishes *Prospero's Book,* a version of Shakespeare's *The Tempest.*

No screen adaptation of *The Tempest,* even Derek Jarman's, could be less orthodox than what Greenaway has in mind, even though he intends to remain faithful to the play's text, trimming only a few of the comedy scenes. He plans to exploit Shakespeare's interest in magic, "something that cinema lends itself to extraordinarily well." Unsurprisingly, there will be magical painterly effects—*trompe l'oeil,* false perspectives, the illusions of classical cinema (Melies and Cocteau) with mirror-imaging and hands disappearing into bowls of mercury. The film is presently shooting in Amsterdam, and post-production special effects will be executed in Tokyo on high-definition video.

Sir John Gielgud plays not only Prospero but all of the other roles— Caliban, Ariel, even Miranda. Gielgud, who has performed Prospero in five different stage productions, and whom Greenaway regards as "the last great classically trained, educated Shakespearian versifier now that Laurence Olivier is dead," will read every line of dialogue. He has always wanted to record his Prospero on film and, at 84, hopes to make some sort of final definitive artistic statement. Appropriately, *The Tempest* is Shakespeare's last play, his farewell to the theater and to illusionism.

With Gielgud handling the dialogue, Greenaway is free to use the whole world as his casting couch. Like Fellini, he can hire dancers, swimmers, Oriental acrobats, tumblers and jugglers, freaks, obese characters, and small children. There are going to be 10 Ariels, starting with a 3-year-old child; as the film progresses, Ariel will get bigger and bigger, and in the final scene, he'll revert to the boy again.

The cast, all masked and miming to Gielgud's voice, includes Alec Guinness, Dario Fo, Isabelle Pasco, Michel Piccoli, Tom Bell, and the English dancer Michael Clark. At the moment when Prospero abandons his revenge, all the characters will take off their masks. "We'll have this big, starry cast revealed at the end—like *The List of Adrian Messenger*—affirming Shakespeare's thesis is that forgiveness can bring alive characters that revenge has killed."

*Prospero's Book* might sound like an excessively genteel Greenaway project, but as soon as it's completed, he intends to return to his *CTW&L* trilogy. "The second one is called *The Love of Ruins.* I want to take feminism to its ultimate, ultimate, ultimate. I want Juliet Stevenson, who performed brilliantly for me as the middle Cissie Colpitts in *Drowning,* to play this contemporary Medea who kills her own child. Again a shocking idea, but I want to try to create a scenario whereby you can get the audience's sympathy for a woman who kills her child, which is an extension of the whole proabortion thing. Does a woman have the responsibility for a life in her womb? And if so, does it extend beyond the womb? Can she therefore kill with ethical justification a 2½-year-old child? There will be lots of other things going on, because I want to use Mediterranean/Roman architecture, an extension of *Belly*.

"The third film is called *The Man Who Met Himself,* which is a continuation of *Zed* in some ways. It's not about cloning or twinning or doppelgangers, but really—what would you do if you met yourself? Would you be appalled? Would you be excited? Would you want to go to bed with yourself? After all, you yourself know better than anyone else what your sexual desires are—who better to know than you? What if somebody else in the world knows all your foul little secrets? What would you do about it? How would you cope with it? It will be an essay in narcissism, our 20th-century disease. I want to explore the idea that we're all born as twins and go through life looking for this other person. Our homosexual or heterosexual bonding doesn't seem to be enough. These ideas are present in all sorts of unrelated cultures—the Easter Islands, Celtic mythology, Plato's Symposium with its notion that we are all originally hermaphrodite. We became too arrogant and so the gods split us down the middle, forcing us to spend our lives chasing our other half. If we start being arrogant all over again, God will come down and split each half in half, and it will take four people to assemble a fifth, making our lives peculiarly, desperately difficult."

Having covered Greenaway's present and future—and, at his request, bypassed personal data due to his conviction that it's the art, not the artist, that matters—our meeting ends. He has another interview and hopes to get to the Hirshhorn before catching a plane back to New York.

But Greenaway has saved one last *coup de theatre*. He reaches for his coat and produces a garment as astonishing as Prospero's mantle, a patchwork cloak composed of velvet diamonds of burgundy, green, and gold—a costume designed by Jean Paul Gaultier for one of Spica's hoods in *CTW&L*.

"Jean Renoir once suggested that most true creators have only one idea and spend their lives reworking it," Greenaway says, enveloping himself in his rainbow cape. "But then very rapidly he added that most people don't have any ideas at all, so one idea is pretty amazing. I suppose I have a concern for this extraordinary, beautiful, amazing, exciting, taxonomically brilliant world that we live in, but we keep fucking it up all the time. That's hardly an original message, but maybe that accounts for my misanthropic attitude toward the characters in my films. At their best, they're mediocre, and at their worse, at their very worst, they are appalling, evil, horrible people. I can't really see that changing either."

# Food for Thought:
# An Interview with Peter Greenaway

GAVIN SMITH/1990

PETER GREENAWAY'S *THE COOK, the Thief, His Wife, and Her Lover* is an aesthetic seduction based upon the spectacle of exquisite decadence and corrupt excess. It is, concurrently, a monument to postmodern Brutalism, an extended formalist metaphor, and a satiric exercise in contemporary social criticism.

Like most satire, the film creates a self-contained world ruled by its own inner logic: a lavishly decorated French restaurant presided over by an enigmatic master chef (Richard Bohringer) and patronized on seven successive evenings by a self-styled gangster (Michael Gambon), his submissive wife (Helen Mirren), and his boorish entourage (most memorably, Tim Roth, who in his time has played young hooligans for Mike Leigh, Stephen Frears, and Alan Clarke). Amongst the other, unindividuated diners is a book reader (Alan Howard) who, with the assistance of the head chef, begins a clandestine affair inside the restaurant with the wife.

Divided into color-coded zones (red dining room, green kitchen, ivory restrooms), the restaurant is not only a temple of human appetite and sensuality but also a metaphorical arena wherein Greenaway posits an aesthetic philosophy, assigning creativity, consumption, and desire their own physical space and character.

Gambon's would-be food connoiseur-thief, an exhibitionist embodiment of rampant appetite and emotional instability, and Howard's bookworm

From *Film Comment,* May/June 1990. Reprinted by permission of *Film Comment* and the author.

historian, representing self-effacing contemplative rationality, are the polar opposites in Greenaway's equation. The cook represents their synthesis in artistic creativity; the wife, the liberation of pleasure-desire that art induces.

The equation is problematic, however; its opposition of art and consumption is false when pushed to its limit. The thief, as a species of "performer," suggests a warped, de Sadean creativity; and "art" is ultimately only a privileged category of consumption, not some precious metaphysical essence. The film sidesteps this through its subtext of social criticism. Its fascination with the aesthetics of excess has a historical function: putting the decay back into decade (try "decade dance" as a Greenaway pun), *Cook, Thief* is about the Eighties. More precisely, it's about Eighties European Style.

An unrepentant formalist, Greenaway understands why the Eighties was the decade of Form; what he's after is an investigation of what happens when Style falls into the hands of the powerful philistine. British and European Style Culture, which emerged in the early Eighties as a youth-oriented, subversive, postmodern response to the banalities of consumerism, was eventually co-opted by precisely the market-led, conservative, elitist establishment it was designed to resist. This was partly because there was nothing egalitarian about it—it was an elitist proposition in the first place, based upon that creaking old fashioned opposition of "cool" and "straight." Style-led radical consumerism was unable to escape from its capitalist orbit. All that was left were the traces of Style itself: imagery and aesthetics could provide sufficient authority to assure power—a truism of the Reagan/Thatcher decade.

At heart, Greenaway is as much a throwback to the English literary and satirical essay tradition of the 18th century—Swift, Sterne, Pope—as he is (to apply his own preferred designation) a painter working in cinema. His films have always displayed his eclectic intellectual-hobbyhorse interests: ornithology, architecture, biology, cartography, numerology, the conventions of artistic representation, etc., etc. They are as much eccentric essays on thematically suggestive topics—a kind of intellectual trivia—as they are British cousins to the European art cinema of Resnais, Ruiz, and Straub.

Born in Newport, Wales, in 1942, Greenaway spent his formative years at public school and then at Walthamstow School of Art. His shaping influences in the early Sixties were R. B. Kitaj's paintings and Bergman's *The Seventh Seal*. After a brief stint as a film critic, he began to work in documentary editing, and in 1965 became a film editor at the Central Office of Information (COI), a government statistics and public-information body in London. He started making short films during this period through the late Seventies, when he received the blessing and funding of the British Film Institute. The advent of British television's Channel Four, with its brief to provide more minority or marginal programming, secured Greenaway's financial future. His last few features have reached out to Europe for co-production finance, consistent with Greenaway's one-foot-in-Britain, one-foot-in-Europe artistic posture.

—G.S.

*How would you say* The Cook, the Thief *differs from your previous work?*
The difference in this film is to do generally with wishing to enlarge my vocabulary and with my anger and passion about the current British political situation. Since this is a movie about consumer society, it's about greed—a society's, a man's. A man who knows the price of everything and the value of nothing. I've allowed much more passion, more concern for an emotive relationship between the film and the audience, than ever before.

   *The Cook, the Thief,* quite manipulatively, is the beginning of a trilogy on very harsh—I'd like to think taboo—subjects. (For which I have a contract with our current producer.) The next, *Love with Ruins,* is to do with the relationships of adults to children. The third, *The Man Who Met Himself,* I hope will build on some of the ideas I didn't develop in *A Zed and Two Noughts.*

*To what extent is this film a critique of your other films' lack of historical context or commentary?*
You use for me quite emotive words—"lack of." I would say just "different from." You're making value judgments I don't accept. There are all sorts of reasons for my aversion to Hollywood methods of making movies, which I find to be, basically, illustrating nineteenth century novels. I think we can learn from the European experience that cinema begins from the ground up. You don't use somebody else's literature, somebody else's play. You conceive the film from the beginning in a sort of Godardian sense. What

happens in America is, properties of another nature, another medium, are taken over in some way.

I began life feeling, and still feel, that painting is the supreme visual image-making process. And I also believe — in a British context, and maybe in a European context — that cinema is dying as a medium for expression. Cinema is quite a local phenomenon; it's not even reached 100 years yet. What I'm interested in is that long tradition of 2,000 years of imagemaking, which has a continuity whether we like it or not. Is it David Puttnam who suggested that even as cinema is dying, that doesn't necessarily mean we all have to cry in our coffee? There will always be some other medium in which to express a philosophy of the world through visual means.

I'm doing as much television now as I'm doing feature films; I've had painting exhibitions since I was 17 or 18, and I've always done masses of writing, although it hasn't necessarily got published. The whole thing for me is an investigative procedure of approaching phenomenology, on a very wide front.

*So what's the relationship between what you do in painting and what you do in film?*
I've always had great problems about methods of collaboration. Even now, in the filmmaking process I'm more entertained, more amused, more intrigued by those times when the film remains very personal — the germination time, when I sit at a desk and conceive the film away from all those collaborative necessities of actors, crew, finances, and so on.

The second most interesting part of the filmmaking process for me is when the rushes come back after we've finished those eight hectic weeks. Using my particular skills as an editor — where I started in cinema — the film becomes mine again. I enjoy myself least during [shooting], which I suspect is totally different from the way, say, Spielberg enjoys himself as a filmmaker. Because it's an enormous collaboration, and most of the time you're not a filmmaker, you're some sort of creche-minder or priest — all those things that have nothing to do with making a film, but just getting a human process on the road and rolling.

*If you were making a film at the level Derek Jarman works at, where he operates the camera, wouldn't that eliminate much of the bureaucracy of production?*

I don't know much about Derek's procedures; I don't think he's particularly keen about my cinema, either. But he has great rapport with people and with actors; he does like that whole process. [My cinema makes it] pretty self-evident that I would rather spend more time with my cinematographer and my art department than with my actors.

The personal origins for this are to do with my disciplines as a painter. That one-to-one relationship a painter has with his canvas seems to me the supreme, exciting, intriguing, most important moment. If there were some way I could make movies entirely on my own with all the professionalism of Spielberg, and with all the personal intent of somebody like Straub, I would be satisfied. I can be as civilized and as charming as is necessary, you know, in order to get on with people.

*But you're a misanthropist.*
My personal obsessions are much more interesting to me than other people's.

*Your films have always felt to me like satires along the lines of Swift.*
Often very savage and ironical; irony perhaps more than cynicism. It's a very English position that basically believes in nothing at all, and has this fatalistic, even nihilistic attitude towards the total environment.

*Satire isn't about being constructive.*
Satire is basically destructive. And I don't think my movies are destructive in that sense. Of course, I obviously *would* say this, but many other people find a great sense of positivism in my movies. They often are about death, but they are very light in heart. I think, in a peculiar way, satire is without humor. Whereas irony has humor.

Cook, Thief, *for me, functioned as a metaphor about the conflict between creativity and consumption, and the way they are destabilized by desire and excess. You can read the film as being about the movie business.*
Yeah, and that's a continuing theme; with some adjustments, that could be said also about *The Draughtsman's Contract* and *Belly of an Architect*. I'm not sure it could be said about *A Zed and Two Noughts*. There is a way in which, if you take the odd numbers, my first, third, and fifth feature films have this attitude you very adroitly summed up, on many levels.

Take the male characters, who are almost ciphers of certain sorts of activity. The perfectionist cook who's obviously the filmmaker, who invites the diners to come and sit down, who invites the viewers to come into the cinema: this is the meal I'm going to prepare for you. He has a sort of patronizing, avuncular concern to tuck the table napkin into your shirtfront. And he provides the spaces for the actors to manipulate and organize. He provides the set, the restaurant; shows you the back room where everything is prepared—part of the self-consciousness of my cinema. Ultimately he nudges the whole thing through and provides the dénouement.

And again, just following your thesis, *Belly of an Architect,* for architect read filmmaker, who has not only an exhibition but also financiers, critics, and the relationship of the private life to a public life, which all creative people have. Also, there's the secret character of Etienne Boulee in the background, a classic example of a man who organized, designed, and thought about some amazing visionary buildings, but they never got built—which, we all know, is very much a filmmaker's position too.

*Your films are marked by surpluses and excesses. Do you see them as being very coherent, or are you allowing yourself the space for an overwhelming of your intentions by other meanings?*
However much you plan and organize, a lot escapes you. It's a part of the human condition, after all. I am very empirically, rationally minded; I'm against mystification and dark areas for their own sake. My cinema is completely different from Tarkovsky, for example, who has this peculiar, woolly, implicit belief in intuition. I think it is a dubious sort of concept.

*I don't agree. Your fascination with orders of reality and grand designs, the creation and maintenance of a specific reality, represent the artist's narcissism—in the sense that we try to conquer external reality by imprinting ourselves on it and reconstituting it in our own image. As a filmmaker, you seem very conscious of that struggle. But you show those intentions and designs defeated by irrational forces that suggest the metaphysical.*
Yes, the systems always collapse. The supreme example is *A Zed and Two Noughts,* where, in a very straightforward parable, all those elaborate systems those brothers believed in, fail. They are saying, science will answer all our problems. And that film is about antagonisms between Genesis and Darwin, ending up to suggest that Darwin, i.e. the scientific method, is just as bogus as Genesis.

Systems are always deeply, deeply faulted—and absurd. Like the alphabet. Our whole lives are governed by this wretched, artificial construct: our medical records, police records, the way we approach our academic life—all based upon this stupid system of A–Z. The whole world is now clued into this—even people who don't use the sort of alphabet we do. It's absurd. The time band system and the lines around the Equator—which are so artificial—have been systemized and empiricized to make chaos somehow more readable. More usable.

*The opposition between art and consumerism is an illusion, though. Art is itself a form of consumption, and perhaps consumption is itself an art. The thief is as much an artist as the cook.*
So is the lover. So is the wife. That's one simplistic viewpoint.

*I don't think it's that simple. Your work shows a relish of transgression, which the thief embodies and exults in.*
It's just full of tradition. It starts with Seneca and goes on through Jacobean revenge tragedy, and picks up De Sade, Bataille, Genet, Peter Brook's Theatre of the Cruelty. And maybe goes on to Pasolini and Buñuel.

This extraordinary excitement or delight in the power of transgression, taking things to the limit; this whole business about evil personified—our humanist tradition cries out to be disciplined and organized, otherwise we'd have total anarchy. It sounds so cliché, but evil is of enormous interest to us all. I wanted to create deliberately, almost in a technical way, a character of great evil, who had no redeeming features. Not like a Machiavelli or a Richard III, who have charisma, which is attractive. I wanted to create a man who *had* to be mediocre. And there's a way that all my heroes are mediocre people. The draughtsman in *The Draughtsman's Contract,* the architect in *Belly of an Architect* are not very talented; those two wretched lads in *A Zed and Two Noughts* are very mediocre animal behaviorists.

*Belly of an Architect* is in some ways a key movie, and I'm only beginning to understand why. It is extraordinarily autobiographical, and contains all sorts of elements in my cinema practice. I can see me using the cinema like a process of catharsis, working things out for myself. On the whole that's probably quite good, because it really does show that filmmaking for me is not some distant, intellectual exercise, but really gut-related.

*Isn't* The Cook, the Thief, His Wife and Her Lover *a Hollywood sellout? It has stars and a story. . . .*
This picture could never be made in America. There's no way its provocations could ever be encompassed by an American sensibility. Don't you believe that's the case?

*Yes, but your vehicle for exploring your preoccupations is as close to a Hollywood model as you've come.*
I disagree profoundly. This is a metaphorical film. There's no way that the American cinema ever deals in metaphor. The only decent metaphorical filmmaker you have here is David Lynch. Americans don't understand what metaphor in cinema is about. They're extremely good at making straightforward, linear narrative movies, which entertain superbly. But they very rarely do anything else. The whole purpose of my cinematic effort is to explore metaphor and symbol.

*How would you describe that effort?*
My cinema is deliberately artificial, and it's always self-reflexive. Every time you watch a Greenaway movie, you know you are definitely and absolutely *only watching a movie*. It's not a slice of life, not a window on the world. It's by no means an exemplum of anything "natural" or "real." I do not think that naturalism or realism is even valid in the cinema. Put up a camera and everything changes. Pursuit of realism seems to me a dead end.

Having said that, I think there's a way in which probably most artists, whatever their particular medium, tend to work according to the other artifacts they like. The artifacts I most like are deliberately artificial and acknowledge their own artificiality, and are made with an incredible amount of self-consciousness. I [don't mean that as a] synonym for self-indulgence, because that is extraordinarily dangerous.

*The Cook, the Thief* opens with curtains opening and closes with curtains closing. It already suggests, in quotes, this is a performance movie, this is a movie about virtuoso performances. It refers very much towards the proscenium arch. When the camera moves, it moves in a very, very subjective, inorganic way. Which again is very much against the general premises of American moviemaking.

Take the color coding. Take the number counts in *Drowning by Numbers.* Take the alphabet count in *A Zed and Two Noughts.* These strategies and systems are like exterior skeletons, very much extra-frame and outside the references of the cinema itself.

*Well,* Casualties of War *clearly announces its artificiality by beginning with the hero falling asleep, having a long dream, and then waking up at the end. It is hyperbolic in the same way your films are. So is* Sophie's Choice, *which expresses the consciousness of its narrator.*
Yeah, but it still uses the attitudes of psychodrama realism, which is a bugbear I'm cynical about. This wretched psychodrama permeates the whole of American culture. My movies aren't remotely associated with that. Once you get over this first little hurdle about "imagination," *Sophie's Choice* is still very, very conventional moviemaking.

*Yes, but those films entitle you to multiple readings. Good filmmakers here can make two films at once.*
Then they are really hedging their bets, aren't they?

My cinema is a cinema of irony and paradox and contradiction. I know that I rarefy activities in filmmaking in a peculiar way. I'm very much subsidized by done cinema; I could not exist at all unless [it existed]. Most audiences, when they're young, come to the products of done cinema. And then maybe when they become dissatisfied with it, they'll start looking in other areas. That's where I come in, along with all other European cinema.

*Your creative control is much like Spielberg's or James L. Brooks's, who don't aim for some theoretical audience. You make films that you would want to see yourself.*
True. But I think Spielberg has a tremendous inkling of who he's making a film for. And that somehow retroactively works back on the [film].

*I think he has the same relationship to an audience that Hitchcock had. Hitchcock made audience films without trying to.*
But from a position of incredible confidence and strength, because he seemed to be able to hit the jackpot nine times out of ten.

*I don't think that matters to Spielberg as much as making pure cinema. His films are as self-referential and self-conscious as yours.*
I'm sure that if his box-office success fell away, his cinema practice would somehow change. If my box office, modest though it is, fell away, there would be no change in my cinematic practice. I do not feel manipulated by my audiences, whereas I suspect he is.

Does he really see *E.T.* as resurrection mythology? Would he think about it like that? There is a way in which *Belly of an Architect* is much more pure Hollywood movie because it has a far less metaphorical front to it. And it does deal in character—Kracklite, played by Brian Dennehy, who's a Hollywood actor. There's a certain sort of psychodrama, a connection between relationships, which is, even though I still find it infinitely removed from a Hollywood tradition, perhaps the closest that I've ever gone in that direction.

A signature or auteur moviemaker has to find some sort of equation whereby he can continue to make movies which are very personal, but also somehow create a certain credibility for him so he can go on making movies. A measure, for me, of my own success is the sense of continuity, especially in an English situation, where there is no auteur or signature movie tradition.

In the last six or seven years, a number of filmmakers have started off very promisingly, like Neil Jordan, but quickly succumbed to commercial filmmaking to some degree, and for me totally dissipated what was interesting. There might be only two, possibly three auteur filmmakers in England. One perhaps is myself, one is Derek Jarman, and thirdly perhaps Terence Davies who made *Distant Voices, Still Lives*. But it's early to tell because he's only actually made two movies. He's already linking up to David Puttnam, which sounds like a very bad thing.

I am still, primarily, a painter who's working in cinema. I think my cinema is best understood in the critical terms normally applied to painting traditions and art history. So sometimes I feel that I am like a hippopotamus in a giraffe race.

My position somewhat as an outsider is a good one for me to hold on to. Maybe that's what's sad about all these other English filmmakers: they have ceased to be outsiders and have become insiders—totally eaten up by this enormous snake, which means that in the end you cannot even be your own voice. I want the biggest audience I possibly can get. But arrogantly, I want them on my terms—though those terms constantly may be changing.

## A Greenaway Inventory

**Death of Sentiment** (1959–62): "About funeral architecture: tombstones, what their imagery was, how people were buried, what the burial service was all about, etc."

**Train** (1966): "The last of the steam trains were coming into Waterloo Station, directly behind the COI, and I spent days on the roof filming them, and then structuring them into an abstract Man Ray ballet mécanique, all cut to a musique concrete track."

**Tree** (1966): "Outside the Royal Festival Hall on the South Bank in London, the center of musicmaking in England, was this blasted tree that had been there for many years and had been gradually surrounded by concrete but still managed to hold out. So I suppose [the film] was a basic ecological message connected very much with the making of music."

**Revolution** (1967): "I was present at the antiwar demonstration in front of the U.S. Embassy—in England, the turning point in the Vietnamese experience. I happened to have a camera, so I shot all those riots and crowds and cut it to The Beatles' *Revolution*."

**Five Postcards from Capital Cities** (1967): "I started traveling in Europe, taking my short films to campus film societies; I took my own 16mm camera and in each capital city shot a lot of footage."

**Intervals** (1969): "Very abstract, an attempt to make a movie without narrative using the figure 13, the harmonic structure Vivaldi used in *The Seasons*. It was made in Venice and combined images from both the Biennale—representing the high culture of painting in Europe—and the Film Festival, largely through graffiti on the houses in Venice."

**Erosion** (1971): "I spent about a month in the South of Ireland and was fascinated by the very ancient landscape. I tried to find filmable evidence of the land eroding—seashores, rock faces crumbling—and put it together with the oldest rocks first and the most recent last. It was very much in response to the Sixties Land Art movement."

**H is for House** (1973, reedited 1978): "I'd just married and had a small kid, and we used to spend our holidays in Wardour; we stayed in a magnificent early 19th century house belonging to a friend. It was the most extraordinary area of idealized, romanticized English landscape, very redolent of Roman Catholic history; all sorts of violent tragedies had happened there during the English Civil Wars. It was a rather shutaway countryside, so it had a sense of great drama and romance—in response to which, I made a series of films, of which this is the first. It was couched in the whole business of naming things—as in the late paintings of Magritte, the confusion between nomenclature, ascribing meanings and words to objects.... I made this enormous list of every single thing I could find in the domestic rural landscape that began with the letter H, which when juxtaposed gave you all sorts of interesting connotations. My daughter Hannah was learning the alphabet and her voice is on the soundtrack repeating and getting things wrong—the wisdom of the innocent. It was also very much to do with concepts of Heaven and Hell and how those are interchangeable. . . ."

**Windows** (1975): "Made in the same place. I had been appalled and fascinated by the statistics coming out of South Africa—political prisoners pushed out of windows, with fatuous excuses like they slipped on a bar of soap, they thought it was the door, etc. I built that into a fiction, trying to find all the possible reasons why anybody might fall out of a window, and compressed it into 3½ minutes and set these appalling facts up against a very idyllic landscape in order to create irony and paradox. I think it sums up everything I've done afterwards: it's about statistics, it's very eclectic, it has a very lyrical use of landscape, it's about death—four characteristics that have stayed with me ever since."

**Water** (1975): "Basically an editing exercise. There were five lakes between Salisbury and Shaftesbury, each with its own character. I was fascinated by the English historian-anthropologist Mortimer Wheeler, who would find a stone beside a road and develop its history; he could invent a history for any given natural object. This was a parody of his technique, which I associated with a whole series of beautiful water landscapes. It was about five minutes and was the basis for:"

**Water Wrackets** (1975): "From my enthusiasm for J.R.R. Tolkein's *Lord of the Rings*. I invented a fictitious early population for that area called Wrackets. The Wrackets belonged in the swamps, the Marriotts lived in the hills, there was another group who lived in the forest; I was going to develop a very serious bogus anthropological-archaeological study of these mythical characters."

**Goole by Numbers** (1976): "I went around this very dull town called Goole in east Yorkshire, where my wife comes from, and simply recorded all the numbers I could find and then strung them all end to end and cut them to a piece of specially composed music by Michael Nyman, whom I first worked with on *H Is for House*."

**Dear Phone** (1977): "About the uses and abuses of the telephone and the problems of where literature finishes and film begins."

**1-100** (1978): "Very similar to *Goole by Numbers* but done in terms of European cities, and much more compressed. I took images from Berlin, Paris, Rome, Florence, and Brussels."

**A Walk through H** (BFI, 41 mins.; 1978): "I've always been fascinated by maps and cartography. A map tells you where you've been, where you are, and where you're going—in a sense it's three tenses in one. It's also an amazing ideogram of information that is very useful and, perhaps most pertinently, also not at all useful. My father had recently died, and the subtitle of the film was 'The Reincarnation of an Ornithologist'—my father was one. Through his life he had amassed an extraordinary amount of information about bird study, and I was very aware that with his death— as indeed with any death—a vast amount of very personalized information had gone missing, was totally irrecoverable. The film is on the journey a soul takes at the moment of death, to whatever other place it ends up— H being either Heaven or Hell. I devised 92 maps to help this particular character get there. The whole film was divided into five sections that represented movement from a very urban landscape to a wilderness landscape, and there were references and cross-references to all sorts of systems."

**Vertical Features Remake** (Arts Council of Great Britain, 45 mins.; 1978): "About the reorganization of the domesticated landscape. In Britain practically every sod of earth has been trodden on a thousand times; we don't have wildernesses here or anything remotely like a wilderness. It's probably one of the most painted and drawn and photographed landscapes in the world, and VFR was very much about this heritage."

**The Falls** (BFI, 185 mins.; 1975–78): "It was really a dustbin, to be blunt, for all the thousands of films I've never made—92 films I've somehow not finished. In some ways it was about 92 different ways the world would end—a very current sociological problem at the time. It was also about bird lore, it worked out all sorts of systems and conspiracies—I suppose I was influenced by Pynchon, Calvino, and García Marquez' 100 Years of Solitude—all those grandiose, encyclopedic works. It was 92 different ways to make a film. It contains many aborted films, films that I'd dreamt of and knew I'd never make, interviews, photographs of practically everybody I ever knew—so it was a personal compendium of my domestic and social relations, a gathering of everything I'd done before. I feel it's the most innovative thing I've ever done; I suppose I didn't realize at the time, but that was important because the next film I made, *The Draughtsman's Contract,* was a new departure."

**Act of God** (Thames TV, 35 mins.; 1981): "I was asked by Thames, a rather reactionary TV station, to make a half-hour program on any subject whatsoever. In my interest in taxonomies and attempts to classify information,

I looked for the most unclassifiable events or phenomena I could think of—which was being struck by lightning. We advertised in the national press for all those people who had been struck by lightning and survived, to come forward to be interviewed—and that's what the film's about. I had hoped to find extraordinary religious experiences, people who felt they'd been punished by God. Most of their reactions were totally banal, but we came across some extraordinary events—girls riding fat ponies down English country lanes and entirely disappearing apart from a pool of cooling fat on the road. I put all these events together and of course every-body thought I had made them up."

**Zandra Rhodes** (COI, 15 mins.; 1981): "She was a Sixties dress designer of considerable influence. I had long left the COI by then, but they wanted me just as I was gathering a reputation to come back and make a sort of personal subjective picture of what she was and stood for. It's an affection-ate critical appreciation of her not only as a fabric designer but also as a media figure, too."

**The Draughtsman's Contract** (BFI/Channel Four, 108 mins.; 1982): "It took on maybe more of the conventional characteristics of an actor's cin-ema. I think that particular sort of stretch really ended with *Drowning by Numbers.*"

**Four American Composers** (Channel Four, 1983): Documentaries on John Cage, Robert Ashley, Phillip Glass, and Meredith Monk.

**Making a Splash** (Channel Four/Media Software, 25 mins.; 1984): "The thesis is simply everything that happens in water, from Darwinian evolu-tion—from amoebae up to sophisticated swimming items like dolphins—and then moving on to everything human beings do in water, such as ath-letics; it ended up with the most sophisticated of the water sports, synch-ronized swimming. Again, all cut to a specially composed Michael Nyman piece."

**A TV Dante—Canto 5** (Channel Four, 15 mins., video; 1984): "A pilot program in collaboration with the English painter Tom Phillips. He was a great Dantean scholar who'd done his own translation privately and also illustrated a book of his own version. *The Inferno* was written in 1300 but he wanted to do it from a post-WWII position. Heaven has changed con-stantly through the ages, but Hell basically has always stayed the same."

**Inside Rooms—The Bathroom** (Channel Four, 25 mins., video, 1985): "The beginning of a series, a wry consideration of how the English use bathrooms. Eventually there was going to be a half-hour program about living rooms, bedrooms, and so on. It never happened. It was an affectionate, ironical, critical look at bathroom design—what people put in their bathrooms, but also what people do in their bathrooms, which is the secret room of the house, where one becomes metaphorically and literally stripped right down to the basics."

**A Zed and Two Noughts** (BFI/Film Four/Allarts, 112 mins., 1985).

**The Belly of an Architect** (Callender/Film Four, 105 mins., 1987).

**Drowning by Numbers** (Film Four/Allarts, 118 mins., 1988).

**The Cook, the Thief, His Wife and Her Lover** (Allarts, 120 mins., 1989).

**Love of Ruins** (pending): "About the Medea myth—the woman who kills her own child. We're in the midst now of an enormous abortion debate. Medea took it even further because the child was 2½ when she killed it; I want to posit that in terms of an independent woman taking the life of her own child for a whole series of reasons that I want to convince an audience are valid. It takes place in ten locations around the Mediterranean and there's a subtext about the very English Romantic concern for ruins. The woman is an archaeologist."

**The Man Who Met Himself** (pending): "Really a reorganization of another classical myth—Apollo and Narcissus, the god and the mortal who competed over who was the best musician. The god won and wreaked a terrible revenge by flaying him. It represents the Apollonian and Dionysian attitude in all of us. I want some ideas I didn't pursue to the limit in *A Zed and Two Noughts,* about what happens when a man meets himself. How would we feel about that? Would we be scared, delighted; would we try and kill him or embrace him? It's a magical, metaphysical film. All my films are pretty *improbable,* but none is impossible. This is."

# Cinema as the Total Art Form:
# An Interview with Peter Greenaway

MARCIA PALLY/1991

BORN IN ENGLAND IN 1942, Peter Greenaway attended
what he calls "a minor English public school that preserves the
worst traditions—fagging, burning the pubic hair of new boys,
that sort of Godawful activity." After completing the Forest
Public School. Greenaway resisted his parents' plan to send him
to university and went instead to the Walthamstow School of Art
in east London. He exhibited for the first time at Lord's Gallery
in 1964. In 1965, he became a film editor with the government's
Central Office of Information where he cut educational documentaries for a decade.

Greenaway made his first films, *Train* and *Tree*, in 1966. By the
time he earned, in the late Seventies, his first 7,500 pounds from
the British Film Institute for *A Walk Through H* (40 minutes), he'd
made over a dozen films while keeping his hand in painting
book illustrations, and novel writing. In 1980, Greenaway made
the three hour *The Falls* for 30,000 pounds of BFI money. It won
the prestigious BFI Award and landed the funding agency in a
crunch. No other organization was likely to finance such kaleido-
scopic, non-narrative works, yet the BFI had obligations to other
up-and-coming filmmakers and to the new Thatcher government,
whose backing helped support it. The controversy about funding
Greenaway resolved when the new Channel Four Television

From *Cineaste*, vol. 18, no. 3, 1991. Reprinted by permission.

agreed to cofinance him with the BFI, provided he kept to a few conventional guidelines. That pact yielded *The Draughtsman's Contract* and Greenaway's career in feature films.

In addition to his commercial movies, Greenaway continues to work on canvas and in television, with programs as varied as documentaries on contemporary composers and dramatizations of Dante's *Cantos.* An exhibition of his paintings has been touring Europe for the last year: the 1991 Berlin Film Festival programmed a collection of his videos, and he is completing a novel, *Fifty-Five Men on Horseback.*—Marcia Pally

CINEASTE: *Since density is such a hallmark of your work, would you talk about how you fill up your screen, how you select and order so much stuff?*
PETER GREENAWAY: It may be banal to say that cinema is an art—certainly in many parts of the world it is not regarded as such. But if it is an art, it should be allowed everything we accredit to the novel, the symphony, and so on. Works of art refer to great masses of culture, they are encyclopedic by nature. I want to make films that rationally represent all the world in one place. That mocks human effort because you cannot do that. But the works of art that I admire, even contemporary ones like *One Hundred Years of Solitude* or any three-page story by Borges, has that ability to put all the world together.

My movies are sections of this world encyclopedia. What I'm manipulating is our cultural illusions—all the very potent, meaningful language of illusions that Western culture has. In *Cook Thief,* I'm looking at cuisine—the very careful effort to arrange and present one of the most primal human activities. It's an effort to de-food food, just like we try to de-chaos chaos. In *A Zed and Two Noughts* I look at creation myths. Genesis and Darwin. Genesis is a nice way of ordering the beginning of things with a very pretty myth. Darwinian theory is a nineteenth and twentieth century myth that's trying to do the same time.

I've always had the desire to organize things—where that comes from I don't know. I'm a lousy mathematician, but I am interested in rationality. I suppose it comes from my classical English education and three years in a rather academic art school. My ten years at The Central Office of Information was spent editing films that portray, supposedly, the English way of life through statistics. How many sheepdogs are there in South

Wales? How many Japanese restaurants are there in Ipswich? It's all about the organization of ephemera.

My early movies are very much about this sort of organizing. That's what art is about, isn't it—trying to find some order in the chaos? That's what civilization is about, some way to understand, contain this vast amount of data that's pushed at us all the time. Even those who do those false arts—the small Cs, couture, coiffure, and cuisine, all with French names, by the way—they look for a way to order their efforts.

The French chef in *Cook Thief* is a deliberate cliché that critiques those small-C arts, but he is also me. With each film, I invite people to my table and I make the meal. I take the cultural systems I admire and try to set them out in one place. I demand, as we all do, some sense of coherence, of order in world. And we are always defeated. This is the human condition.

CINEASTE: *Some artists respond to the need for order by clearing everything away and drawing the one necessary stroke. Your impulses are quite the opposite. Your screen overflows.*

GREENAWAY: I do hope that all the objects and events in my films are germane to the content. Obviously, in a film where I examine cuisine I would examine how other artists have used food in their work. The cook presents cuisine as a piece of civilization. In seventeenth century Dutch painting, which I refer to in *Cook Thief,* food was also thought to reflect the civilizing forces of that era, the power and wealth of the high bourgeoisie. It declared the success of the political and economic structures emerging at that time.

I think the most successful of all painting has been that of the Dutch golden age—I refer to it in much of my work—because it was done when each individual painter was most understood. It's very bourgeois, not the privilege of the church or state. It was the time when art became most democratic and so most understood by the most people on both its literal and allegorical levels. A woman who holds a mandolin with three broken strings probably means she's had two abortions. If she's not wearing shoes it means she's a loose woman. All that language has been lost to us but it was commonly understood by the bourgeois Dutch, by the people who commissioned the films ... er, paintings ... sorry, Freudian slip. It was their language. Painting today has again divorced itself from mainstream activities and become a rather rarefied object.

Anthony Higgins, Alastair Cummings, Anne-Louise Lambert, and Hugh Fraser, *The Draughtsman's Contract*, 1982

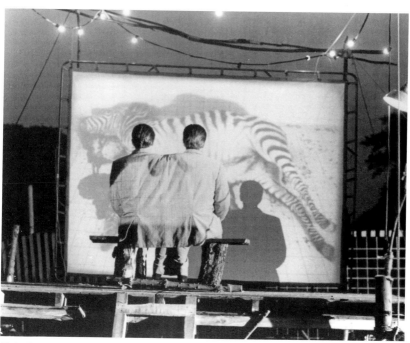

Eric Deacon and Brian Deacon, *A Zed and Two Noughts*, 1985

Brian Dennehy, *The Belly of an Architect*, 1987

Bernard Hill, *Drowning by Numbers*, 1988

Back row: Richard Bohringer, Ewan Stewart, and Ron Clark; front row: Alan
Howard, Helen Mirren, Michael Gambon, and Tim Roth, *The Cook, the Thief,
His Wife, and Her Lover*, 1989

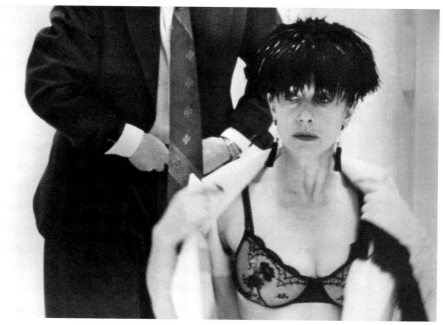

Alan Howard and Helen Mirren, *The Cook, the Thief, His Wife, and Her Lover,* 1989

Isabelle Pasco and John Gielgud, *Prospero's Books*, 1991

Nils Dorando and Julia Ormond, *The Baby of Macon*, 1993

Vivian Wu, *The Pillow Book*, 1995 (Photo: Mark Guillaumot)

Vivian Wu, *The Pillow Book*, 1995 (Photo: Mark Guillaumot)

I would like my movies to work the way Dutch painting did, on literal and metaphorical levels. If you've got that as a premise it's no problem at all to find all the information that ought to go in the frame—all the cultural, allegorical material.

CINEASTE: *How do you choose the organizing art or science for each film?*
GREENAWAY: I try to choose them to be germane to the thematic material. It's very important for satisfactory art that there be a very happy marriage between form and content. Take, for example, *A Zed and Two Noughts.* It's a film about twin scientists who try to organize the plant and animal universes, the beginning of things. One of the central organizing structures of the film is the alphabet, which I chose because most cultures use it as the basic template for organizing information.

I use number series for that reason as well. *Drowning By Numbers* is about game-playing: I begin the film with a little girl counting to a hundred because counting is one of the basic ways games are organized. The film is filled with number games. For instance, the coroner's son is named Smut, which begins with the letter S. So there are one hundred things in the film that begin with S. You don't have to know that to see the film, but it somehow enriches the fabric of it, makes the film again encyclopedic by nature.

Symmetry is an important element in *Belly* because the problems of construction—or civilization—and decay are seen from the point of view of a classical architect. It makes sense to express civilization with the sorts of constructions he'd be most familiar with. The only time the symmetry collapses is at the end of the film when the architect dies and the audience sees the film on the diagonal. It suggests, I hope, that the Apollonian universe that he tried to maintain has been destroyed.

In *Cook Thief* I wanted to use color as an organizing principle in addition to cooking because color has become so divorced from meaning in twentieth century painting. We no longer have to paint the sky blue simply because we observe it to be blue, so color has become decorative, even cute. I wanted to make a film where each color had a meaning within the language of the movie. The room where the thief eats, where the violence happens, is red. The car park is blue because it's the cold nether regions of this world. I made the lavatory white obviously with some irony. The book depository is golden to suggest the golden age of books, the gold color of old book bindings.

The kitchen of the restaurant where the cook works is greenish because it suggests safety and vegetation, where food comes from. Because it is a grey-green, stony color and a very large, cavernous room, the kitchen can also be seen as a cathedral. The cook sits at a kind of altar in a rounded apse area. The kitchen boy has a nimbus around his head and sings the 51st Psalm, which is about being an unworthy sinner—which the thief certainly is—and is the low point in the Catholic year.

There are other religious references in the film. The lovers who make love naked amid the food and foliage of the kitchen recall Adam and Eve. When they leave, they go to the book depository, the Tree of Knowledge. They are driven there in a van of red rotting meat, which can suggest their journey through hell. The van can also suggest the Trojan horse myth. Since the van belongs to the thief, he has unwittingly provided that way for his wife and her lover to escape him.

All these minute references rely on the great cultures—Western civilization, the Greco-Roman, and the Judeo-Christian, which has tried to order and explain the world to its inhabitants for over 2,000 years. These devices should emphasize to viewers that they're watching artifice, a construction overlaid on the world. It is not natural, not slices of life. *Cook Thief* opens with curtains and closes with curtains. It is a performance. The very effort of placing cultural artifacts into a filmic frame is an attempt to order them.

I'm in no way a neo-realist. Neo-realism and naturalism in cinema is a chimera anyway. You can't be real in cinema; you make a decision about form and artifice for every twenty-four frames per second of film. All those theoreticians who concern themselves with realism in cinema seem to be barking up the wrong tree entirely. I think the most satisfactory movies are those which acknowledge their artificiality.

I'm looking for ways of structuring films that coexist with my thematic material but that also have their own identities and interest. In some ways my films are more satisfactorily explained by the esthetic one brings to painting than to movies. The sense of distance and contemplation they require has much more to do with painting. When you go into an art gallery you don't emote, by and large, like people do in the movies. I know my work is accused of being cool and intellectually exhibitionistic. But I'm determined to get away from that manipulated, emotional response that you're supposed to have to Hollywood cinema. Human relations are considerably harder and harsher, and much more to do with contracts than with any glossy ideas that are so much in the current media package. Most mainstream cinema tends to glamorize, deodorize, romanticize, and senti-mentalize. I'm very keen to not do those things.

My other bugbear about Hollywood cinema is that it's based on the nineteenth century psychological novel, and the psychological novel represents only a tiny space in two thousand years of European cultural game-playing. I want to investigate some of those other forms, like Jacobean drama or landscape painting.

CINEASTE: *In most of your films, men are the civilizers, the people who com-bat chaos. Women give birth and murder. Your sympathy seems to be with the men—until your last film,* Cook Thief, *where for the first time you give the woman the civilizing efforts.*

GREENAWAY: My films have been accused both of misogyny and of championing the supremacy and confederacy of women. On one hand, women always end up as the dominant force—especially that last line in *Cook Thief* when the wife forces her husband to eat the body of her dead lover. "Why don't you eat the cock?" she says. "It's a delicacy and you know where it's been." It's seen as the final humiliation of the male. In *Drowning By Numbers,* which is about impotence, the central man desper-ately tries to express his sexuality, and he fails.

On the other hand, I'm accused of misogyny because I force these women to go through such humiliating experiences—as though the fact that they win is just my copout for all the rest. I don't think I'm a misogynist; I hope I'm not. In *Cook Thief,* the woman begins cowed and bullied, and ends by finding strength—and she is motivated by love. After all, *Cook Thief*—though this surprises many people—is motivated by love, not hate or misanthropy. She ends up triumphant, though there is an irony to her triumph. She has to use the violence of her husband to turn it on him and win.

You know that Helen Mirren and Michael Gambon have played together numerous times on the British stage and their best success was in *Anthony and Cleopatra.*

CINEASTE: *Who played Cleopatra?*

GREENAWAY: The twentieth century male has desperately to reorganize his sexuality in terms of the emancipation of the twentieth century female.

We all know we have a hell of a long way to go. In my films, women make the decisions that make the action. Men may be vile and barbarously destructive or they may make attempts at civilization, but the women make the decisions that count.

CINEASTE: *But there's been a change in the sorts of decisions your women make. In* Cook Thief, *the wife kills the thief in the name of civilization. The women in* Drowning *tolerate men only as long as the men give them sex and children, and then murder them by drowning—all that womblike water. This is the primal view.*

GREENAWAY: One of the projects I'm working on now is a twentieth century reconsideration of the Medea myth. It is a monstrous idea that a woman would murder her own child, but I want to try to place the audience in sympathy with her. Her action will have to do with a bid for absolute freedom without any trammels whatsoever. Medea was a powerful woman who organized her life and fate. She also represents woman as witch, an idea that has permeated all European culture. Men are so shit scared of female activities, especially if they are clandestine.

My movies are cathartic attempts for me to work out certain problems. My characters are the same age as me; as I get older, they do too. I want to make movies for people who have the same anxieties, hopes, fears, and ambitions that I have as a man approaching middle age.

The most personal movie I ever made was *Belly of an Architect*. For architecture, write film: for architect, write filmmakers. The architect in *Belly* is trying very hard to put something up in the world, but he's very doubtful so he's doing it by proxy—by mounting an exhibition of the work of an architect who lived hundreds of years ago. He believes that we can make ourselves immortal by creating one grain of sand on the beach of civilization—not by religion, which fades, and not by politics, which fades very rapidly, but through art. Though we know very little about Egyptian religion or statecraft, for instance, we do have their art. It seems to survive as a talisman that's passed on. Man has been able to make these magnificent structures which do seem worth preserving.

The irony of *Belly* is that this guy, who's put all his efforts into making art, loses out. He loses his wife, his child, his health, and, ultimately, his life. Many architects end up as paper architects: they never make the final product they've been dreaming about. This is also true of filmmakers.

Moreover, the financiers, critics, politicians, and producers are all apparent in the form of a film, in its architecture and perception of the world.

I'm first now understanding how personal my films are. There's a way in which all my films are about my father; he died of stomach cancer like the architect in *Belly*. He was a huge man, an anti-intellectual businessman who lived in London and had a great desire to be an ornithologist. He prepared to take early retirement and go to the country with a pair of binoculars, but just at that moment he went down with stomach cancer.

I'm in the extraordinarily fortunate position of being allowed to make signature movies. I have many more ideas—eighteen or twenty scripts lined up to be done. I feel that ultimately I'll be defeated, that there won't be the time to do them.

At the end of *Belly*, the audience hears the cry of a child, which might indicate that the best way we can be immortal is through the female ethic— even if bearing children for the male is mostly an involuntary process. This may sound like a very corny, clichéd attitude, but if we're concerned with immortality—and I'm sure all of us fear the vacuum of not being here—then we are concerned with that Picasso idea of leaving a stain on the wall.

My films try to address that problem for myself. What is all this about arcane cultural information that I'm trying to construct into a film? What am I doing looking over my shoulder at past ages and dragging all this past culture into some organization, some art, for the present day—this post-modernist concern with trying to make history and culture relevant to now?

CINEASTE: *Do you have children?*

GREENAWAY: Two daughters. My purpose on earth was finished a long time ago. I do believe in that Darwinian idea that we are here as sperm and ovum carriers.

CINEASTE: *It's fairly common today to believe that men and women can contribute both children and work—art or science and so on—to the world. Do you disagree?*

GREENAWAY: The Medea character in my new project is an archeologist. Archeologists are concerned with organizing history in a very empirical way. Maybe there's an answer to your question in the future.

The Medea film is not the very next project: that I hope will be a version of *The Tempest*. We're calling it *Prospero's Books* but we're using the Shakespearean text. Gonzalo throws some books in the bottom of Prospero's boat, and the rest of the film is seen through those books. It's as though books maketh man. *The Tempest* suggests that ultimately books led Prospero the wrong way. Again, the film is a concern with organizing, learning, and knowledge — especially for an old man.

There are basically only two subject matters in all Western culture: sex and death. We do have some ability to manipulate sex nowadays. We have no ability, and never will have, to manipulate death.

CINEASTE: *Do you feel frustrated trying to pass on knowledge through your films?*

GREENAWAY: I get a kick out of the pursuit of knowledge. The sheer garnering of information, the collecting and collating, the finding, reading, and research is of great interest to me. I enjoy it and it's the stuff I want to use to make my movies.

Borges once said it's much more difficult to read a book than to write one. In a peculiar way, he was right. Think of what a work of art demands of an audience. It's OK for me because it's my world: I made it. It's much more difficult for you to inhabit a world of my making.

For instance, my relationship with my father was never a happy one. I'm sure I'm reprising aspects of it in my work. But to make autobiography work for anybody else, it has to be refashioned into something less personal and self-indulgent. I dislike the psychological approach to art. It's too limiting. For instance, do we really know more about Van Gogh's painting of sunflowers because we also know that he cut off his left ear and gave it to a prostitute? Is it important that the author make himself very apparent behind the work? I have the feeling that the work is itself important and what you know about the author doesn't necessarily throw more light on it. It's a terrible misalliance of appreciation.

Psychoanalysis is also used to blame our parents and our heritage for everything that goes on, as if to absolve us of personal responsibility. I object to this a great deal. I have to make my films somehow readable to an audience and financially responsible. Fortunately they have so far been successful enough at the box office, in European terms, for me to go on making them.

CINEASTE: *How are your films financed?*

GREENAWAY: A Dutch producer, Kees Kasander, financed *Zed, Drowning,* and *Cook Thief.* Most of the money comes from European sources—for example, the organizations contributing to *Drowning* include Film Four in England, the Coproduction Fund for the Dutch Broadcasting Corporation, Elsevier Vendex Film, Prokino in Germany, BAC Films in France, Progres film in Belgium, and so on.

The films are made extremely cheaply. *Cook Thief* for instance cost something like $2.8 million. And they are organized very economically. Everything is written down: even the smell of flowers is marked if it needs to be there for the actors. Initially, we break even, and after perhaps three or four years we gradually slip into profit.

CINEASTE: *Do you get BBC funding?*

GREENAWAY: I never have. It's always been Channel Four, till *Cook Thief,* which they found much too tough for British television. I've always had very large input from French sources. I think my best audiences are French because they are great delighters in the accumulation of knowledge and they understand what I'm doing.

We still have that anti-intellectualism in Britain. The recognized channel for intellectual information in Great Britain is the theater. You can do anything you like there, but not in films. Tom Stoppard, for example can get away with anything. Should you attempt a cinematic essay on grand ideas, there's a feeling that film can't hold it together. It's a form of snobbism that ends up as anti-intellectualism.

CINEASTE: *Anti-intellectualism in the U.S. crosses all art forms: there's no out for theater.*

GREENAWAY: You have a fantastic cultural Puritanism over here. For example, all the attention you pay to frontal male nudity in films. It's too bad for me, really, since the nude-naked nexus is one that interests me. There are a great many issues about the body besides the sexual one—like vanity, for instance. From the European perspective, it seems quite pronounced in America—this coy concern with youth, all the jogging and harsh dietary regimens. It has to us an arch feel, as though you feel guilty about yourselves and are unable to accept what mortality is all about.

I don't know if the recent popularity of Puritanical restrictions—in all the fundamentalist movements we see nowadays—is linked to the panics that traditionally develop at the end of millennia. I'm writing a novel, *The Historians,* about the second between the year 1999 and 2000. It describes three centuries, past, present, and future. It's really about all of history. I'm fascinated by the panic around the Western world when the year 999 became 1000. People were jumping off cliffs, slitting their wrists and so on.

Fundamentalist religions are a shield, of course. Without imagination or effort, it solves all the unanswerable questions. It pushes the responsibility somewhere else, which is what's so incredibly dangerous. Fundamentalism is also part of the anti-intellectual ethic—the denial of rationality and imagination. To be an atheist you have to have ten thousand times more imagination than if you are a religious fundamentalist. You must take the responsibility to acquire information, digest and use it to understand what you can.

Cinema is an ideal medium to do that in. It can contain metaphorical, allegorical, and literal meanings. It's the system Wagner always dreamt of, the total art form—and already it's dying, technologically and socially. The statistics in England say that in the 1950s every family used to go to the cinema at least three times a week. They hardly go three times a year now. There are other indications that we're picking at the corpse. It seems every city in the world now has a film festival. And there are thousands of critics, which is always terrifying. It's like ballet: as soon as the critics become more numerous than the dancers, you're in great danger.

No one can do anything about this death of cinema. *Draughtsman's Contract* was paid for by television money and I was bitterly disappointed when I saw it on a television screen. It just didn't work. But there's no use complaining. I thought cinema was a vocabulary that had all the letters of the alphabet. Television has only vowels—primary colors, simple soundtracks, large closeups, no wide shots. Keep the picture moving, don't hold a still.

It's also disastrous as a capitalist vehicle. In Great Britain, the Sixties and Seventies saw the Golden Age of television. Now we're on this slippery slope to get the highest ratings. The quality goes down: monopolies of the media are held in more and more banal hands. Attempts to be innovative, exploratory, or investigative are disappearing.

I don't want to get too carried away talking about the death of cinema because of television. Cinema is related to 2000 years of image-making in Europe. When the electronic media get switched on around the world, there will still be painting and draughtsmanship—that goes back to the caves. The continuity of the effort continues, only the tools change. If you look at painting at its prime, it is a form of visual philosophy. Its crucial elements can still happily be contained in cinema and television. Now we're into holograms and so forth, but I don't think that matters. These machines are only as good as the imagination that uses them.

Cinema is about one hundred years old. If you examine the West's large cultural movements, they all last about one hundred years. Fresco painting did, easel painting, and so on.

CINEASTE: *In the face of social or technological change, there's always alarm that the new technologies will never be what the old ones were.*

GREENAWAY: Nostalgia. We're always so frightened of the new—people put wallpaper in their caravans. John Cage used to say there's a fifteen year gap between the cutting edge of culture and when even the highly educated follow on. The general public has just about caught up with Impressionism.

In Jane Austen's time, people complained that the young learned bad moral impulses from the novel. Exactly the same arguments were used in the 1920s against cinema, and again today about television. It's part of that silly "They don't make 'em like they used to" cry, or the ridiculous notion that now, today, it's worse—more decadent, more corrupt—than it ever was. Of course this is what every generation says.

I always thought my children would know what Jericho and who Hercules were. There is some indication that these two main mythologies of Western civilization are fading and need to be replaced. OK. What is replacing them? Superman? Batman? When you have no idea of what culture preceded you, you're limited to what can be invented at the moment.

On one hand, our knowledge about the past always diminishes. Content always atrophies. Poussin's paintings, for instance, are rather recherche in their classical references and most people don't know what the hell they're about. Yet we still admire and enjoy a Poussin painting. The form exists long after the content fades. On the other hand, Judeo-Christian and Greco-Roman traditions determine so much of life today—from our legal system to our buildings and streets—that if you know very little about them you inevitably know little about the forces that run your life.

CINEASTE: *How do you find the time to make films, television programs, write novels, paint?*

GREENAWAY: I don't do all that much research, and what research I do gets done after the fact. I write the script and then collect the background. For example, I know only the architecture that was necessary to do *Belly*. I don't employ researchers. I read the architectural magazines and take what's necessary from the general culture.

My films often start with some quite minor characters whom I fantasize about and make my own. One impetus for *Belly* was my interest in an eighteenth century architect whom I studied marginally in art school. The other impetus was a painting by Bronzino of a man called Andrea Doria, a Genoese statesman, age 45, done in the nude. I was intrigued that this 45 year-old man of great social standing would want to have himself painted so vulnerably. I began looking for someone who looked like Andrea Doria. I was very lucky to find Brian Dennehy.

There are also certain cultural traditions that I use repeatedly in my films because they are very important to Western civilization—like Dutch painting—or because they are especially germane to my themes of order and decay, like Jacobean Theater. It was the theater looking over its shoulder at the grand Elizabethan age of exploration and comparative financial success. England is still looking over its shoulder at the loss of empire. The Jacobeans had a great sense of melancholia—think of the funereal colorations of the poetry of people like John Donne. There seems to be a parallel in contemporary Britain—a peculiar nihilistic fatalism, as if to say, "These are simply the way things are."

I'm also interested in the theater tradition of the evil character. There are very evil characters in *Draughtsman,* for instance, and there are a couple of lines in *Cook Thief* where the thief gives away his desperate, vile identification with people like Mussolini. He keeps his tiny private army of cronies who dress up in pseudo uniforms and parade themselves very much like some swaggering, emasculated army. He associates grandiosity with the bully's figure.

CINEASTE: *Are you making a connection between dying civilizations and bullies who try to goad power where there is none?*

GREENAWAY: Perhaps. Think of all those evil, late Roman emperors or those larger-than-life terrorists of the late French revolution. Is this characteristic of late twentieth century Britain? It's certainly uncharitable to think so, though the current Tory party in Britain has made one or two adjustments in that direction.

Another tradition that reappears in my films is food and the uses of food in centuries of theater and painting. Eating tells you a great deal about people—like all those young middle class people, the yuppies, who go out to eat all the time at places where it's more important that the tomatoes match the wallpaper than it is that the food tastes good or is nourishing. They don't go out to eat so much as to show off their clothes or the way they can handle a knife, fork, and wine glass. Food is a very good way to critique the people who eat it. Today's dining critiques a society where consumerism has run riot.

Certain technical, painterly problems also keep reappearing in my work, like the problems of masking that first appeared in European table paintings—arranging people around a table so that no one is obliterated by anyone else. Or the problem of choreographing characters in the space of a film, and the physicality of bodies.

Cinema usually uses people as personalities rather than as bodies. You do see a lot of naked people but usually to reveal something about sexuality. Since I spent a lot of time drawing nudes when I was in school, I want to see the physicality of an actor, the size, the bulk, the shadow they cast on the wall. Brian Dennehy was especially good for this as the architect in *Belly,* where his considerable figure moves through all those fixed architectural spaces.

So there are cultural traditions and disciplines that always interest me and there are the specific triggers for a film, like the one about Andrea Doria that I mentioned.

When you publish this, will you edit for clarity and such? I'm concerned with being absolutely clear. When people sit around and talk as we have, information tends to get disorganized, so when you edit this . . . I do want to be clear.

# Anatomy of a Wizard

## HOWARD A. RODMAN/1991

TOKYO, THE SHIBUYA DISTRICT. On a sunny midday in February, the streets are dense with purposeful pedestrians. But if the image is Japanese, the text is English: Signage—massive, outsize, in paint, in neon, in pulsating arrays of electric-bulb dot matrix—shouts out Coke, Amtrak Discotheque, Newport Beach Fashion's Island.

Just across the avenue at the edge of Yoyogi Park, in what can only be described as a human dot matrix, 49 young Asian men in pompadour hair-styles, arrayed in a 7-by-7 grid, execute rockabilly dance moves in strict unison to the beat of American rock-and-roll songs—perhaps older than the dancers themselves—played loud on an enormous radio.

Just behind the dancers, cutting into the Tokyo skyline, is the imposing headquarters of NHK, the Japanese broadcasting giant. And inside the NHK corporate fortress, in the corridors of the west wing, an equally delirious clash of cultures is being played out. Here, against a backdrop of (literally) millions of dollars' worth of high-definition video equipment, Peter Greenaway, the English writer-director of such art-house classics as *The Draughtsman's Contract* and *The Cook, the Thief, His Wife and Her Lover,* is at work on a film. Looking donnish indeed in a blue blazer and casually draped woolen scarf, Greenaway is engaged in conversation (via an interpreter) with a crew of young Japanese men and women in identical (and very nifty) bright red "Team Hi-Vision" warm-up jackets.

Greenaway is here to orchestrate the postproduction of *Prospero's Books,* his latest and most ambitious work, an adaptation of Shakespeare's *The*

From *American Film*, November/December, 1991. Reprinted by permission of author.

*Tempest* at once fanciful and exact. Shot on film in Holland with a multi-national cast headed by Sir John Gielgud, *Prospero's Books* is being edited on videotape here in Japan in one of the world's most advanced high-tech postproduction suites and later will be transferred back to celluloid for release.

The visual image on the high-definition monitors is thrillingly dense: Actors vie for screen space with superimposed calligraphy, Muybridge-like animatics and all manner of body parts. Greenaway's trademark long lateral tracking shots—now a seminaked women skipping rope, now a tableau from Hals or Vermeer, now a very young boy urinating with gleeful (and artificially enhanced?) abandon into a swimming pool where Sir John is bathing—compete for attention with cadenced drops of water, rhythmically pulsing balls of fire and, above all, the lovingly rendered scrape of pen against parchment.

Greenaway has a formal, rigorous, near-algebraic approach to film narrative—"there's a way in which the scripts themselves are almost constructed on a grid," he says—that is almost always belied by a luxe, painterly richness. But here he pulls out all the stops. Layer upon layer upon gorgeous layer of text and image float across the screen, like a 1940s MGM montage gone mad, a Slavko Vorkapich fever dream.

It's a process fraught with possibilities—as the film's producer Kees Kasander says, "perhaps too many possibilities." On this electronic island—of which, one supposes, Greenaway is the Prospero—anything can happen. Adding another metaphor, another layer of meaning, becomes just a matter of tweaking a slider on the Sony HDS7.

While the Team Hi-Vision technicians are taking their lunch break, Greenaway—who speaks rapidly, articulately, in complete, cadenced sentences and well-structured paragraphs, his speech peppered with words like *shan't* and *albeit*—puts forth a version of his history as a filmmaker and how he came to make *Prospero's Books*.

"Shall I just talk about the barest bones?" he asks. "Well, I suppose I've made about 30 films. The earlier ones were made under very noncommercial circumstances, of which I suppose *The Falls* is the ultimate one—the encyclopedia that would bring everything together.

"That initial, sort of very private approach to filmmaking," Greenaway says, "which obviously had extremely restricted audiences, was much more appreciated, I suppose, by the painterly fraternity—semioticians, theoreticians of the cinema—perhaps more than by the general public.

But that's a period I still look back fondly upon and often regret in some cases I can't get back to. 'Cause it's extremely open-ended, requires comparatively little collaboration—and I'm not, on the whole, a very good collaborator."

He pauses as if to indicate a new paragraph. "Now, all the time that I was making these films, though, I was also engaged in the making of television work. I sincerely believed that if cinema could command a full vocabulary which was made up of 26 letters of the alphabet, there was a way in which television could only handle vowels. I since have come to believe that that's not true and that television has its own alphabet. I made about six or seven programs in television which I tried very hard to turn into what I would call *television* television. Deliberately against the language of film. And a program called *TV Dante,* I suppose, was finally the opportunity for me to get my hands on comparatively sophisticated, if ultimately low-tech, technology.

"There are, obviously, tremendous frustrations about working for television, only one of which—not necessarily the most important—is the question of scale. My frustrations about making very complex pictures on television for *Dante* and not being able to see them in high quality on a big screen, where there's a mass of information that comes rushing at you, hundreds of events, bang, bang, bang, bang. . . ." He smiles. "All that explosion on the tiny screen was very frustrating.

"So. Having made *The Cook, the Thief,* which was CinemaScope, widescreen, taking it to the other extreme if you like—big screens, lush cinematography, rich use of all the vocabulary of cinema—and also playing, I would like to think, at the cusp of what television was all about, television language, I dreamt somehow of bringing these two together.

"And this, of course, is why we're here in Japan."

Well, as it turns out, not *quite* Japan.

Though the NHK facility is square in the heart of Tokyo, the edit suite—and the electronic Paintbox suite down the hall, connected by an imposing snake of co-ax cables—is not officially part of the country at all. By way of explanation, Greenaway points to the sign in Japanese on the door.

"Well, I think it's something like, All strangers are forbidden in this room. And that is because we're under a certain interdict which suggests that our program is erotic, if not pornographic. You're probably aware of the Japanese sensitivity about pornography, yes? There is a law which says, Thou shalt not show pubic hair. Which I take, by the way, to be a pseudonymous way of saying, Thou shan't show genitalia on the screen.

"Shakespeare wasn't particularly known to be highly erotic—or if he was, by inference rather than by direct fact. We, however, have made a treatment of a Shakespeare work whereby there are a considerable number of naked people."

Greenaway continues, moving his hands in small, precise gestures as if wielding a pointer or baton. "The whole of this studio is bonded; that is to say, we are not officially in Japan per se, but rather, in what is considered for these purposes an adjunct of the customs shed at Narita airport. Officially, we are not here because we are pornographic. It's a rather curious situation.

"This means that everybody who works in this room is supposed to walk around with a little badge allowing official entry into a bonded area. You see I'm not wearing one," he says. "But that's only because I'm carrying it in my pocket."

Kasander—a handsome, unflappable Dutchman who used to produce the Rotterdam Film Festival—is as excited by the editing process as by the work: "Celluloid is so limited and so conventional nowadays, so badly organized—the large crews, the way it's shot, the cameras, so many problems, so stupid, so back-to-the-Middle Ages—that it's time to leave all that behind and do something different."

Greenaway concurs. "The very reasons I became interested in the cinema or television were because of the extraordinary opportunities to play with images, to play with words, to play with their interactions. I started my career as a painter. And I still believe painting is, for me, the supreme visual means of communication. Its freedoms, its attitudes, its history, its potential. And if you look at twentieth-century painting, it's been 10,000 times more radical than the cinema has." He pauses. "Cinema," he says, "is a grossly conservative medium."

He sweeps his arm as if to invoke Kasander's nightmare vision—the world of celluloid and its heavy-metal apparatus. "The cinema is conservative because vast sums of money are necessary to make it. And it's conservative because it is a very large collaboration. If you look at the twentieth-century inventions in painting, from cubism onward, there has been absolutely nothing comparable in cinema. So the cinema, you see, seems to be an opportunity to expand on those things which my rather small painterly talent would never allow me to.

"I desperately think," he says politely, "that cinema needs a savage jab in the arm."

That jab in the arm is being administered, in this case, by a not-so-savage array of Hi-Vision equipment (Hi-Vision being NHK's proprietary name for high-definition television, which offers a film-style aspect ratio and several times the resolution of standard TV).

How it works: In the Paintbox room, Eve Ramboz enters images into her computer via a high-definition video camera. The images—plundered from a variety of books featuring the work of da Vinci and Muybridge, among others—are then treated by Ramboz: colorized, resized, rotated, enhanced. As Ramboz works the images, Greenaway looks on and offers suggestions: "A deeper red, a burgundy. No, it's the same color as the letter. Maybe something blue, but not the ED blue. Can you make the dots bigger? There's still some black in there. Good!"

The Paintbox images are then ported down the hall to the edit suite, where layer after layer of superimposition is tested, tailored, adjusted, combined. At every turn, Greenaway seems preternaturally certain about what he wants to see—as if the film already existed inside his head, the task now being but to coax out those images from the bank of switches and devices. He speaks to his *equipe*: "I want to have 15 frames fade in, hold it for five seconds, 15 frames fade out. I want the fade-in to begin the very moment that the face disappears."

The engineers reroll tape, stare at the frenetically rewinding image on the monitors, pull sliders, twirl knobs. Now Greenaway views the results of his instructions. "It's too long. Can we make it four seconds?" he asks editor Marina Bodbijl. He views the new cut. "Now let us try three seconds." They make the edit, play back the tape. "Good," says Greenaway, a smile playing at the corners of his mouth. "Now. Can we reconstruct 'The Anatomy of Birth' according to this new ratio? Would it be at all possible?"

*Prospero's Books* is, in essence, a set of perpetual translations.

The first is Greenaway's "interpretation" of *The Tempest,* in which one line of Prospero's—"knowing I loved my books, he [Gonzalo] furnished me from mine own library with volumes that I prize above my dukedom"—is made to serve as the metaphor for the whole enterprise. Green-away then assumes that this library contained some 24 books and pro-ceeds, one by one, to invent them. The 24 books—like the 12 drawings in *The Draughtsman's Contract,* the sequential digits in *Drowning by Numbers* or the color scheme in *The Cook, the Thief*—provide Greenaway with his grid, his armature.

"I'm often thought of, by those critics who hate what I do, as being incredibly anal-retentive," says Greenaway. "But I would refute that. I think that I can quite honestly say that I'm open to a serendipity.

"Besides," he adds, "this is the first time I've actually used, as it were, somebody else's screenplay."

The second translation is the technological one, that of film-to-tape-to-film: Shot on 35mm film (by the venerable Sacha Vierny; who contributed his talents to such modern classics as *Belle de Jour* and *Last Year as Marienbad,* as well as several previous Greenaways), *Prospero's Books* was then trans-ferred to 1125-line high-definition wide-screen video. Superimpositions, special effects and opticals were added in the video domain and then transferred back to film to be married with the original celluloid. (In con-ventional film-to-tape editing, the tape version is too low-fidelity to be transferred back to film—the end product of those devices is, rather, a computer-generated Edit Decision List, whose numbers can be used to con-form the celluloid to the videotape edit.)

And third, underlying all, is the translation whereby Prospero becomes Shakespeare and Gielgud becomes Prospero—with Greenaway perhaps hovering above all.

Greenaway explains: "*The Tempest* [has been] a fantastically popular play for the past 10 years or so." He speaks briefly of Paul Mazursky's *Tempest,* of Derek Jarman's *Tempest* and of *Forbidden Planet,* that wonderful '50s science-fiction chestnut in which Walter Pigeon plays Dr. Morbius, the Prospero of Altair-IV, with Robby the Robot as his Ariel.

"For me," Greenaway continues, "*The Tempest* is extremely self-referen-tial, and I always tend to feel the most sympathy for those works of art which do have that sort of self-knowledge, that say, basically, 'I am an arti-fice.' I very much like the idea that when somebody sits in the cinema and watches a film of mine, it's *not* a slice of life, it's *not* a window on the world. It's a constant concern of mine to bring the audience back to this realization.

"*The Tempest* is somehow an ideal medium to play this game. To start, there's a way in which Prospero himself is a portrait of Shakespeare. Although first person isn't used all the time—he's not saying, 'I, I, I'—there are inferences, certainly toward the end of the play and certainly in the epilogue, which say, 'I am an artificer, I have spent most of my life making tricks for you; if you like them, well and good, but if you don't, no matter, I'm now taking my leave.' Taking leave of you, the theater, the world of illusion. And supposedly, it is Shakespeare's last full play.

"Obviously, what clinched it was the opportunity we were offered to have the last grand classic English Shakespearian actor, Sir John Gielgud, to play what presumably is the last performance of his life—he's 86. So we can have an identity cross-referencing Shakespeare, Prospero, and Gielgud. And I've tried very hard to do that, so that Gielgud *is* Shakespeare, so much so that, as the film progresses, we actually see Gielgud/Prospero as Shakespeare writing *The Tempest*. Self-referential, and it brings us back to text again. Because we see the text written.

"Well, a cynic, of course, might say, This is all highly fashionable, it's very postmodernist, part of that phenomenon. And, of course, I would not deny it. Gielgud is not Action Man, but he does have the most magnificent voice and an extraordinary ability to use it. And since there is a way that Prospero is both Gielgud and Shakespeare, we have got Prospero himself to invent the dialogue for all the other characters. And as you see Gielgud/Shakespeare/Prospero writing the dialogue, so you see Prospero, as played by Gielgud, trying the dialogue out. Ultimately, Gielgud's voice is everybody. But, since this is a Jacobean play, there is a feeling that this originally might have been a classic revenge drama—something like [seventeenth-century playwright John] Ford's *'Tis a Pity She's a Whore,* on which I based, in fact, *The Cook, the Thief.* But unlike that film, this is a broken-backed revenge tragedy—because it doesn't end in revenge. It goes to a certain point, then suddenly doglegs in a different direction.

"And I've used that crucial point which suggests that forgiveness brings alive that which revenge can only keep dead. So all the characters, who have been previously voiced by Gielgud, at that moment of forgiveness suddenly speak for themselves."

But if Prospero (and perhaps Gielgud) has renounced his artifice, it's not at all clear that Greenaway is about to renounce his. Though the cross-cultural, cross-technological project was not without its difficulties, a basic sense of goodwill exists among these comrades in electronic arms.

Greenaway and Kasander love jousting against celluloid and found NHK a stunning benefactor (the postproduction time and services furnished to *Prospero's Books* would be worth, on the open market, perhaps $4 million). Says Kasander, "It works for us, it works for NHK. 'Cause we do the research for them. We did perhaps 80 percent research and 20 percent the real work. In exchange, we can do everything for free." Kasander says that he and Greenaway pushed the limits of what Hi-Vision could accomplish. "We asked so many things from them; we sent back the first [tape-to-film] transfers; we refused almost everything because it was not good enough. But now it's good. It's one step forward."

The transfers were done at Imagica, the leading Japanese film lab. Although the *Prospero* material presented formidable obstacles — due, in part, to Greenaway and Vierny's insistence on high-contrast chiaroscuro film-style shots, with no concession to the lowered contrast range of video — Imagica managed, by assiduous tweaking, to produce video and video-to-tape images without grain and with full, rich blacks.

NHK seems content, as well, to let Greenaway — and, on a slightly earlier project, Wim Wenders — have their days on the Hi-Vision playing fields. Wenders, says Hi-Vision technical director Hideichi Tamegaya, became fascinated by the grain artifacts that appear on the screen when HDTV tape is fast-forwarded or rewound at high speed on digital recorders. "I tell him, 'This is not an actual effect, this is noise.' But he thought it was very good." Wenders ended up using the hi-def noise artifacts extensively in his film *Until the End of the World* for dream sequences. "We developed," says Tamegaya, "a special system as a means of dealing with strange images."

Greenaway sighs about some of the constraints of this postproduction. "I'm a guest in the country, and I'm grateful for what's been offered, but I'm used to very sophisticated Western video houses, where you move very fast — not least of all because it's incredibly expensive. It took 3½ weeks to do 8½ minutes of film. And the actual degree of complexity I don't think is that astonishing. It's a combination of unfamiliarity with the approach, the inexpertise of the technicians — which is not their fault, they just haven't had the experience. I suppose the third factor which must be taken into account is that the machinery is well-nigh prototype.

"Retrospectively, I wish we'd been more ambitious. But this whole exercise—like every film you make—opens so many doors. Now we're looking out the window to the next ocean. And that's very exciting."

Greenaway smiles. "You know that [Jacques] Derrida quotation which says, The picture always has the last word? A great little epigram. And here I am taking this renowned text and turning it into images. Now, I don't want this to be an English intellectual playing with the tools, as I did in *TV Dante*. But even if we have created something unsatisfactory, I shan't cry copious tears over it, because I can see now the potential."

Once more, Greenaway describes the precise sequence of dissolves and superimpositions he'd like for a particular sequence. Now, as the red-jacketed engineers find the right section of tape, Greenaway—assured of perhaps 10 minutes during which he will not be called upon to make a decision—retreats to the corner where, seemingly oblivious to the multilingual play of voices in the edit suite, he types out a scene for yet another film on his laptop computer.

"There's a project," he says later, "I'd like very much to do, called *Prospero's Creatures*, about what happened before the beginning. Sort of a prelude to *The Tempest*. And I've also written a play called *Miranda*, about what happens afterwards on the ship on the way home. It's about what happens to innocence and how it has to be destroyed."

# The Book, the Theater, the Film, and Peter Greenaway

DYLAN TRAN/1991

IT WAS THE COOK, *the Thief, His Wife and Her Lover* in 1989 that finally catapulted the British independent filmmaker Peter Greenaway into the spotlight of Hollywood cinema. The attention was not without irony, however. The film emerged in the midst of the debate on censorship of the arts that year, and was cited by many in the far Right camp to be a prime example of a work whose "pornographic" sex and violence demoralized viewers without any redeeming quality or family values. But Greenaway's artistic merits were impossible to ignore and the critical acclaim attributed to the film, along with Philip Kaufman's *Henry and June,* placed Hollywood in the uncomfortable position of having to re-evaluate its own X-rating system. Nevertheless the unfortunate context of sensationalism remained a permanent scar and Hollywood branded the director with the infamous seal of "controversial" filmmaker in the minds of many U.S. viewers.

Followers of Greenaway's prolific body of works, which actually span almost three decades, know that the films extend beyond the lush surface decor into complex issues of class, myth, sexuality, and politics. From *A Walk Through H* (1978) to *Draughtsman's Contract* (1982), *A Zed and Two Noughts* (1985) to *Drowning by Numbers* (1988) and *The Cook, the Thief,* the thread that weaves throughout these pivotal films is not only a fascination with the artificial systems by which man organizes his world, and with which Greenaway structures his films, but also how the intrinsic absurdity

From *High Performance,* Winter 1991. Reprinted by permission of *High Performance* and the author.

of these categories are perceived. What is not easily realized, however, is that these highly symbolic systems often critique current political realities in an imaginative, although sometimes indirect, fashion.

Greenaway has always demanded that his audiences work as hard as he to question the artificial construct of cinema, to question what we name and take advantage of as truth, knowledge and reality. And work they must for his current film *Prospero's Books*. Even though the text of the film is familiar—based on Shakespeare's *The Tempest*—and the plot is predictable, Greenaway has again managed to abandon safe ground and subvert all expectations. Aesthetically, the film is a stunning visual layering of images, aided by the cutting edge technology of the Graphic Paintbox, that reflect the depth of Shakespeare's language and provoke new meanings by nature of its superimposition. This structure also provides a convenient vehicle for the framing and re-framing motif in the film, as well as instigating the transition from "words making text, text making pages, pages making books from which knowledge is fabricated in pictorial form." Greenaway is thus able to reveal several narratives at once, manipulating at will the characteristics of time and space, fact and fiction, illusion and reality. It's interesting to note that U.S. independent filmmaker Gus Van Sant's *My Own Private Idaho* also manipulates Shakespeare's text from *Henry IV* in much the same manner, although relying more on conventional editing techniques and introducing the inventive device of narcolepsy. But whereas Van Sant uses the text to point out the relevance of the plot to past history. Greenaway poignantly shows the relevance of *The Tempest* to the crises at the end of the 20th Century.

Although Greenaway has admitted that there is a deliberate cross-identification between Shakespeare, Prospero, and Gielgud, the star of the film, it's no small task to be the master manipulator of these three. So how does Greenaway see his role as the filmmaker in that equation?

"Well, it maybe ought to be whispered up against the reputation of these three. But it would be naive to also suggest that there is little input from me because we did take certain amount of license with the text, the invention of the 24 books, for example. Although Shakespeare mentions the books, he doesn't exactly say what they are, and he certainly doesn't describe them. The strategy is not only getting Gielgud to speak the part of Prospero but to also voice all the other people on the grounds that Prospero is like the marionette master, the puppet master, who controls everybody, which of course is exactly what Shakespeare did because he invented everything. We just took the stage a little further so to speak."

In the film, Prospero's absolute vision brings about a political reality in which the natives on the island have no freedom of speech or expression. The metaphorical situation is a familiar one, and can be applied to everything spanning British imperialism to the National Endowment for the Arts. For Greenaway, the key to resolution is based in compassion.

"It is interesting that Gielgud as Shakespeare as Prospero communicates to both us, the audience, and the other characters in the film through writing words on a piece of paper. It's as though he's writing memos to everybody. The first memorandum to him is written by his own servant Ariel. He is treated to his own means of communication, which makes him ultimately change his mind and forgive everybody. Of course everyone then springs to life through the situation that forgiveness brings to life those characters that revenge could only keep dead. I think that's one of the interesting things about *The Tempest* that makes it a very contemporary drama because it's about the end of the 20th Century, the end of the millennium. It's a play about endings and beginnings, about rebirth, about forgiving your enemies to start all over again, which I think makes it particularly pertinent to now.

"It's a play and therefore a film about knowledge. We're all now so incredibly knowledgeable, we have access to so much knowledge. We can manipulate DNA, we can interfere with embryology, we have the secrets to the H-Bomb, we can annihilate the world, which makes us in some senses, magicians. But then what do we do with that knowledge? Do we use it for good reasons or do we use it for bad, do we want to revenge ourselves and our enemies or do we want to try to create a universal suffrage or reconciliation? There's one thing I would take issue with Shakespeare on: in the end he destroys his books, which I find very painful indeed. We can't unknowledge ourselves, we can't turn away knowledge once we've got it. There is a line in the original text that suggests he drowned his books. I've also suggested in the film that they were also combustible so that when they hit the water, they burst into flames to remind us of all those times in the twentieth century when people burned books."

Prospero's books aren't just any books. These 24 volumes contain all the knowledge Prospero needs to execute his magic. Shakespeare does not bother to mention the quantity of the books in passing, but Greenaway

has seized upon this minor detail and made the central narrative periphery. But why only 24?

"The first and rather glib answer is it's a self-reflection of Godard's suggestion that cinema's truth is 24 frames a second. But that's if you're a little
fanciful. Prospero, of course, lives in a pre-decimal age when the basic
mode of counting is based on twelve and not on ten. We have around two
dozen books. I presumably could have made a lot more but I thought that
would just be the right number of books in order to suggest all the different types of knowledge, all the different types of books that would have
been available not only to him but to us. So you have the whole world of
theology represented by a theological book, the whole world of natural
history represented by a bestiary, the whole world of erotica represented
by one pornography, and so on. They are a summation of all the knowledge at that particular time, which was about the year 1611 when the play
was first performed in London."

"It's quite extraordinary to think that man can organize his world
around just 24 volumes."

"Right. Well, I guess you really could say it's 24 library shelves, or 24
libraries indeed. The whole thing can go from there on. But the books are
fascinating and very magical. Imagine a book that supposedly is dedicated
to motion and dance and in fact does dance on the library shelf, or a book
of architecture that when you open it, out springs Rome. I mean maybe
who knows, in 100 years time, we might have books like this."

Greenaway's use of the Graphic Paintbox is revolutionary in its ability
to manipulate images, time and space. I asked Greenaway to talk about
this process and its potential for future work.

"I started my career off as a painter. Painting is a radical visual vehicle
for the expression of ideas. Twentieth century painting has leapt ahead
and left cinema way behind. Cinema hasn't even reached its Cubist period
yet. This tool is a way to resurrect the relationship that maybe an artist has
with film or with tape. I can make mocks on a TV screen now with a pen,
pencil, or brush, much like a painter does. The Quantel Paintbox is able to
produce 17 million colors whereas I think the human eye alone can only
recognize about a 1,000. So in a way, it can extend the potentiality of a
painter's color range, for example. But I can manipulate the world. I can
change things just like a painter does: I can erase, I can brush out. I can
reverse, I can negativize, and I find that very exciting. Eisenstein, the great

Russian director, suggested the greatest cinematic artform is animation because you are in complete control. I'd like to think we can somehow take animation out of the prerogative of children's cinema and use it perhaps for sophisticated, complicated, complex adult situations, and to also make it part of our general vocabulary. I'd like to imagine that *Prospero's Books* for me is the beginning of a massive investigation of a cinema that could make use of all these extraordinary new technologies."

Greenaway the filmmaker, painter and writer is extremely eloquent and articulate about his art, having thoroughly worked out the process to immaculate detail. He admits to favoring a systematic Classical approach, finding it very useful in saving time and money as an independent filmmaker. But no matter how outspoken he is about his work, he is adamantly shy when it comes to discussing personal motivations. Perhaps this is due to the fact that he refuses to acknowledge an artist's biographical background as a necessary tool to understanding the work, or rather it's because he despises the Hollywood psychodrama that predicates actions on simplistic personal motivations. In any case, Greenaway the man is much more softspoken and reflective about his philosophical attitudes. He is not the artist/activist we are accustomed to, even though his films are very political. When I confronted Greenaway with the censorship controversy that surrounded *The Cook, the Thief,* he responded, "I don't know if you'll believe me when I say this, but the American situation is very different than the rest of the world. We had no censorship problems at all in Europe with this film, or even in Japan, who obviously have certain sensitivities about forms of eroticism. It only seemed to be in America that we came across this problem of censorship, and of course the debate that ensued was interesting for me but I never in any way wanted to manipulate or calculated it to be particularly sensational. However, I do believe that cinema should be provocative and I do think it should push form and content, and examine sensitive areas."

When we spoke last September, there was already growing speculation that *Prospero's Books* would meet a similar fate in its U.S. release. Speaking on the eve of its premiere at the New York Film Festival, Greenaway enthusiastically defended the film against all criticisms: "Well, I suppose [the controversy] has to do with all those uhh . . . nude bodies in the film. But they're very asexual, they're very desexualized. They're very much part of the general light and dark chiaroscuro of the picture, part of the landscape, part of a scholar's mind in 1611, who had been brought up on Renaissance painting. They represent the clay or the loom in which he makes and organizes all his magic from. They also represent all those hundreds of mythological spirits that were part of the early baroque period. But you know how in most dominant cinema people take their clothes off to have sex. This sort of contrived expectation is in no way realized in the film. The body in all its forms, either fat or thin, old or young, so-called ugly or so-called beautiful, is portrayed here; I think that no body's ugly. There is a way in which this represents mankind, if you like. It's presented in a very asexualized or desexualized way (if at all you can view the body without some sexuality), and I would have thought it to cause no offense."

"I'm interested in finding out what's the response to your work in England because your films contain very scathing critiques of the political situation there."

"*The Cook, the Thief* did very well. It broke all box office records at the theater. It ran for about 18–20 weeks in London. And the only film making more money right now in London than *Prospero's Books* is *Terminator 2*—"

"That's quite a remarkable argument for artistic integrity in the face of commercialism."

"Well, I don't know how long that will last of course, but it is indicative that there are a large number of people entertained and intrigued by my sort of cinema. I do of course have violent detractors who hate what I do: 'impossible, recondite, intellectually exhibitionist' and all those other things. But I think society very often considers that intellectual, complicated, sophisticated ideas about drama are legitimate in the theater but somehow not legitimate in cinema, which I find very strange."

It's this hypocrisy that Greenaway characterizes as part of the anti-intellectual ethic. It's also the challenge he has chosen to wrestle with in bringing Jacobean drama to *The Cook, the Thief,* and Shakespeare to *Prospero's Books*:

"This isn't exactly a straightforward version of the play. I wanted to do more than just tell the story very well. I wanted to really examine and experiment, invest some interest in the actual sheer poetry of the extraordinary text, the last play of Shakespeare, who was moving into extraordinary new ground that prophesied all sorts of theatrical ideas of the future."

# Prospero's Books — Word and Spectacle: An Interview with Peter Greenaway

## MARLENE RODGERS/1991

Many years ago I wrote a script called "Jonson and Jones," about the relationship of Ben Jonson and Inigo Jones in making masques for the Jacobean court. I suppose they made something like thirty masques in a period of fifteen years, but apparently all the time they were quarrelling. They were professionally—and in their private lives—very antagonistic and jealous of one another. But I think over and above these niceties, basically Ben Jonson was interested in the word, and Inigo Jones was interested in spectacle. And there's a way they had to fashion their two opposing interests to make a coherent whole, in order to present their masques. And in a way that is also the quandary of cinema...it's very interesting to try to find a filmmaker who can bring the word and the spectacle together.

—Peter Greenaway

VERY EVIDENTLY, GREENAWAY HIMSELF is this filmmaker. The marriage of word and spectacle informs every moment of his latest film, *Prospero's Books*. Greenaway's sixth feature is operatic in its use of music, song, dance, and the choreography of scores of extras. Against opulent settings of Renaissance architecture, naked spirits form tableaux based on classical mythology or Western art. The spectacle is further enhanced by the density of the images. Greenaway uses both conventional film techniques and the resources of high-definition television to layer image upon

From *Film Quarterly*, vol. 45, no. 2, pp. 11–19, Winter 1991-92. © by The Regents of the University of California. Reprinted by permission.

image, superimposing or opening out a second or third frame within his frame. At the same time, the film is highly literary and self-referential in its constant reminders that *The Tempest* is text: Greenaway conceives the play as Prospero's own creation, and we see the pen of the magician-play-wright as it moves across the parchment, leaving baroque, calligraphic lines of the text in its wake.

Language and text are further emphasized by the authoritative voice of Sir John Gielgud—as Prospero, author of the play, he speaks all the dialogue until the final act. The magical force of his words conjures his characters before our eyes in elaborate dumb shows, played out in long extended takes. Only when Prospero forgives his enemies, realizing that "The rarer action is/In virtue than in vengeance," do the characters he has created come alive and speak in their own voices.

Perhaps Greenaway's most imaginative strategy in adapting *The Tempest* is his use of Shakespeare's brief mention of Prospero's magical books. Greenaway creates fantastical volumes that encompass the vast knowledge Prospero required to create his island utopia. The twenty-four books, which punctuate and structure the narrative, include anatomy texts with organs that throb and bleed and architectural texts with buildings that spring out, fully formed.

The realization of *Prospero's Books* has not exhausted Greenaway's creative engagement with *The Tempest*. He is publishing a collection of images from the film under the title *Ex Libris Prospero* as well as a novel, *Prospero's Creatures.* Additionally, he is writing a play called *Miranda,* which forefronts Prospero's daughter as the characters of *The Tempest* journey back to Milan.

Greenaway was in Toronto for the Festival of Festivals and I spoke to him about *Prospero's Books* and his very evident interest in the seventeenth century. Greenaway's latest film is now the third to bear a relation to that period. His first feature, *The Draughtsman's Contract,* is set in the Restoration, in 1692; *The Cook, the Thief, His Wife and Her Lover* is strongly influenced by Jacobean revenge tragedy, particularly John Ford's *'Tis Pity She's a Whore*; and *Prospero's Books* is set in 1611—the year that Shakespeare wrote *The Tempest.*

PETER GREENAWAY: For some reason, the seventeenth century is an extraordinary period, it's a transitional period—you must remember that the Renaissance came to England very late. So by the time the High Renaissance had run its course in Italy, we were only just beginning our sense of Renaissance. Sometimes it's curious to imagine Shakespeare as an equivalent figure to somebody like Michelangelo; it's strange to think that they are both figures of the Renaissance but that they are posited in completely different worlds. I always think of the Jacobeans as being much more Renaissance-conscious than Shakespeare—although the first Renaissance influence in England came in the reign of Henry VII. There was a man called Torrigiano who created the tomb for Henry VII, so that was the first evidence of the Renaissance spirit in northern Europe.

There is a way that late Shakespearean drama has certainly excited and been a profound influence on a lot of my cinema for a long time, but I think that *'Tis Pity She's a Whore* has somehow been responsible for my interest in both the beginning of the seventeenth century and the end. I saw a production of that play when I was an adolescent and probably very impressionable, and I was immediately taken with all its themes and ideas—its violence towards women, its concerns with examining very dangerous taboo areas like voluntary incest, its gestures that are almost too melodramatic to be true, like the cutting out of the heart, and so on. Jacobean drama basically has to do with translations of Seneca coming through France and the Low Countries to influence English drama. There is an alternative tradition, that starts with Seneca and goes on through Jacobean drama to be picked up later by people like de Sade, and then much later by people like Genet, Bataille, and it even continues with Ionesco's Theatre of Cruelty and Peter Brook's Theatre of Blood, and perhaps it is also picked up by filmmakers like Buñuel and Pasolini. So I'm fascinated by an alternative examination of cultures, which I suppose basically examines the center of the human predicament by going to the edges, to the extremes, to see in fact how far one can stretch the examination of various forms of aberrant behavior. It's obviously a tradition that I'm interested in, as exemplified by the extremes of the both literal and metaphorical examination of cannibalism as an idea in *The Cook, the Thief....*

MARLENE RODGERS: *In the past you've talked about the seventeenth century having correspondences in our own times. In what ways to you feel* The Tempest *is particularly relevant now?*

*The Tempest,* of course, is a play all about beginnings and endings, which makes it perhaps very relevant to the end of the century, the end of the millennium. Miranda is given those words which Huxley used, "O brave new world/That has such people in it," which is an extraordinary state-ment for the future and optimism. I think that I saw about six performances of *The Tempest* on the stage in London last year, and there's now appar-ently a Danish animated film about *The Tempest* going around, and of course there's the famous Peter Brook that is now travelling the world, so it seems to be a very, very useful and contemporary piece to play with.

Another nice thing is that Shakespeare begins to eschew narrative [in the last plays], he's not worried about all those narrative niceties any more. He jumps time, he changes locations very dramatically, all those sorts of things which I'm interested in. Because I'm not particularly interested in contemporary psychodrama—with all that pseudo-supermarket Freudian analysis of character which becomes so boring—that has now been going on so long, especially in dominant cinema, which itself seems to be simply an illustrational medium, illustrating novels all the time, not even twenti-eth-century novels but nineteenth-century novels. I mean, what film can you see that's actually taken cognizance of James Joyce, for example? I've made comments about cinema not reaching Cubism yet, but there hasn't even been an awareness of Joyce. When these other art forms have taken great imaginative leaps, cinema tragically has remained very conventional and backward-looking. You can see why, of course: great sums of money are necessary, great collaborative efforts, distribution and exhibition sys-tems that are very moribund and reactionary. So, as you can see with my cinema, I'm trying very hard, maybe overambitiously—for myself as well as for any other purposes—to begin to explore these sorts of examples that exist cross-culturally.

*What is your own theory of character, given that you're not interested in the tra-ditional psychological exploration of character?*
You know the novels of Heinrich von Kleist? There is a way in which this writer, who is writing about the eighteen-twenties, had a great sense of de facto examination of characters, so that there was never any attempt to explain. Characters were given characteristics and there was no attempt to delve into Oedipal problems and the traumas of childhood and all that sort of association. And there's a way that I really like that approach.

Another thing that I'm trying to do—since Prospero has become an industry—I've written a novel called *Prospero's Creatures,* which is about all
those allegorical creatures that dart about in the penumbra areas of the
film. Because I've been interested for a very long time in allegory. Allegory
is very largely not important to us anymore. We have Father Time with the
attribute of the scythe, and maybe Blind Justice holding the scales, but
compared to the plethora of allegorical figures that inhabited the seventeenth-century imagination there is no comparison to be made anymore.
And all those characters in the tracking shots behind the title, I've tried to
find as many characters as I could who had an allegorical reference to
water. So, just to name a few, you get Mr. and Mrs. Noah with their ark,
you get references to Moses in the bulrushes, there are examples of Leda
and the Swan, there are examples of Icarus falling into the sea—all those
mythological allegorical figures that have some association, since it is *The
Tempest,* with water. And I use this sort of idea elsewhere according to
whatever else is happening on the screen. So . . . an examination of characters as ciphers, characters carrying the weight of an allegorical significance.
*The Cook, the Thief, His Wife and Her Lover*: the very title implies all cooks,
all thieves, all wives, all lovers. It's like Chaucer's *Canterbury Tales,* the so-
and-so's tale, the so-and-so's tale, and the so-and-so's tale. And these
characters are all brought together into one particular situation. I've often
been castigated for not wishing to develop the characters in a three-dimensional sense, but I'm not really interested if their grandmother was called
Grace and had a dog called Fido. So quite readily, without apology, characters for me have to hold a weight of allegorical and personifying meaning.

*Yet there were a lot of psychological insights into character to be taken out of*
The Cook, the Thief, His Wife and Her Lover.
Inevitably, inevitably. You could work up great theses about the sexuality
of Albert Spica, for example, and his interest in the lavatory rather than
the bedroom and his concern for the sexual apparatus being so near the
digestive tract and all that. Of course that was there for those readings, but
I would also like all these other readings to be apparent.

*I want to come back to the water imagery in* The Tempest *you were talking of
earlier. This is obviously a very strong element in the play, but it seems that
water imagery has had a special fascination for you in your other films, too.*

*Most obviously in* Drowning by Numbers, *but also in other films, including your short,* Making a Splash, *which was a sort of ode to water.*
Well, on a practical level, water is fantastically photogenic. But of course, the world is four-fifths water, we're all born in amniotic fluid, water is a big cleansing medium whether it's literal or metaphorical. On another, pragmatic level, water provides almost a legitimate opportunity for people to be seen nude, in the case of *Twenty-six Bathrooms,* for example. But it literally is the oil of life, it is the blood of life, which splashes, dribbles, washes, roars—it's a great friend and a terrifying enemy, it has all those significances. And there is a way in which somehow water is the unguent, the balm, the cooling agent of a lot of the dramas of all the films. And I suspect I should go on using it, too.

*You suggest in your notes to* Prospero's Books *that the books Prospero has on his island are responsible for making him the paradoxical character that he is. To what extent did you actually use the books as a means of reflecting on Prospero's character?*
On a slightly facetious note, if *The Cook, the Thief . . .* was a film about "You are what you eat," *Prospero's Books* is a film about "You are what you read." We're all products of our education, our cultural background, which very largely is perceived through text. Text is so desperately important in this film. All the images come out of Prospero's inkwell, as though the inkwell were a top hat, with the magician pulling out the scarves, image after image. And there's a way in which each time a book is brought forth, it indicates a slight change in Prospero's behavior. Because sometimes he is a stern grandfather, sometimes he is rather avuncular—he has an avuncular relationship with Ariel. Sometimes he is a dictator, wearing the hat of a doge, representative of a maritime power. Sometimes he is a beneficent magician. Sometimes he is worried about his daughter's virginity. His character changes all the time, so we introduce a book which might, as it were, explain the cultural references that made him the man he was.

So the books are working on that level, as well as introducing the vast plethora of Prospero's knowledge. In some senses the whole film is going on in his head; there are all the masses and masses of knowledge that a scholar accumulates, some of it quite wasteful, some of it quite bad. There are images obviously from Michelangelo but also from nineteenth-century salon painting, there's high art and low art. You know this post-Warhol attitude towards the elevation of kitsch into something more significant. Although the film is posited in 1611, Prospero has—as a magician—foresight. He embraces the art of the future, as well as the art of the past.

*A narcissistic desire for omnipotence drives a lot of seventeenth-century protagonists, as well as some of your characters, like Albert Spica, for example. They crave the kind of godlike power that Prospero possesses. It is ironic that at the end of* The Tempest, *Prospero relinquishes that power by destroying his books.*
I have a great antipathy to that ending and would take up a quarrel with Shakespeare, if I could be so bold in my humble position as an eccentric English filmmaker at the end of the twentieth century. I could never imagine that there would be any great significance gained by throwing away knowledge—I don't think you can throw away knowledge. And the correspondence for our present reality that is important to me is that we have invested ourselves with so much knowledge that I think we ourselves have almost become magicians. We can alter nature's course almost, with our creation of the atomic bomb, and with all the investigations into embryology and DNA and so on—you know this whole business about genetic manipulation of continuums. I don't think you can de-knowledge yourself, you can't un-knowledge yourself, so the gesture of throwing books away is a peculiarly wasteful one. It's also a very selfish one, too, because even if we cannot use the value of those books ourselves, other people can, so somehow it's almost not just denying knowledge to himself but to everyone else too.

There is, I suppose, even one more gesture after the throwing away of the books. You must remember the last two—a collection of Shakespeare's plays and *The Tempest*—are preserved. Otherwise of course I wouldn't have the wherewithal to make the film itself. That's a typical post-modernist self-referential gesture at the end. Also, Caliban, the image of the negative aspect of the island, so-called, is the savior of the books, which is I think a nice ironic gesture. But even when that's done, we still see the final, almost apocalyptic release of Ariel, the final gasp or release of the spirit. So you see them [the Ariels] running, through fire and water, through the main elements towards us. Finally there is the little child who runs to the audience almost like a child would run so that you could embrace it, catch it with a great sense of innocence and pleasure. But then he too escapes our grasp—*whhht*—and goes flying up into the sky. And all that we're left with is the equivalent of a safety curtain that has come down between us and this whole world. This whole universe now gradually disappears and all we're left with is a few scribbles, some animated graffiti. And then finally we hear on the sound track this huge splash and we're right back again at the beginning of the play, which began with those single drips. So—the final release of the spirit when you've thrown the knowledge away.

*In divesting himself of power and of knowledge, Prospero is of course preparing for death—even though he is going back to Milan.*
There's that beautiful, very last thing he says before the burning of the books, "And thence retire me to my Milan, where/Every third thought shall be my grave."
    Prospero feels a strong sense of inevitability. There's a way in which he wants his power back again, and he could conceivably return to Milan fully fleshed as the Duke. But by bringing Miranda and Ferdinand together, he does hand over the power—he's passing it over to the next generation. He's finally resigned himself to the fact that he is no longer significant, that the rod of power had already by that gesture passed on.

*This sense of reconciliation is a common thread in all of Shakespeare's last plays. The other interesting thing that they have in common is that the men abandon their quests for power and domination and make some peace with their own vulnerability and the contingencies of the natural world. The fathers, like Prospero, rely on their daughters to carry on their identities through bearing children, rather than relying on their sons to maintain their honor through deeds and achievements.*
The fallback Darwinian position—where we are all basically just carriers of the genetic material and we're only here in some senses just to pass it on. The corollary of that, which is terrifying to some people, is that if you do not pass it on, you're valueless. So that if you don't have children, your purposes on earth are invalidated, which is quite a terrifying sentence for all those people who have no wish to procreate, or no desire, or no opportunity. I've done my procreation—I'm idling my way between now and death, my purpose on earth has been completed.

*Unless we believe that our civilizing projects, art and so on, are worth doing.*
Well, there's a way in which maybe that's only merely decorating the nest.

*You've said before that in* The Belly of an Architect *one of your questions is "Is art worth doing?"—and this is perhaps one of the questions Prospero's gesture suggests at the end of the play.*

*The Belly* has become retrospectively very, very sensitive material for me. There is the central argument between a public and a private life, which is very important for a creator—and the film makes lots of personal references to myself and my family and my offspring and my next of kin. But also, it does really examine this question of "Can art make you immortal?" It's posited in Rome, the city of eternity. That title suggests that it's the longest-living, the longest-existing—certainly architecturally—city that there's ever been in the Western world. But also one must remember that Rome, both in the ancient empire and certainly in the Second World War, was the home of fascism. Ultimate power, ultimate narcissism, personified in someone like Mussolini, taken to extremes. And Rome is full of monuments to death and glory, ruins, enormous pyramids to Sestius, triumphal arches representing slavery, representing colonization of the rest of Europe. So Rome itself is the most extraordinary image of all these power crises: it has kings, it has republics, it has democracies, it has Garibaldi, it has emperors like Napoleon, it has oligarchies, it has the most extraordinary range of political systems. And that Roman power and glory and might and narcissism—and the political ideas taken to extremes—were all part of what was represented by Stourley Kracklite, the architect who comes from Chicago, which Upton Sinclair described as the city of blood, meat, and money. Those descriptions can perhaps be used for Rome, too.

The film is also about the way that man reproduces himself. At the beginning we see a lot of three-dimensional sculpture, one way of man reproducing himself, a very complicated and expensive and time-consuming way. A little later on we begin to examine painted representations of man at that bathhouse scene, and then there's that representation of man through photography, and finally the most banal of all, through photocopying. Now there are more photocopies in the world than there are photographs, there are more photographs than there are paintings, and there are more paintings than there are sculptures. There is a way in which we have increased the banality in proportion to the accuracy with which man actually finds a picture of himself. Because after all, a photocopy is supposedly an exact reproduction of the original that you put into a machine. But all these things fail, all these attempts to continue man in sort of an artistic sense or a search for immortality, and the film ends with the cry of a child. Rather clichéd, rather contrived, how the actual birth of his child happens at the selfsame moment as the artist himself, the architect, throws himself out the window. Suggesting that this is the only way we can ever conceivably imagine any sense of immortality. Which throws an enormous question on the significances not only of civilization but of all cultural pursuits. So it's still a question for me—am I doing something which is valuable, is this a total waste of time, what am I doing, what do I think I'm doing, and all those problems. In that sense it's a very, very personal film.

*Your work seems to address this tension again and again, the tension between the desire to control the world, whether through force or through ideas, and the reality of our own vulnerability to chaos and the natural processes of decay.* Without necessarily in any sense attempting any consoling solution to the matter, because it is to continue an ongoing debate. But that's perfectly true. There's also a way that all my heroes are mediocre people. The Draughtsman is a middling artist, capable of making a likeness but hardly very profound and not very intelligent; he gets completely hoodwinked by these rather intelligent women. The two behavioral scientists in *A Zed and Two Noughts*—again not particularly bright in the head—mediocre sorts of people in some senses. And Stourley Kracklite is easily hoodwinked by the Italians. It's so Henry Jamesian, the naive, pioneering, blustering American who goes to the old world and gets completely controlled and manipulated. I suppose the coroner in *Drowning by Numbers* in some senses is also part of that, a man who just cannot get it together. *Drowning* is very much about male impotency, and for that read mankind's impotency in controlling the circumstances, what he likes and dislikes. And Albert Spica, of course, is a totally mediocre man through and through. He takes mediocrity to a high art form and uses it for terrifying ends because he's such a philistine. I don't know quite what you would make of that. I suppose they're all self-portraits of a sort, shades of feeling about whether one has the apparatus to control or organize these power plays, or these principles, or this continual discussion about immortality.

It's also interesting that all these people are creators. I suppose one could say, "the filmmaker's contract" or "the belly of a filmmaker." It's obviously too close to home to do that, so I slightly remove it. But there's a way in which the whole of *Belly* could be said to be not so much about putting on an exhibition as making a film. Because the producers are there, the critics are there, the people who finally take the product away from the artist are there. In a sense, building a piece of architecture is like making a film. It has to satisfy certain sorts of audiences. It has to be practical. It has to fulfill aesthetic obligations, it has to return its money to its backers, and in some senses it has to have a stake in mortality, insofar as buildings are meant to last for a long time, and I sincerely believe that somehow films need to last at least over several generations so that several people can view them and use them and address themselves to them.

*Stylistically it seemed to me that* Prospero's Books *was very close to* TV Dante, *in which you were also bringing together your images and a very renowned literary text. However, the technologies used in* Prospero's Books *and* TV Dante *were obviously very different.*
There is a way that *Prospero's Books* is *The Cook, the Thief*... meets *TV Dante*— the two big vocabularies of film and television that I'm trying very hard to bring together, which is so exciting. The opportunity I had to work with a number of Japanese backers was instrumental in making *Prospero's Books*. There's no way I could have used the low-tech television that's represented by *TV Dante* and put it up against 35mm without embarrassment, because the quality's so bad. But with the new technical equipment of high definition, we have 100-percent improvement, because there are twice as many lines on the television screen. Very obviously this is like a picture in the newspaper—the more dots you have the higher quality the picture. There's still a long way to go because the technology hasn't been fully perfected yet, but it did give me the courage to feel that a TV picture finally could be put up against a 35mm picture of excellent quality. I could finally consider a marriage between the two—and I want to go on and on doing this because I think it's very exciting.

*What's the next project?*
*Fifty-five Men on Horseback,* which I suppose is sort of a *Les Liaisons Dangereuses* [set in the mid-eighteenth century], but communicating a courtship not through letters but through the sending of horse portraits. Rather strange and eccentric, and it's putting a load of information on the horse as being a symbol of virility, energy, sexuality, status, all those things that are often put on the contemporary motor car. And 1760 represents perhaps the height

of attention being paid to the horse, and the horse and carriage. It's the beginning of road building in England, and the very first road in England was the road from London to Newmarket, where young bloods could rev up their horses and have races. The film is about fact and fantasy in courtship, so the parts of the film that have to do with fact are probably going to be shot in CinemaScope black and white, and for the parts to do with fantasy I'll try to use highly colored television techniques. I still haven't quite worked out a way to combine the two elements, especially since I want to try to reproduce a very careful kind of landscape that's relative to the paintings of George Stubbs and possibly Gainsborough as well. So on the aesthetic level, beyond the use of content, the film will try to bring together these ideas of the fact and fantasy of courtship.

*What's happened with the trilogy that was going to come out of* The Cook, the Thief . . . ?
Those films are certainly there; the scripts haven't been completely fin-ished yet, but I could certainly finish them very quickly. One is based on the Medea myth about a woman who kills her own child — *The Love of Ruins*. It is almost a technical exercise to see if I can convince an audience or make an audience sympathetic to a woman who kills her own child. Which again is delving into those same taboo areas that I did in *The Cook, the Thief . . .* — into cannibalism and going back again into the incestuous areas that are dealt with in *'Tis Pity She's a Whore*. And the last one is based on the myth of Apollo and Marsyas, who had this competition about who could make the best music, and of course Apollo won, and the punish-ment was that Marsyas had to be flayed alive. It's based very much on that last painting by Titian, *The Flaying of Marsyas*. But the title of the film is *The Man Who Met Himself* — what would we do if we actually met ourselves, not a twin, not a clone, but ourselves. How would we react — intellectu-ally? sensuously? sexually? What would happen? Because it's only us who know, or think we know, what is best for ourselves.

# Peter Greenaway

S U Z A N N A   T U R M A N / 1 9 9 2

S U Z A N N A   T U R M A N :  *In terms of inspiration,* Prospero's Books *certainly seems unlike your previous films, in that the initial subject came from someone else.*

P E T E R   G R E E N A W A Y :  Unlike all of the other feature films I've made, the actual initial idea for this project did come from Sir John Gielgud, who's spent nearly 75 years in the theater. As you probably know, he's a great contemporary of Sir Laurence Olivier, who's managed to put quite a number of Shakespearean roles down on film, and I think that Sir John Gielgud himself often wished he had made the same sort of contribution.

S T :  *Was he familiar with your past work?*

P G :  Yes. He was one of the very first visitors to the cinema in London which was showing *The Draughtsman's Contract.* And he was there at the front of the queue, tapping on the box office glass with a coin. He had, in fact, for the past two decades, been considering the possibilities of making a film version of a part which he somehow always thought was his own, and had approached film directors like Kurosawa and Bergman to see if it was possible. He tells me that the first question he was asked under those circumstances was, "How much would it cost?" That was a question that I could answer very quickly. It would have to be made for very, very small sums of money, because we'd want to try and create a somewhat radical approach to the project. I think there's not any particular purpose, per-

---

From *Films in Review,* March/April 1992. Reprinted by permission.

haps, in simply recreating a Shakespeare play; certainly this is not the Zeffirelli *Hamlet*.

ST: *And the cost was—?*
PG: The hard-core money available to make this film was £1.5 million (about $2.7 million), which is extremely cheap. But we were given considerable help by NHK in Tokyo—facilities, personnel, and studio time—worth probably the same amount of money again. Some critic in London suggested that *Prospero's Books* was *Terminator 2* for the art house market, with 3% of its cost. I think when I mention these figures, people just don't believe me; they just think I'm lying.

ST: *Every time I've heard you mention it to audiences, they applaud. But do you ever have financial people or distributors trying to pressure you, trying to tell you what's going to sell?*
PG: Well, to hell with that. I am in a rather privileged position. I have this extraordinary producer, Kees Kasander, who does create a space for me to make films I want to make.

ST: *A Shakespeare play doesn't seem to be what one might expect from you.*
PG: I think it ought to be said that there's something very special about this extraordinary last play by Shakespeare, which does offer the opportunity to make interesting explorations. There is a way in which *The Tempest* is a completely different sort of play from *Macbeth* or *Richard III,* which are more confrontational dramas involving a much more traditional approach. I always find it very interesting that those last works of the great geniuses—and this is surely one; analogies could be made with the very last paintings of Titian, perhaps the last quartets of Beethoven—somehow take an enormous leap and lurch into the future, and with these last works create whole new worlds and universes worthy of exploration, which maybe only come fully to fruition many, many years after the death of their creators.

The original play was supposed to be first performed in London in 1611, and saw, in terms of English history, the transition from the Elizabethan age to the Jacobean age. It is also curiously believed to be the only original scenario that Shakespeare ever put together, and was based mainly, as I understand it, on a sort of newspaper item about a shipwreck that happened apparently in the Bermudas, so perhaps this could be said to be the first drama about the Bermuda Triangle.

It's an area of late Shakespearean drama, early Jacobean drama which I am comparatively familiar with, and I think the collaboration with Gielgud worked extremely well. You must remember, he's played this part at least five times on stage before, the very first time at the remarkable age of 26.

S T:  *How was it working with him?*

P G:  He was a first rate collaborator. To explain the strategies, which I would like to think are legitimate, is to first of all consider the possibility that since this is Shakespeare's last play, it is in some sense Shakespeare's farewell to the theater—and this might well be Gielgud's last grand performance. So this may represent his farewell to magic, farewell to theater, farewell to illusion. So using that as a central idea, there was my wish to find a way of uniting the figures of Prospero and Gielgud and Shakespeare. From that, everything else follows, using it deliberately as a vehicle for that magnificent Gielgud voice, so that not only does he play the part of Prospero, but he voices all the other parts as well, at least for two-thirds of the play. That's exactly what Shakespeare did: by creating the words, he created the characters, and the events and the ideas that flow from them, so that the recurring image of the inkwell is like a magician's hat, where everything comes from, always acknowledging the Shakespearean original text.

S T:  *It was interesting to have the emphasis on the books and the text of the play.*

P G:  The book is still the unit of knowledge, certainly in Prospero's time, and also our own, despite the fact that we live in a computer generation. I think also what makes it relevant to this particular time is that it's a play about knowledge and the uses of knowledge. We are all so knowledgeable now and there's so much knowledge available, that in some senses, we, too, have become magicians. There's obviously a moral position about reconciliation, but also a palimpset of knowledge and what it means. We are now in a position to manipulate DNA and work with the secrets of the H-bomb, and so on, and maybe this sets up all sorts of interesting questions about how we ourselves in the 20th century can handle these problems.

s t :   *Your inventions of the books themselves are wonderful.*

p g :   Although Shakespeare doesn't tell us what those books are, I would like to think that they were magical books which could be associated very much with the year of the first performance of the play in 1611. In some senses they could be described as fantasy books, like the book of motion that jumps up and down on the library shelf, and the book of architecture which when you open, out springs Rome. I would like to imagine perhaps that maybe in a hundred years we shall certainly have books like that. But each book is supposed to represent a whole area of knowledge which would be applicable to the imagination of a post-Renaissance prince such as Prospero. And there is also a little facetious joke about the 24 books—Godard suggested that cinema was truth 24 frames a second. The whole phenomenon has become a sort of industry for me, because I've also written two books, one of which explains Prospero's library in much greater detail.

s t :   *And I heard you were writing a sequel as well?*

p g :   Yes, because I'm so unhappy about the wretched position of Miranda. I've complained so bitterly about the female in cinema, either being a passive sexual object, or at very best a catalyst for male behavior. And, lo and behold, Miranda exactly fulfills those two stereotypes! So I've written a play about Miranda, and she completely changes things on that boat going back home—a whole different twist to everything.

s t :   *You're certainly non-sexist and even-handed with the nudity in the film.*

p g :   Americans always ask about nudity. There are many rationales for it, but primarily I'm trying to create here the imagination of a late Renaissance mannerist potentate, who would almost certainly have as his background classical imagery. So that his pictorial landscape, I'm sure, would be formed by the classical nude as seen in paintings by Titian, and Giorgione, and late Bellini. I'm interested in the debate about sensitivity to the nude in some senses, which was certainly started with me in the last film I made, *The Cook, the Thief, His Wife, And Her Lover,* which you might remember. Normally, contemporary American cinema, indeed, contemporary world cinema, presupposes that when you take your clothes off, it's a prelude to sex. This landscape of the nude and the naked in *Prospero's Books*—it's a very de-sexualized, or un-sexualized concern. There is a proposition here that the body, the clay, the lode of Prospero's magic is represented by this huge population of people, both young and old, masculine and feminine, so-called beautiful and so-called ugly—though I think, in context, a body can hardly ever be described as being ugly.

ST: *But do Americans usually ask you to justify the nudity?*
PG: I think they're perplexed. Those sensitivities are obviously interesting to contemplate and examine. Anybody in New York can go to the Metropolitan Museum of Art and see nudes galore, but they are in the context of art. Now, what happens if I think that cinema is art? Can my audience acclimatize themselves to the fact that I'm using the same language that exists at the Metropolitan? I think these things need to be debated.

ST: *Are you aware that there has been a debate going on in the U.S. regarding the propriety of funding art, if it should be distasteful to the general public, usually hinging on sexual content?*
PG: Really? Who decides? That's artistic fascism, isn't it? You're all so Puritanical. There are criticisms—and maybe with a Puritanical nation like America—a suspicion of excess, which is crazy, because the Americans are the most excess-ful nation on earth.

ST: *The other aspect of the film which is arousing a lot of interest is the high-tech innovations that you were using.*
PG: I've done as much work in television in the U.K. as I have done in films for cinema, and I rapidly became aware that there are two very sophisticated but very different vocabularies. In television that is primarily not in the actual instigation of the image, but in the manipulation that's possible in the post-production situation. And I wanted to somehow find a way of bringing these two languages together and make a co-ordinated whole. But I also wanted to hang onto all those chiaroscuro characteristics of the brilliant cinematographer I worked with, Sacha Vierney. So 90% of the original material was in fact shot in fairly conventional methods of 35 mm, and then began a long process of high-tech post-production. So this is a very complex amalgamation of these two vast vocabularies, and certainly for me it suggests enormous opportunities for making future movies, and I think we're beginning with something very, very exciting indeed.

s t :  *Is it safe to say that you're more interested in form and format than plot?*

p g :  Let me make one statement, which people have a lot of difficulty understanding. I sincerely believe that in all cultural activity, content atrophies very rapidly, and all you're left with is form and strategy. Then there is a way in which the form and the strategy themselves become the content. I don't think you can get away from the fact that anything that moves through time has some sort of narrative. One, two, three, four, five, six, seven, eight, nine, ten, is a narrative—beginning, middle, and end. But I have a great distrust of narrative. I can write stories extremely easily, and I feel that narrative writing is extremely facile. I have an antipathy to the psycho-drama, too, which I think is too easy. I do feel that we ought to look for other ways of explaining the human condition, apart from this sort of pocketbook Freud—it isn't even Freudian, because it's still stuck somewhere in the middle of the 19th century, or associated with Jane Austen, for God's sake—

s t :  *Hey, I like Jane Austen!*

p g :  I do, too! I suppose the European novel took an interesting turn with her writing, but I still feel that cinema basically is illustration of the 19th century novel, ways and mean of examining the world very much in the way that perhaps Dickens organized his narrative scheme. And, you know, American cinema is a bit like telling children stories, to placate them— make sure the moral code is all right, and now we'll tuck you up in bed, and everything will be all right, give you a kiss, goodnight, see you in the morning. It has that sort of self-satisfied smugness about it, that feeling that all the characters will walk happily into the sunset, hand in hand in hand [sic]. No! This is just not the case! That is not satisfactory exemplum of our human condition.

s t :  *That reminds me of the Dorothy Parker retort, when she was working on a screenplay and Goldwyn, I think it was, complained that she always had unhappy endings, she stalked out saying that in the whole history of the world, there has never been a happy ending.*

p g :  And the other thing is, there has never been an *ending*. My films are incredibly open-ended, though maybe *Prospero's Books* is a little different from that. But generally, the narrative schemes of the end of the 20th century in cinema in some senses haven't developed much more than D.W. Griffith's. But I think the beginnings for me here with this dual language of the two technologies used in *Prospero's Books,* bringing together the characteristics of the television medium and cinema, is just the beginning of a vast exploration that I certainly hope to continue.

# Interview with Peter Greenaway:
## *The Baby of Macon*

### M I C H E L   C I M E N T / 1 9 9 3

M I C H E L   C I M E N T :  *Of the eight full-length films you've made, three take place in the past, and this past, it's always the 17th century: its beginning with* Prospero's Books, *its middle with* The Baby of Macon, *and its end with* The Draughtsman's Contract. *It appears that this is a period that attracts you.*

P E T E R   G R E E N A W A Y :  Absolutely. In a certain sense, it's the first century of intellectual and artistic maturity in England. On the other hand, I don't claim to be focused on this period or to want my films to be a mirror image of it. For me, historic films are like science fiction — they offer a freedom to the imagination that one cannot find to the same extent in films that take place in the present. Since I employ a cinema of metaphor, of fable, of symbolism, I have more room when I distance myself from the contemporary, from the mimetic quality of surrounding reality. My dialogue is intentionally declamatory, artificial — it has nothing to do with conversation. I feel more comfortable with the literature from the period starting with Shakespeare and concluding with the theater of the Restoration, which facilitates tirade, word play, enigmas, allegory. Undoubtedly, this is another reason for my fascination with that century. And, of course, there's the baroque and all that it involves. The end of our own century appears baroque to me from two points of view: first of all, in the excess of details, the mass of information [that characterize it], and, secondly, in the idea of illusion and its corollary, deceit, with its parade of propaganda, be it political or promotional.

From *Positif,* January 1994. Reprinted by permission of *Positif* and the author. Translated from the French by Judy Schroeter-Deegan.

M C :  *Two of these three films aren't situated in England.*

P G :  *The Baby of Macon* had to have a Catholic setting because the super-
stitions, the beliefs that it shows don't belong to a Protestant society. Our
Mannerist period in England was later, it corresponds to Newton's time.
He was born in 1615, I believe — that is, four years after the time of *Prospero's Books*. The 17th century was culturally, politically, socially, a thrilling
period of transition, that heralded the era of democracy. With Cromwell,
we had the beginning of parliamentary government.

M C :  *Although you weren't aiming for historical accuracy, your treatment of the
costumes, of the decor, is different in relation to these three different periods from
the same century.*

P G :  I would like for each frame of film to refer back to the basic concept.
In *The Draughtsman's Contract,* it was necessary that the characters be
affected, mannered, both in their clothing and in their language. It is
natural to work within the limits of our notion of these periods, but this
nevertheless leaves one a good bit of latitude. For *The Baby of Macon,* we
had color schemas that we played with. The problems of style bring me
an intense pleasure — just like the study of history. One might say that history doesn't exist, that there are no historians. In this sense, I would like
to be an historian.

M C :  *The* Baby of Macon *is the first of your films that plays with the idea of a
spectacle within a spectacle, an idea that has interested you for a long time now,
with your project on Inigo Jones and Ben Jonson.*

P G :  I've thought about it recently. In a certain sense, another project,
*Augsbergenfeld,* which I intend to be my next film, is another variation on
this central idea in the film on Inigo Jones and Ben Jonson, which opposes
spectacle and speech — a major point of argument between Jones and
Jonson, and which presages the dual nature of cinema, the cinema of words
and the cinema of show. Is it possible to unite them? This is a question
that has not ceased to interest me because I attach great importance to text
but also to image. How to combine Ophuls and Fellini on the one hand
and Rohmer on the other? The idea of a scene within a scene also refers
back to the baroque. Cinema is an ideal form of the baroque — it plays
with shadows and illusion, it combines several means of expression. If you
go into the basilica of St. Peter in Rome and sit through a service near the
high altar of Bernini, you will experience a synthesis of stone, light, music,

incense. It is a form of total art, which is what the cinema of the 20th century was supposed to be, even if it only rarely lives up to this ideal.

MC: *To what extent did your experience with new images and new technologies during the filming of* Prospero's Books *influence your approach to* The Baby of Macon?

PG: I've always wanted to make long films—if you recall, *The Draughtsman's Contract* was originally four and a half hours long (and the cuts were set aside for safekeeping, so I could always restore them)—I would love to make a movie eight hours long. But I have to be practical and accept the idea of the two-hour film, which is imposed by the distributors and movie house operators who want to put on three shows each night. Even Scorsese and Spielberg have to comply with this rule. With *Prospero's Books,* I satisfied my desire to say more in less time with the use of three-dimensional images [and being able to] work on several visual and narrative planes at one time. After all, Shakespeare, too, confronted the new discoveries of his time, the changes in perspective ushered in by the Renaissance. I would like to take up an old text, *The Tempest,* and set it against the second information revolution, [the revolution in] communication techniques—a revolution just as significant as the revolution which Gutenberg introduced was in Shakespeare's time. I also wanted to confront directly one of the phenomena of our time: the overload of [visual] images, a visual "overkill." I've realized that this excess has been literally indigestible for many viewers. Younger viewers, those used to videos and new images, were capable of "taking in" *Prospero's Books* but the challenge proved too great for other generations.

The direct influence of *Prospero's Books* on my subsequent work can be seen in *Darwin,* a relatively modest production for which we got a lot of money. There is something contradictory and perverse about a film that was shot in cinemascope to be shown on television! I got a great deal of pleasure out of the filming. There were in all 18 scene changes for a length of 50 minutes. I wanted to find an equivalent for Darwin's perception of the visual world and I got the idea of *tableaux vivants,* which correspond to the 19th century taste for wax figures like the presentation, after Gericault's *Raft of Medusa* shown in Liverpool, of the same scene in the form of three-dimensional figures. For *Darwin,* we had only one set, which we transformed 18 times. We took extremely complicated camera shots and we almost completely dispensed with any editing. It was thus a different, even an opposite experience, from *Prospero's Books*, even though it grew out of that earlier experience. I wanted to replicate this experience with *Baby of Macon* even if there wouldn't be actors and narration to the same degree as in *Darwin*. I also didn't want to forget that *Baby of Macon* was originally an opera, and we find in it the same notion of a chorus, as well as the same structure—a prologue, three acts, an epilogue, two intermissions—as in the grand operas of the nineteenth century. This form reminds one of the last part of *The Cook, the Thief, His Wife, and Her Lover*, which is also very "operatic." This concept, along with that of the *tableaux vivants* in *Darwin*, and also the desire to take three steps back from the new technologies before plunging back in with my next film *Augsbergenfeld* (which will be shot in black and white, in unsaturated colors and in full colors using all the resources of high definition) are the formal sources for *Baby of Macon*.

M C :  *How did you go from the concept of an opera on the theme of* Baby of Macon *to a film?*

P G :  In the middle of the 1980's, I talked about it with Michael Nyman. We didn't get very far. Then I returned to the project with Louis Andriessen, who was going to be working with me on another opera the following year, *Rosa*, about a composer who writes music for Westerns and wants a serious artistic career. But this opera was set in Argentina, with its gaucho stories a la Borges. We came to the conclusion that opera was not an appropriate medium for expressing the complicated ideas of *Baby of Macon*. Thus, two years ago, we mutually decided to abandon the project—but the idea of it remained in my head and I had the desire, almost immediately afterward, to make a film of it that retained the notion of the ceremonial, of the artificial decor associated with the opera of the 19th century, and, of course, the music, but the music of the period.

M C :  *What was the initial inspiration for* The Baby of Macon?

P G :  In 1988, not far from Nevers where Resnais filmed *Hiroshima Mon Amour*, my daughters bought some French magazines, and in an issue of *Elle*, I discovered a photo of a 14-year-old girl, very pretty, with a virginal air and very nicely dressed, holding a baby in her arms in the manner of the Virgin Mary. The eyes and hair of the child were in no way similar to those of the young girl. The point of the photograph was to portray the child in the same way as a fashion accessory. During that time period, one also saw postcards of highly virile men holding infants in their arms. The "new male" was supposed to be tender. This was also the period of the infamous Benetton ad that showed a newborn covered with blood and which shocked the entire world. Afterward, I had a show in Rotterdam on the "Physical Self" and I had the opportunity to view numerous Nativity scenes from the thirteenth, fourteenth, and fifteenth centuries. I want to discuss these phenomena and [in so doing] explore our attitude toward children at end of the twentieth century.

At the same time, we're seeing more and more stories in the newspapers about children being sexually abused, often by their own parents. In most cases, it turns out that the parents are innocent, but this mass hysteria surrounding the ill treatment of children puts me in mind of the witch trials. Today, everybody, from Madonna to Roseanne Barr, goes around talking about how they suffered maltreatment in their childhoods—it's all become very banal! People seem to regard it as a badge of honor that they were mistreated as young children. Only six months ago, I discovered that the photography in *Elle* was the work of Olivero Toscani, who was also responsible for the Benetton ad. There is, then, a web of significant connections between the sale of images and the exploitation of children. Certainly, there is an exhibitionistic side to Toscani, but at the same time he brings to light some very interesting questions. The world of advertising is very constricted. We are presented with the best of worlds, where everyone smiles, where all problems can be resolved by buying a car or a detergent. It excludes death, dirt, poverty, the suffering of which we are all aware in our daily lives. Toscani has introduced these things into his ads and has thereby profoundly disturbed people. But, after all, he has done no more than push a little further the tendency already present in advertising, to tie together two things that have no connection: a naked woman and selling a motorcycle, for example. Toscani has opened the floor for debate.

MC: *With this Nativity theme, you introduce a pictorial reference until now absent in your films, that of Flemish painting at the time of Van Eyck or Van Der Weyden.*

PG: The infant embodies all our optimism—and this applies also to *The Belly of an Architect*. The infant represents the possibility of a new beginning. In Flemish painting, the infant is seated in the middle of the painting, surrounded by the holy congregation, his halo radiating over the entire scene. I wanted to portray other figures, not just the mother holding the child, and also to portray the [mother and child's] exchange of looks, since in the paintings the [child's] eyes are directed toward the viewer. There is also [one particular] canvas that inspired me—by an obscure fifteenth century painter, Crevalcore. It shows a decapitated head—the head of Saint Catherine, I believe. I've always been fascinated by decapitation and moreover have plans for films about Salome and Charles the First of England. I was also guided, in my visual research, by the paintings of Naples by Monsu Desiderio, with their extremely elaborate architectural structures, their innumerable details, their representation of fires and explosions in cathedrals. Sacha Vierny and I have had many discussions about these canvasses. We had a great deal of trouble finding a church. We started in Spain and southern Italy, but were unable to obtain the necessary authorizations or, else, simply find what we were looking for. Finally, we hit upon the old cathedral of Amsterdam, which belongs to the Reformed Church and which we remodeled. The owners gave us permission, on certain financial conditions, to shoot the film there. Before that, we had planned to use the cathedral of Cologne, but two days before we began our preparations, *The Cook, the Thief, His Wife, and Her Lover* was shown on German television and the archbishop immediately forbade us from entering the cathedral site!

One source of inspiration for *Baby of Macon* is the Miracles as they were represented in the Middle Ages. This was an age of great piety. But we transposed the setting to the time of the Reformation, when piety was replaced by religiosity. We are in a world of pretenders. It is probable that Cosimo de Medicis believed in God and life after death, but it was a different attitude that had more to do with the relics of the saints and the institutions of the Church than with Christian faith. I was interested in the differences.

M C :  *Is Macon somehow connected to this history?*
P G :  Macon has a small cathedral; it played a role in Burgundy of the 14th century but, since then, has been forgotten by history. I thought this would be an ideal setting for this story. I also read that, around 1212, at the time of the Children's Crusade, a holy child came to Macon who was later crucified in a desert to the north of Jerusalem. But this is probably a ficti-

tious tale. In any case, the name Macon pleased me: one wonders about the reason for this city—there's something mysterious about it.

M C :   *You establish an analogy between the Church and theater. Both have as their purpose to inspire belief through . . . spectacle.*
P G :   What difference is there, in effect, between these two ceremonies and the strange people in strange clothing who ask you not to doubt? If you look back at ancient Greece, you see that theater was born from religious ritual. For me, this film is not a criticism of Catholicism in particular. It talks about power, all ideologies that pretend to guide the thought and imagination of the social body, and what happens when one defies them. The Church finds itself deprived of the opportunity to exercise [power] in its own domain, that is, the domain of miracles, and it reacts forcefully, taking vengeance in an atrocious manner. It annihilates this woman, just as, for 2,000 years, it has consistently treated women in a terrible fashion.

M C :   *How did you get the idea of having an old woman give birth to a child?*
P G :   I had to find a way to suggest to the public that the sister of this child could have born it. The dilemma facing the son of the priest was in effect this: if she gave birth, she couldn't be a virgin; if she was a virgin, she couldn't have given birth. The solution presented itself in the form of this old and ugly woman. She is the agent of the miracle, which is all the more striking in that a beautiful child is born from a deformed being. No child is present at the beginning of the film because it was said that no woman had given birth in the last five years. The film is set off by the image of illness—which some have identified with syphilis. But which could simply be the plague. Man is treated in the same way that he treats the planet. This refers back to a scenario I wrote a very long time ago, *The Quadruple Fruit,* which was inspired by Robbe-Grillet's *Jealousy* and his scenario *Last Year at Marienbad.* That was the period of the sexual revolution, when everyone was having sex all over the place. I envisioned an opposite situation, the negative reverse of it, in which it would be difficult to conceive and give birth.

M C :   *You show different social classes.*
P G :   It's a little bit schematic. There weren't really very many bourgeois at that time yet—the main social division was between the peasants and the

nobility. Nevertheless, I wanted to show all three classes reacting to the
spectacle, some of them believers, others not, but everyone in the last
analysis cynical. Another thing that interested me was that the spectators
could move about. We accept that movie audiences must remain immo-
bile, but I like to imagine a room in which the spectators can walk around,
view the film from different angles. There have been experiments of this
sort in the theater over the last twenty years. I want to develop this idea in
a series of shows titled "Stairs": the first will take place in Geneva next
spring and the series will progress one city at a time. All of this is related,
in our time, to the progressive erasure of the line between the actor and
the public. Didn't Andy Warhol say that everyone will enjoy fifteen seconds of fame? Moreover, the advent of video, of cameras, has made of
everyone both an actor and a spectator. I'm thinking now about the *Rocky
Horror Picture Show* and the Christmas pantomimes of our childhood, in
which everyone watched yet at the same time participated in the show.
Nowadays, people are very passive most of the time, but during the Restoration period, for example, they reacted constantly. Here, [in my film],
the public counts the contractions during labor (an echo of my interest in
numerology), screams out numbers.

M C :   *Cosimo de Medicis can be found among the public.*
P G :   I wanted a chorus whose function would be to serve as an intermediary between the audience and the actors. I've been fascinated by a book
by Lord Acton, *The Last of the Medicis.* Cosimo was inspired by a real historical figure. Along with the girl and the child, he is one of the three
innocents in the film who believes he can stand up to the power of the
Church. Cosimo is an innocent believer. He knows the litanies and the
religious precepts by heart but he doesn't have the practical experience to
understand them. All his notions of compassion and pity have been grafted
onto his limited knowledge of life. One has the sense that his entire circle
of friends and acquaintances is pushing him to exact the terrible punish-
ment inflicted on this young woman who has annoyed the Church. And
he knows that in the end he will be pardoned. The classic Catholic situation. The story takes place in 1659, the year of Cosimo's 17th birthday. He
was raised by his mother, a very religious woman. His father was a sup-
porter of people like Galileo. Thus, Cosimo was reacting against the
interest in the new sciences embodied by his father. He is also at odds with

the son of the priest, who, likewise, is interested in the world of scientific knowledge. Shortly afterward, the dynasty of the Medicis would crumble.

M C :   *He is chubby, stout, and looks like an albino. This is a type that attracts you. We find the same type in* Prospero's Books *and also in* The Cook, the Thief, His Wife, and Her Lover.

P G :   Each time, they are innocents. They are manipulated by others. They represent those members of the public who come to shows without prejudices, without advance instruction. And in one sense, Cosimo is the first spectator of the religious melodrama that unfolds before everyone and that seems to be above all intended for him to see. Most movie audiences today are between 16 and 25 years old and it is from the movies that they learn their manners and morals, just as in the nineteenth century one learned from novels. Cosimo is in some sense one of these viewers. We have, I believe, much sympathy for, for example, the young kitchen boy in *The Cook, the Thief, His Wife, and Her Lover.* The boy behaves like us, he is treated as we are, attacked, manipulated.

M C :   *Isn't the character of the theater director a direct descendant from* Prospero's Books?

P G :   It is a deliberate reference. He is dressed in almost the same way. He also represents me. It is the director who invites you into the theater to watch the performances, who prompts the actors with their lines when they forget them and who speaks for the child, the main character of the drama. He also sings, which refers back to the operatic origins of *Baby of Macon.* He holds an enormous book on his lap, an encyclopedia that contains everything; finally, he claps his hands, revealing that all of this was nothing but a game, an illusion, and he summons the dead. Some rise, others don't. But this proves nothing, they could rise later. When it comes to spectacle, all is manipulation, and there are two things I have never believed in showing on film: copulation and death. This film plays with both propositions. Think of the thousands of actors who earn their living playing dead people. It's like showing rape. Recall the debates over the film with Jodie Foster, *The Accused,* which the actress declared to be so difficult to play and how the whole crew was on her side, how they cried during the rape scene. This was nothing but bluff, but it underscores how delicate and how taboo the subject is. I think we've gone much farther with *Baby of Macon* in devising a scene played with shadow-theater figures, where the spectator imagines the action based on sound effects.

M C :  *The character Famine, who opens and closes the film, complements that of the director. He, too, comments on the action and draws a moral from the story.*
P G :  This appearance of Famine was inspired by a photograph of a malnourished man taken by Joel Peter Witkin, a Mexican who works in the United States.

M C :  *One thinks of syphilis, especially when one sees the progression of the illness between the first and last images.*
P G :  One of Famine's speeches, where he speaks of men and women who no longer sleep together, is echoed in the director's comment about his memory of experiencing ecstasy, as if there were once a golden age of sexuality that has now ended. These two characters are in effect two sides of the same coin.

M C :  *The auction of the child's limbs reminds one of the scenes in which he is dressed and undressed.*
P G :  There are three major ceremonial events that I had the pleasure of filming in very slow motion. This ceremonial can be seen in the large canvases of Carpaccio. In the fifteenth century, the ceremonial was an artistic form in painting and it heralded the famous saying of Shakespeare's: "the world is a stage." The procession was there to demonstrate the social hierarchy and it passed through the streets and plazas as if on a "teatro mundi." In Great Britain there is an expert on the Jacobean period who has written about Paracelse and the Rosacrucians, about all the phenomena of the theater of Memory, and on which I based a character in a novel I wrote, *Prospero's Creatures*. The character serves as an assistant to Prospero and creates 100 allegories in their House of Memory.

M C :  *There is something blasphemous about the child's body being divided into parts like the body of Christ is in communion.*
P G :  "Eat—this is my body." This phrase is uttered several times in *The Cook, the Thief, His Wife, and Her Lover*. It is like a theological acceptance of cannibalism, in the figurative sense, of course. There are numerous examples of saints' bodies being cut up, not only by peasants but by the eccles-

iastical elite, in order to transform the bodies into relics. We also know that you could construct thirty crosses out of the pieces remaining from Christ's Cross and that there are enough pieces of foreskin from the circumcision of Christ to create a whole population of babies! It is an aspect of Catholicism with which we are all very familiar. For me, the film is a dark parable, but is it possible that as an atheist I could be a blasphemer?

MC:  *In its theatricality,* The Baby of Macon *resembles* The Cook, the Thief, His Wife, and Her Lover.
PG:  In my view, the film is closer to *Prospero's Books*. This last film had as its subject the power of the mind, of knowledge. In *The Baby of Macon,* the subject is religious power, and in my next film, *Augsbergenfeld,* it will be military power, the power of war. They will thus form a trilogy united also by the time period they are set in, the first half of the seventeenth century.

MC:  *As in* Prospero's Books, *you highlight the movements of the crowd.*
PG:  I enjoy constant camera motion, all the choreographic preparations, the relationship between the movements of the actors and those of the camera crew. No doubt this enjoyment will soon push me to want to stage a play or an opera. Certainly the psychological examination of characters a la Chekov is not what interests me most. I am more concerned about the relationship between human figures and light, space, architecture. This is the painter in me. But it's also true that I am finding it increasingly gratifying to work with actors who have great cinematic intelligence, such as Michael Gambon in *The Cook...,* Gielgud in *Prospero's Books,* and Philip Stone in *Baby of Macon.*

MC:  *In your last films, there are fewer close-ups than there were previously.*
PG:  Here again, this is my painter's side [coming out]. I don't like the quick succession of different scenes that one finds in American cinema. I am an admirer of Poussin, I like to place my characters in their environment. This is related to my taste for historic paintings, from the Venetian school to David and Gericault. In *The Anointing of Napoleon,* for example, I admire the way the painter has made it possible to see every one of the marvelously defined characters just as clearly as the entire scene. Perhaps the last historic painting ever done is Picasso's *Guernica.*

M C :  *Sacha Vierney once again outdid himself in* The Baby of Macon.

P G :  We wanted a dominant theme of red and gold. We had done a lot of studying of medieval painting. I wanted every act to have a special color, as I had wished, in *The Draughtsman's Contract,* to have a succession of red, black and white, but had been unable to due to lack of funding. Once again, our costume budget was not sufficient for us to push the idea to the limit and we were obliged to make some compromises.

# Beyond Cinema

## SABINE DANEK AND
## TORSTEN BEYER/1994

*In the last several years you have given more and more attention to curating art exhibitions.*

PETER GREENAWAY: These are comparatively new things for me. I'm almost as excited about this whole phenomenon of making exhibitions as I am about the opus of cinema. I have had the opportunity over the last four or five years to put on various ones. The first was at Rotterdam, an exhibition called "The Physical Self." It examined my interest in physical reality, corporeal reality. Except for the physical images of childbirth, of lactation, the early years of a child's life were exemplified by early fourteenth- and fifteenth-century paintings. I found several of these in the Boymans van Beunigen collection in Rotterdam. I juxtaposed them with the famous Toscani image for Benetton that affronted so many people. Perhaps the most interesting project of all was called "100 Objects to Represent the World," which I realised in Vienna. I received lots of invitations to take this same shopping list of 100 objects to Rio, to Tokyo, to Beijing, to St. Petersburg, to Johannesburg. I will carry my shopping list to these different cultural venues and reinterpret it.

*What are your new exhibition projects?*
There is a whole series of them. The first one began in Geneva in May this year, a project called "Stairs." It is, I suppose, an examination of my disenchantment with some of the issues of cinema. It breaks up the contemplation

From *Sight and Sound*, July 1994. Reprinted by permission.

of cinema into ten separate areas. They have literally given us the city of Geneva. We lit locations throughout the city — the cathedral, the fountain in the lake, the opera house, the art gallery, and other major buildings. We have erected 100 staircases, grand staircases, each of which has a viewing platform on the top that frames up some part of the city. In some cases the viewpoints are very touristic, sometimes banal, sometimes quite surreal and sometimes, maybe, even dangerous. There are exactly 100 of these, which relates neatly back to *Drowning by Numbers*. I carry the number 100 like a piece of cultural baggage.

The phenomenon of framing has been part of my last three or four films. They were very much about how plastic art since the Renaissance has been so keen to discipline the world in a frame, whether it's the proscenium arch in a theatre or the picture frame. This was not necessarily true before the sixteenth century, but it is certainly true in cinema and television. For me this investigation will take the concept of the frame out of cinema and put it into a more public situation. I'm very frustrated by making two-hour films. This exhibition will last 100 days. At 100 sites, I can make 100-hour, 100-day films . . . whole days and nights. In essence, here in Geneva I have a 24-hour continual viewfinder. You can imagine it narrated in sequences. You would see a man taking a dog for a walk. On another day you might see the dog biting the man. On the third day you might even see the man biting the dog.

The second exhibition is to be held in Barcelona, Madrid, and Bilbao. It is intended to create an audience of 1,000 seats, right across Spain, again for 100 days. There will be three performances every night and all the seats will be numbered. This project again is very much about the audience. One of the seats is King Carlos' throne and another five seats stand in the football stadium of Real Madrid. At six o'clock you know that you are sit-ting down in an audience of 1,000, looking not just at one phenomenon but at a whole series of phenomena across Spain. I have other exhibitions which will take place in Prague, Sydney, Warsaw, Beijing, probably one in Tokyo and the last in association with the Guggenheim Museum in New York, in the year 2000.

*It really seems that you are losing interest in making movies.*
The whole question for me is to get away from the set cinema situation where the people sit in the dark, look in one direction, see an illusionistic

object on a flat screen—not to mention all the related problems of distribution and organization. The straitjacket way we watch films. It is also because of the fact that film has no materiality, has no viable history, and has the passive association of the director having created the time frame. When you look at a painting, you can look for three seconds, three hours, three days.

*Have you ever thought about working as a theatre director? Your exhibitions are theatrical, but in a special way. They remind me of Robert Wilson, when in the '60s he played on seven days and on seven hills in the desert.*
It's interesting that you mention Wilson. One of the composers he worked with was Louis Andriessen from the Netherlands. He and I have made two television films together and the Amsterdam opera house commissioned us two years ago to create a new opera for November of this year. At this moment I'm not particularly interested in doing work in the theatre, but certainly I will remain involved with music theatre in some sense. *The Cook, the Thief, His Wife, and Her Lover* has been turned into a play by a New York theatre group. And Lee Strasberg has asked me to make a theatrical version of my last film, *The Baby of Macon*. I'm deeply goaded by this. What will I do about the baby, the cow, and the audience? Some interesting solutions are possible.

*In some of your earlier films you have been concerned with baroque garden design or landscape paintings. Are you also interested in modern ways of dealing with nature, like land art?*
Very much so. I was still in art school when this phenomenon was around and people like Finlay and Long were occasional visiting lecturers. So I am closely associated with the thought behind this movement. I am fascinated by the extraordinary *Lightning-field* of Walter de Maria.

I too did extravagant experiments with the English Ordnance Survey, which was one of the first and most sophisticated mapping systems in Europe. My experiments took place in a particular area of Salisbury, where I used to spend a lot of time making films, like *Windows*. I wanted to reconstruct the grid that is laid on the landscape. A group of us found out where these particular gridlines intersected and dug enormous holes in the ground and buried very large, old ball bearings in them. I think in the end we buried

100 over about five square miles. It's totally hidden land art—there's nothing to be seen. We had great difficulties because some of the points were in the middle of a pond, or a farmyard, or tarmac.

*The composition of your films is closely related to the tradition of European painting.*
There are a lot of direct quotations. We were deliberately trying to recreate *The Art of Painting* by Vermeer in *A Zed and Two Noughts* as a parallel to the art of filmmaking. Godard suggested that Vermeer was the first cinematographer because he used the *camera obscura*.

*The French painter Georges de La Tour seems to be especially important for your lighting.*
Yes, I think so. Perhaps even more than Caravaggio. De La Tour holds a lot of Caravaggio, holds a lot of the period. Caravaggio's painting is very much about dramatic lighting, whereas de La Tour's work is much softer. It has a more religious spirit. The image is much more static, the figures look as though they have been standing there for years and years. I was also influenced in my last film by the Venetian painter Crevalcore, who was working in about 1450. There are only six known paintings by him. Another influence was that rather strange, I think German painter, who lived in Naples under the Italian name of Desiderio. He painted the interiors of churches in a very melodramatic style. One is simply called *Explosion in a Cathedral*—it sounds like a modern title. Some sort of unspecified miracle is happening and the whole cathedral is being blown into the picture space. It looks like a frozen moment, a long time before frozen moments were possible photographically—the quintessence of a drama. About two years ago, I found that a new book had been published on Desiderio. The bookseller told me, "You shouldn't buy this book, because it's too dangerous." He said that anyone who doubted Desiderio's work was in for bad luck. A Frenchman wrote this monograph and three days after the publication he was run over on the Champs Elysées. Then his wife was mugged in a taxi six weeks afterwards. And then his publisher had a miscarriage. It was one year ago that I bought it.

*You use art-historical quotations to reflect on the difference between fiction and reality—a theme that all your films deal with.*

The two big themes of contemporary cinema in the last decade have surely been death and copulation. We see enough death in the documentary tradition, but not in dominant cinema. It is obvious that actors don't die. This is the big dichotomy. In *The Piano* an actor and actress copulate, but outside the genre of pornography. This doesn't happen in dominant cinema either. What I did deliberately in my film *The Baby of Macon* was to push these two things to the extreme in order to confront the circumstances of this double act—the oldest play in cinema. For me the most disturbing moment of the film is when the actress playing the daughter jumps backwards out of her role and becomes an actress. But she is forced to play. She is forced to suffer the humiliations of her character. Yet even in that moment, when you think, "Oh God, is this really going to happen?," even then she is not playing the part. As an actress she is going to be raped, yet you know all the time that it isn't the case, because she is an actress.

So how can we sustain—how can the cinema sustain for us—these two opposing attitudes? One of the reasons why the Baroque is so important in my work is that it is centered upon the suspension of disbelief in its most extreme form: it uses all the details, all the decoration, all the light to that end. Bernini's fountain in Rome manifests, re-creates a desire for a miracle. And cinema portrays something of the same kind. Hollywood cinema tries to find the pie in the sky, it tries to find solutions. My films don't offer solutions, they don't offer intimacy, they don't offer condolences. They are removed from the phenomenon, they watch it without judgment. They go against the grain of a deodorising, romanticising and sentimentalising attitude towards sex and death.

*In* Prospero's Books *you used modern post-production technologies like Paintbox. Are you still interested in these new ways of composing pictures?*
We are considering making a special version, a sort of reconstructed version, of my first feature *The Draughtsman's Contract*. If I remake it as a CD-ROM there would be the possibility of selecting from the out-takes and things we didn't use. In addition we can maneuver off into areas such as fruit symbolism, basic background material, literary devices and so on. All that can be organized in a present tense, so to speak. We will also make at some time in the future *Augsbergenfeldt* as a film and CD-ROM that will use some of these extraordinary post-production techniques again. We are going to shoot in black and white and monochrome colour. One of the

subtexts of the film is the idea that history doesn't exist, but is created by historians. So there will be a relationship between the perspective of the historians and what is foreground, what is middleground and what is background. But I am a little alarmed at the possibility of remaking things—there are still so many new ideas I want to work on.

# Blasphemy in Cinema:
# An Interview with Peter Greenaway

## JOHN PETRAKIS/1997

IT HAS BEEN SAID that director Peter Greenaway is a filmmaker as one might be a modern painter or an experimental novelist.

Born in London in 1942, he was initially drawn to painting and attended the Walthamstow College of Art. He later attempted to enroll at the Royal College of Art Film School, after undergoing the "Road to Damascus" experience of seeing Ingmar Bergman's *The Seventh Seal,* but was turned down. Undaunted, he landed a job as an editor with the British Film Institute, where he was able to screen their impressive collection of classic experimental films. Inspired, he purchased a 16 mm Bolex camera and commenced making his own short movies.

His move to features came in 1982 with the remarkable *The Draughtsman's Contract,* and since then, he has turned out an eclectic assortment of unique efforts, most of them praised and reviled with equal fervor by critics. They include *A Zed and Two Noughts* (1986), *The Belly of an Architect* (1987), *Drowning By Numbers* (1988), *The Cook, the Thief, His Wife, and Her Lover* (1989), *Prospero's Books* (1991) and *The Baby of Macon* (1993).

Greenaway was in Chicago recently to promote his latest effort, the strange and beautiful *The Pillow Book,* which is currently playing at the Music Box Theatre.

It is a visually challenging cinematic experience, inspired by a tenth century erotic journal, or Pillow Book, which is also the inspiration for

From *The Chicago Tribune,* July 1997. © John Petrakis. Reprinted by permission of the author.

the film's main character, a beautiful Japanese woman named Nagiko, who searches out lovers to draw on her body, (just as her father drew on her face when she was a girl), before becoming the artist herself, using her lovers as canvases.

Though Greenaway is considered to be one of the most brilliant and innovative contemporary filmmakers, no less a director than fellow countryman John Boorman has attacked Greenaway's "cruelty, coldness, and awesome sterile certainty."

Q :  *You are one of the few filmmakers working today who has been called blasphemous. Is there a place for blasphemy in cinema?*

GREENAWAY:  I'm sure there is. Because it indicates the alternative position, the question of dogma, the opposition to rhetoric, the concern that pyramids of construction of human intent must be examined and reconsidered in order to break up the power blocks. Blasphemy's got nothing to do with God. It's got to do with the church, who feel threatened by outsiders or by critics.

Q :  *You've been quoted as saying that "it is very arrogant to suppose that you can make a film for anybody but yourself." What is your take on modern cinema?*

GREENAWAY:  I feel that the cinema we've got after 100 years is in some cases not a cinema at all, but a history of illustrated text. *The English Patient,* for example. Why do people bother? Why do they spend money, patience, time, and activity perverting one work of art into another? We know cinema is very hybrid, very mongrel, and still hasn't found an autonomy for itself. But I don't think it should be used simply to illustrate literature.

I sincerely believe that cinema desperately needs revitalizing. It hasn't done anything interesting, as far as I'm concerned, since the Germans way back in the 1970s. The last radical investigation. Fassbinder, Herzog, Wenders.

Q :  *Tell me about* The Pillow Book.

GREENAWAY:  It's a story about a woman who wants her lovers to write on her body. Every time you see sex or flesh, you see text. Every time you see text, more or less, you see sex and flesh. So in a sense, it's a dissertation on sex and text, my two favorite subjects.

Q: *Your films are filled with lists, numbers, architecture, and games. How does the text in* The Pillow Book *follow suit?*

GREENAWAY: Many years ago, during my art studies, I came across Oriental calligraphy. I was fascinated by the notion that the calligraph, the hieroglyph, the character, was both an image and a text. When you read it as an image, it is a text. The history of Japanese painting is almost entirely synonymous with the history of Japanese literature. So here was the possibility of metaphor for a new sort of cinema.

Q: *Why do we need a new cinema?*

GREENAWAY: Because I don't think cinema is a good narrative medium. If you want to tell a story, become a writer. Don't get involved in cinema. Cinema is about other things. I know we excuse cinema because it's not very old, but one of the great things about the twentieth century was the taking away what for many years had been regarded as the main props. So, melody's been taken away from music, figuration's been taken away from painting. And there's a way, I feel, that narrative should be taken out of cinema, so it can get on with what I believe it can really do.

Q: *Which is?*

GREENAWAY: I'm looking all the time for alternatives to storytelling. My films are very much based on horizontals and verticals. It's a grid situation. Also lists, number counts, and alphabetical counts. Not that I believe intrinsically in any particular magic in these systems, but they are well-defined, well-wrought systems of organization. Go back to Petrarch or the paintings of Giovanni Bellini in Venice, where all the world is structured according to a series of ceremonies and processions.

Q: *It seems that the structure of your films is just as important as the substance. Sort of a marriage between style and content.*

GREENAWAY: You know how French philosophers have deliberately told us that the world's not just in front of us, it's all around us? There are experiments we can play that will pick up ideas of cubism, for example, which cinema's never really entertained, in order to create a fragmentation of experience, which I would argue is much more like the way we live in the world.

Take *Casablanca*, for example. It is the ideal, coherent, narrative structure, with beginning, middle and end. Preordained characters. Systems of representation. It is extraordinarily artificial. There's no such thing as a narrative in real life, because we all live in the present tense. But our minds and our memories are working overtime to make sense of that present tense. I would be fascinated to see if we could find an equivalent for that fragmentation in terms of cinema. One way to possibly do it is with this multiple use of different sorts of images. I mean, if a painter wants to emphasize the narrowness of a giraffe's neck, he uses a long narrow frame.

Q : *Does all this begin to suggest television more than film?*
GREENAWAY:  In some senses, it is a television language, but I would like to think it's going further. Antagonistic French intellectuals might regard *The Pillow Book* as a CD-ROM and not as art at all. But three cheers for that.

Q : *Despite all the technological advances, however, you still use traditional narrative devices. The childhood story takes place in black and white, and you make it clear when we are hearing excerpts from the original Pillow Book.*
GREENAWAY:  A remark like that is so pleasing to me, because so many people are jumping onto new technologies with total abandonment of all we've learned. I constantly look over my shoulder to find old strategies to try and make them work again, so there's a continuity. But as John Cage once said, "If you introduce even 20 percent of novelty to an art work, you immediately lose 80 percent of your audience."

# Peter Greenaway: An Interview

## LAWRENCE CHUA/1997

A FEW YEARS AGO at the Toronto Film Festival, a press screening of Peter Greenaway's *Prospero's Books* had been scheduled first thing in the morning. It was the kind of festival planning that almost guaranteed an intensely grumpy, sleep-deprived hangover for the rest of the day. Fueled by coffee fumes, shielded by sunglasses, we dutiful critics nonetheless filled the tiny theater in seconds and rolled our heads back as the lights dimmed. The flood of images pushed some of us into sleepy reveries; others into alert antagonism. After the screening, I ran into a Taiwanese critic, one of the most important opinion makers in world cinema today. "I liked it," she said, then added confidentially, "I fell asleep. But that doesn't mean it wasn't a good film."

Today I recognize the architecture in Greenaway's films (*The Draughtsman's Contract, A Zed and Two Noughts, The Belly of an Architect, The Cook, the Thief, His Wife, and Her Lover,* among them) as the kind of fantastic worlds that I wanted to escape into when I used to sneak into revival cinemas as a high school student to watch Pier Paolo Pasolini's *The Arabian Nights* or *The Canterbury Tales*. Both Pasolini and Greenaway have given expression in their films to an architecture of dreaming, a place where space can escape the demands of narrative, where interior and exterior flow together, structure combines with surface, dreams with reality, flesh with technology. These were the rooms, the palaces, libraries, bodies, and worlds I wanted to inhabit. The spaces where, it seemed, anything was

From *Bomb* Magazine, Summer 1997. Reprinted by permission of *Bomb* and the author.

possible—the possibility of telling one's own story outside of the often pretentious stories unfolding on screen, of falling in love with whomever one wanted. Anything.

*The Pillow Book* is no exception. Like any film by Peter Greenaway, the images in *The Pillow Book* are sensual and rich enough to sustain many narratives. One is the story of Nagiko (Vivian Wu), a young woman who passes into agency through writing. Another is an Oedipal fantasy of her father, a successful novelist, using her skin as a writing surface. Yet another is her involvement in a love triangle with Jerome (*Trainspotting*'s Ewan McGregor) and his lover, a handsome but unscrupulous sex- and literature-hungry Publisher (Yoshi Oida). Set in Kyoto and Hong Kong at the edge of the twentieth century, *The Pillow Book* is also an "Oriental-philic" homage to the diary written by Sei Shonagon, a noblewoman at the Heian court a thousand years ago. The historical *Pillow Book* was a highly mannered vernacular "fuck journal": a collection of reminiscences, amorous adventures, lists, and literary quotes related in a laconic, almost modern style. In Greenaway's hands it becomes a work of science fiction as he investigates, through his own fetishistic attachments, the allure of the written word. He has captured the lushness of the page, the seduction of reducing the body to a text. Our dreams to a book.

LAWRENCE CHUA: *What was your emotional attachment to the narrative in your film,* The Pillow Book?

PETER GREENAWAY: It's a rather strange question for me since I'm not very interested in narrative in the cinema. I don't think the cinema is a particularly good narrative medium. My interest, I suppose, would concentrate on other notions that the film represents. If you want to be passionately attached to narrative then be a writer, not a filmmaker. But this is indeed the second film I've made which has the word "book" in its title. So I'm certainly very interested in metaphors like "the body is a book, the book is a body," but a book can be about a myriad of things other than narration. There is a way in which I have no particular support for the idea of dramatizing a work of literature, so I'm always surprised that after a hundred years, when cinema perhaps ought to know better, we can still award a movie like *The English Patient* nine Oscars. What on earth is the point of translating a work of literature, which sits perfectly well on the page into a cinematic illustration? Why do we have to have text before we can have image?

My cinema has been trying very hard to invest a lot of energy and imagination into the notions of strong and effective pictorial communication, and *The Pillow Book,* I hope, is another example of that. The story is very reductive, very simple. It can be summed up very quickly in the suggestion that it is a fable about a young woman who wants her lovers to write on her body. The origins for me don't rely in any particular desire to make a storytelling activity, but to be interested in the metaphor.

In Asian calligraphy, we have the possibility of an image being a text, a text being an image at one and the same time. Wouldn't this be a good way to consider the possibility of a reinvention of cinema? I believe that cinema is in need of reinvention. In the West we have continually separated the image and the text, and one would imagine that cinema would be the ideal place in which to remarry these two notions. But alas, it does not seem to have been the case. *The Pillow Book* is another attempt to readdress my particular anxiety or disenchantment about a cinema which is primarily text before it can be image.

L C :  *You've been very critical of a kind of cinema that's based specifically on conventions of the nineteenth century novel. How is the relationship between text and body different in* The Pillow Book? *In showing the pleasures of the text, aren't you also running the danger of reducing the body to a narrative?*
P G :  Maybe drawing an intense concentration onto the conditions of cinema and its relationship with a notion of image and text is a good way to do the very opposite. Perhaps we have to progress slowly. John Cage suggested that if you introduce more than twenty percent of innovation into any artwork, you immediately lose eighty percent of your audience. He suggested this might remain the case for a subsequent fifteen years. He was being optimistic. We have to travel slowly, since I want to continue making movies. They're expensive. I don't know why they have to be so expensive, but that's the way things are. They're also complex collaborations. I can't make movies on my own. I think we have to travel at a certain pace, to accommodate the introduction of radicalism or exploratory ideas embracing both old and new technologies.

L C :  *Yet narrative is not easy to abandon. I'd question also if it's even worth abandoning. I know that narrative is often used as a kind of dull sword against intellect: a Cartesian battle between the matter of storytelling and the mind of*

*ideas. But isn't there some other way to imagine narrative that doesn't interfere*
*with ideas or aesthetics? That is somehow true to its complex interdependence on*
*those things. There is a story to* The Pillow Book, *regardless of...*

P G :  Yes, there is a very reductive, fable-like story that doesn't have much
truck in some senses with notions of well constructed narrative. It doesn't
fit the general circumstances of what we would call the Casablanca narrative syndrome. But yes, there is a story. I would aim for a cinema which
tries to be non-narrative, but just like the obligation to believe in virgin
birth if you are a Catholic, a filmmaker is obliged to believe in narration if
he pursues cinema. Most audiences around the world go to the cinema to
be told stories. I don't necessarily think that that's the best way to organize
the cinematic experience, but as of now that is the cinema that we are
saddled with. I ought to also acknowledge that among many writers and
authors around the world there is a large reconsideration of what we mean
by narrative. So authors and writers who are not even remotely interested
in cinema are certainly readdressing those problems in terms of world
literature.

L C :  *You've said that one of the ideas that fueled this reductive story was a*
*fetish, perhaps a sexual fetish. How do you imagine and image that fetish, because*
*for me the fetish is something that, like the novel, emerged entwined with the*
*history of colonial expansion. You can see that throughout* The Pillow Book. *On*
*a very superficial level Nagiko and the Publisher take pleasure in the white body*
*of Jeremy and not in other black bodies. Certainly not in the body of the photog-*
*rapher, Hoki, whose dark skin Nagiko dismisses as unsuitable for her calligraphy.*
*For me, the fetish that is expressed in* The Pillow Book *is a residue of the colo-*
*nial encounter. It's a reminder of how text has been used to distinguish the civilized*
*from the savage mind.*

P G :  I think there's also a subsidiary text in the notion of the Madame
Butterfly complex. The film sets off an association with the Western fetish
for the notion of the Oriental, which was not only relative to the celebrated
opera but to general nineteenth century ideas of sexual exploitation of
colonial imposition. I would like to think that we have negotiated that
particular hurdle by indeed throwing the idea of the Western exploitation
of the East on its back. We start with a heroine who begins as the page, but
she indubitably ends up as the pen. She takes the responsibility into her
own hands and reverses the strategy on her predatory masters, developing

a knowledge of her own identity. Those notions may be relative to your theory of colonization.

There's a suggestion here that we have impoverished ourselves in the West for all sorts of reasons—good, bad, indifferent, accidental, and intended—of the notion of the calligraphic text. The calligraphic text is essentially made by the body. There are many arguments in French philosophy in the last forty years that have constantly demonstrated that it's the body that makes the text. I have ironically suggested, if the body makes the text, then the best place for that text is back on the body. It is suggested we should preserve that particular relationship where the body, through its brain, shoulder, arm, hand, pen, and paper makes the calligraphic gesture, and if we break that particular relationship, as indeed perhaps we have done ever since the invention of printing, and certainly now at the end of the twentieth century when most people develop their ideas on a keyboard, we have quite savagely broken the umbilicus between the notion of the body and text. Maybe at our peril. We have a film that deals with a very new television language examining a very old calligraphic language, which is at least three thousand years old—and embodies all of our contemporary anxieties about the idea of severance of body and text.

LC: *Or body and mind. I was struck by the way that you understood Sei Shonagon's original text. You were talking about how many writers in world literature today are challenging the idea of what the story is, of what narrative actually is, and Sei Shonagon's text predates the arrival of the nineteenth century novel by almost a millennium. In many ways it may be the first form of Japanese vernacular literature. At a time when Japanese literature was written almost entirely in Chinese, Sei Shonagon wrote in this very vernacular form for which she was mercilessly critiqued. How does the vernacular inform your idea of cinematic language?*
PG: There are resonances. For example, we use just one Yiddish word in the film, when Jerome writes the word "breasts" on the appropriate anatomical part on our heroine. It's interesting also that Yiddish was a nineteenth century vernacular language, which in the latter part of the century began to develop a written form. That has certain parallels with the creation of the Japanese language. There's something about Sei Shonagon's use of the diary form with its continual fragmentation of narrative ideas which is so completely different from her exact contemporary Murasaki who wrote the famous *The Tale of Genji,* which in some senses precedes the notion of

the English, French, or Russian grand saga novel. So I suppose if we were to regard *The Tale of Genji* being more associated with Tolstoy or Zola, we could think of Sei Shonagon as much more related to Baudelaire. We tried very hard in the film to represent this fragmentation in the different ways we used black and white, high color, low color. We borrowed not just the notions of the creation of a new language as she was doing in the year 995, but also made correspondences to what the creation of a new language would be about.

So the film itself is very much a palimpsest of what's happening now at the end of the twentieth century with the fragmentation of the relationship between cinema and all the post-televisual medium: the CD-ROM, the Internet ... French intellectuals have criticized the film, saying *The Pillow Book* is not a film, it is a CD-ROM. I could think of no higher compliment. There is a way that our contemporary vernacular in the business of making images has become television. Godard suggested that there is a disasterous cultural snobbism about television. Indeed, we physically and metaphorically look up to cinema but look down at television. But in terms of what MTV has to offer with the video clip, with the use of the talking head, that continual change of perspective of time, event, idea, action, and intended use of tense, there is a brand new vernacular language which is being developed day by day almost incidentally and accidentally, much as I suspect in the way that the early Japanese language was created by Sei Shonagon. She was often accused, certainly by her contemporaries, for her excessive use of Chinese quotation. Television certainly recreates or reprises or "quotes" the celebrated so-called *fossilized* forms of cinema. Television, shall we say, takes cinema as the Japanese vernacular did the Chinese language of the tenth century. We have new languages that are attempting both to erode the old languages, but also to deliver like a phoenix, knowing that the new languages have to be a combination of the old and the new.

L C : *But that process is not unique. That hybridization, mestizaje, dialectic, whatever you want to name the process that makes language, is continual. In describing those languages as "new," aren't you also reinscribing this idea of a linear notion of history and language?*

P G : We must indeed be careful when talking about newness and novelty. As Borges says, everything new immediately creates its own predecessor.

There have been many examples: Abel Gance's fragmentation of image and continuity in the multiple screens of *Napoleon* 1929, Alain Resnais's in *Last Year at Marienbad* and *Hiroshima Mon Amour*. The one completely novel characteristic in this film is the reconsideration of the aspect ratio. I was trained as a painter. A painter's language allows a painter to select his own aspect ratio, proportion, size, and frame according to content. By and large that has not been possible in the cinema, perhaps even more impossible in television, but with the new technologies we can address that problem. Gance certainly knew what he was doing, considering all sorts of very expansive vocabulary, treating the past, present, and future all in one plane, considering the notion of the close up, the wide shot, the portrait, the still life, all in one frame. There's a way in which particular technologies in 1929 didn't allow him to continue. We now have the technologies which would make this particular manipulation possible, and in terms of fashionable concepts like "multi-media" and "interactivity," these ideas are in some strange way embraced by the potentiality of not simply reproducing the syndrome of one finite frame which repeats its format chronologically from a beginning to an end, but gradually insisting that the cinema screen should break up, fragment not only in terms of pace, of architecture, and of space, but in the whole lateral way of thinking which is becoming endemic of our attitude towards the notion of ideas at the end of the twentieth century. So away with the notions of linear cinema, let's embrace the potential of a much more lateral thinking cinema. I'd like to think that not only this film, but the film we made two years ago, *Prospero's Books*, was also an attempt to consider these ideas.

LC: *I'm interested in how your ideas of a lateral cinema have reconfigured ideas about architecture and space. In* Prospero's Books *interior and exterior flow together. In* The Pillow Book, *structure and surface are integrated. Have these televised vernacular languages we've been speaking about opened up new ways for you to think about space and architecture in the frame? Is it the technology that's opened up those ideas for you?*

PG: I think the prime interest is just the new ways of conceiving the notion of cinema. The cinema of the future is going to look much more like the pages of an encyclopedia. It's going to be much more concerned with interactions, rather like sophisticated forms of vernacular advertising which are now extremely adroit at putting image and text together. The cinema of the future is going to embrace these notions and continually develop that sophistication of the comic strip which already influences the Internet page. All the film we've seen so far that have been influenced by the comics are in some senses remarkably naive. They haven't taken what the comic book can really offer us, which are ideas of changing aspect ratio, of interaction of text and image in very sophisticated ways. This vocabulary has been developed all over the world in terms of the American, French, and the Japanese comic books, but they have not been embraced in cinema. So there is maybe another example of a local vernacular developing itself slowly to become a major language. All these pursuits are very much alive for me. I planned *The Pillow Book* with lots of diagrams—I was always going to fragment the screen in various ways—but as soon as we transferred the original super 35mm film onto tape and edited the whole movie on an Avid computer system, I was immediately struck by what the software could offer me. The diagrams for the original script became remarkably redundant because the complexities of the new languages were offering me so many other potentials. Since the information was undifferentiated, "objective" and infinitely maneuverable backwards, forwards, together, apart, segmented, chronology became irrelevant. Does the past have to come before the present? Does the future have to be ahead of the present? Literature is familiar with the experiments of James Joyce and Borges. Since cinema is so conservative and so slow, these notions already have been preordained in other media. So in some senses, despite my anxiety about cinema copying literature, we must keep our eyes and ears open to find other tropes and strategies in order to reinvest cinema with new, exciting late-twentieth century life.

LC: *There is a moment in the movie where the writing slips, where the paper that the texts are inscribed on shifts gender and Nagiko becomes the writer and passes into a kind of agency. At the Digiforum in Rotterdam last year, you talked about the erosion of the artist, where not art but communication stands at the center of the creative endeavor. Could you talk a bit more about what you meant by that?*

PG: I suppose it's to do with the idea of audience participation and interactivity. I've chosen to put most of my ideas of the last fifteen years into cinema which is a very passive medium. Far more passive than literature for example. There is a way that now the western world ascribes to notions

of democracy. There is a way in which our art, our culture is still remarkably concerned with notions of absolutism. Renaissance ideas of the artist
as king. So we still genuflect before figures like Picasso and Le Corbusier
and Stravinsky, whereas our general political systems are far more sophisticated in terms of interactivity. I do think that one of the things that these
new languages will give us is a necessary shift away from the notion of the
artist as some Nietzchean supergod and we'll make the whole process of
cultural rapport far more democratic. We ought to consider this seriously
and not hide behind the notions of artist's egotism and embrace these
notions of interactivity not frivolously, but very seriously indeed.

L C :  *I'm not a big fan of democracy. It tends to obscure as much as a word like
interactivity does about social process. Can you say more about what you mean
by "interactivity?"*
P G :  We keep talking about interactivity, but I still don't think that we
exactly know what we mean by these terms. It is a particular word for
which everybody has their own particular interpretation. We all know for
example on it's basic level if I give you a film with five endings, your choice
is predetermined by me. Maybe there is a point when in fact quantity
becomes quality, but I'm not quite sure how we circumscribe those things.

L C :  *For me the potential of* interactivity *is more about dialogue, a response to
perfect translation, a space between the screen and the audience where antiphony
is possible.*
P G :  The cinema we have now has precious little space for dialogue. There's
a way the audience bows before the screen and puts their imagination in
the hands of the cinema maker. I suppose my particular anxiety also is
related to the phenomenon that you can look at the *Mona Lisa* for two seconds, two minutes, two days, two hours, two centuries if you so feel fit,
which gives you, the viewer, the circumstances for a true contemplation,
rumination, expansion of your imagination. Having been trained as a
painter I can understand that view point, but having spent so many years
being a cinema practitioner I can see the opposite, and have found it to
be so unsatisfactory. Many activities I would now take into making three
dimensional cinema by curating exhibitions. I'm fascinated by the idea of
a film as an exhibition, and the exhibition as a film. It brings in notions of
time and space in ways which the cinema cannot possibly handle. My

enthusiasm is for the notion of the exhibition as an art form in itself using the new technologies and an expanded cinematic vocabulary. A lot of people are engaged in this in lots of ways, sometimes on the periphery, sometimes as a prime concern. Very shortly the notion of *Jurassic Park* and *Mission Impossible* will certainly end up looking like an early nineteenth century lantern-slide experience.

# It's So Hard to Be Humble, But I Try . . .

## JONATHAN JONES / 1998

SOMETHING STRANGE HAS HAPPENED to Peter Greenaway.
The film director is famous for being abrasive, but when I meet him at
Manchester's Cornerhouse, where a retrospective of his art has just opened,
he is expansive, charming, even self-critical. It's an almost unthinkable
nineties rebranding—a warmer, more human Peter Greenaway.

The root of his transformation seems to be a wounding experience. Almost
as soon as we sit down. Greenaway refers with a shudder to *The Baby of
Macon,* his 1993 film that was severely panned by most of the critics in the
world. Culminating in a 10-minute sequence in which an actress is raped
to death by more than a hundred soldiers, the film nauseated many who
saw it. Rejection embitters some people; in Greenaway's case, it appears to
have goaded him to reach out to his audience. His next film, *The Pillow
Book* (1996), an exploration of the related pleasures of sex and calligraphy,
was an arthouse and video hit. He presciently cast Ewan McGregor just
before he went off to make "his Scottish film," as Greenaway calls *Trainspotting.*

All this meekness is a startling rebirth for someone whose arrogance has
been mythified over the years to monstrous proportions. One interviewer
asked Greenaway if he had ever met his hero, Alain Resnais, the director
of *Last Year in Marienbad* and was told without a trace of humor: "No, it's
a mistake to meet your heroes—rather like you meeting me." Nor was it
just Greenaway's personality that irritated *New Yorker* film critic Terence

From *The Guardian,* 26 October 1998. Reprinted by permission.

Rafferty who compared watching his films to being trapped in a "night-mare art history seminar" with a lecturer who sneered at anyone who questioned him. Fellow British director Alan Parker has publicly foamed at the mouth at the British Film Institute's support for Greenaway.

That was in the days when Greenaway was promoted as the last word in British film. Today, after a decade that has seen the emergence of Ken Loach and Mike Leigh as internationally acclaimed auteurs, Greenaway's status is very different. He's an unfashionable presence in British cinema. He's been accused of being pretentious, but that's not true. He pursues his ideas with total conviction. On the Continent, he is acclaimed as the last great European intellectual. He moves from city to city, curating exhibitions and mounting installations. When we speak, he has just flown in from Berlin where he'd been directing an opera at the prestigious Staatsoper.

One key to understanding Peter Greenaway is that he's a painter who makes films. He was trained at Walthamstow College of Art in the early sixties, and has continued to paint throughout his career. He paints in hotel bathrooms. He paints on set. Above all, he paints on screen; his films are sensual, violent, animated tableaux rather than coherent narratives. Like the stories told on altar pieces in medieval cathedrals, Greenaway's film's are overwhelmed by a rich accumulation of images. The eye lingers on detail and we lose the plot.

Yet Greenaway's slow move from painting to film directing may also account for the personality that has so grated in the past. He made his first feature, *The Draughtsman's Contract,* in 1982, his 40th year, and saw himself acclaimed for exposing the mean-spirited heart of Thatcherism. Before that he had led a strange divided life, making short experimental films in his spare time while filing images of sheep for a living. His day job from 1965 to 1980 was as a film editor and finally a director for an Orwellian-sounding government department, the Central Office of Information. This entailed compiling documentary footage on aspects of British industrial, agricultural, and cultural life to show in classrooms all over the Commonwealth. You can see how such a strange bureaucratic life might have driven Greenaway to make anti-realist, anti-narrative films.

Greenaway's escape from this rational world is documented in his exhibition in Manchester, bringing together art works he has done on paper and board, with pencil and paint, since the early sixties. It's a draughtsman's autobiography. The curators present Greenaway as an important painter of the late sixties and seventies; they relate him to the high-brow Pop artist RB Kitaj, to the English landscape tradition. The show isn't convincing on that level. As a painter, Greenaway is almost too good a draughtsman, too lucid a thinker. But in the early seventies, he started creating the gorgeous, mad, painterly collages that also appear in the exhibition. The moment Greenaway starts to work in collage—to cut up, fold in, overpaint—his work takes on a new energy. Suddenly there are no clear ideas: thought is messed up.

Greenaway's films replace the narrative pleasures that we expect from cinema with the static visual ceremony of painting. "For me the most successful painting is non-narrative. Why can't we adapt those sorts of excitements and put them into cinema? The experiences of people when they go to the cinema are not about plot; they're about ambience, atmosphere, performance, about the glance." Greenaway hates narrative because he claims it's reassuring, "a bedtime story." So, instead of storytelling, his films discover alternate systems of meaning. *The Draughtsman's Contract* is a game of sex and architecture with a savage secret at its core. *A Zed And Two Noughts* (1985) juxtaposes symmetries and doubles. *Drowning By Numbers* (1988) is organised as a numerological game. His new film currently in post-production, *Eight and a Half Women,* emulating Fellini, features eight-and-a-half male heterosexual fantasies. "Let me see if I can remember them all. There's the idea of having sexual relations with a nun...the woman who rides horses...the idea of having sexual relations with a pregnant woman..."

Greenaway's films are also deranged collages, interfolding different fields of imagery and knowledge; the Central Office of Information is replaced by information overload. Greenaway lets heterogeneous images, words and bodies clash, entangle and collapse into one another. In *Prospero's Books* (1991), his first attempt to complicate cinema with digital technology, he grafted his own iconographies over Shakespeare. He admits it got out of hand. "I am guilty of visual indigestibility. We showed the first five minutes of *Prospero's Books* at the Venice Film Festival; it was received with rapturous applause. I then took the whole two hours to Cannes and by the time people came out, they were sweating and bored."

His best films are full of social and political satire and have a mythic narrative power. In *The Cook, the Thief, His Wife, and Her Lover* (1989),

Greenaway translates the Hobbesian viciousness of the eighties into a gory, luxuriantly wrathful film. His previous features had conformed to his ideal of a cinema that is pure art. But in *The Cook, the Thief* there is no pure art. Finally, the artist-chef serves up a kind of revenge, forcing moronic gangster Michael Gambon to eat the bibliophile he has murdered.

In the nineties, Greenaway is no longer the arthouse god he was in the last decade. "I'm a million miles away from the traditional English film-makers who are determined to put over a politically accentuated notion of reality," he says. "I don't think you can get reality." In the new climate of realism, he's a misfit: *The Cook, the Thief* was his biggest hit in 1989, but by 1993 he was being torn apart at Cannes. Yet his films of the nineties have more pertinence to their cultural moment than they're given credit for. *The Baby of Macon* engages, in a darkly hilarious way, with the central theme of contemporary cinema—the shrinking space between fiction and reality.

This much-maligned movie depicts a masque about a miraculous child being performed to a seventeenth-century court. A baby-faced prince makes bizarre interjections, as if he can't tell it is fiction. "It's a seventeenth-century production of a twelfth-century miracle play," says Greenaway. "In the middle ages, everybody would have been truly pious, but by the seventeenth century, you had to show off your religion." This sense of being disconnected from its time makes *The Baby of Macon* the director's most surreally troubling, uncanny film.

The film's savage reception repeated the inability to distinguish art and life that Greenaway mocks. *The Baby of Macon* wickedly touches on nineties sensibilities, about pornography, censorship, and the influence of cinema violence on spectators. It parodies cinema's current addiction to reality. "It's so miserable and so easy to keep slamming *Titanic*—I'll shut up," says Greenaway. But the obsessive verisimilitude of *Titanic, Saving Private Ryan* or—at the arthouse end of the market—of Leigh and Loach is the lifeblood of nineties cinema. Perhaps it's not such a good thing that Peter Greenaway should go soft. We need someone to carry on giving us full-on fantastic cinema, to provoke us by asserting that cinema is dying out but painting will last forever, and to tell us that realism can be an oppressive ministry of information.

# Luggage Stories

## SABINE DANEK/1999

GREENAWAY PROJECT: FIVE FEATURE films, a TV
series, several CD-ROMs and a Website—the current project of
director Peter Greenaway is a multimedia spectacle. Under the
title *Tulse Luper's Suitcase,* the British director follows the life of
the Swedish diplomat, Raoul Wallenberg, who during WWII
saved the lives of a great many Jews and disappeared under mysterious circumstances in 1945. In connection with this historical
figure, Peter Greenaway resurrects his alter ego, Tulse Luper. The
cultivated, many-sided ornithologist, who appears in Greenaway's
work from its beginning, journeys with the film team in search of
Raoul Wallenberg over the whole globe. Filming begins this June
in Colorado and so also does the website. Every day a new story
will be placed on the internet just as in *A Thousand and One Nights*
Scheherazade spun another story for her King. Greenaway has
already written over 700 legends and sagas with more to come as
filming proceeds.

Filming only for the big screen ceased to interest the director
long ago and he has turned to other fields with increasing energy.
In the weekly TV series, one will be able to follow the diplomat's
fate, on the CD-ROMs in Tulse Luper's suitcases one can search for
trails and signs. Through the various media, any interested indi-

From *Page* (Hamburg), May 1999. © 1999 *Page.* Reprinted by permission. Translated from
the German by Vernon Gras.

vidual will be able to construct his/her own Wallenberg legend. Greenaway has never pursued the conventional methods of story-telling, as perfected by Hollywood films. In films like *The Cook, the Thief, His Wife, and Her Lover* and *Drowning By Numbers,* he structured the films via number series and colors, and in *Prospero's Books* with the help of new computer techniques, he created a new synthesis of text and image. In *Tulse Luper's Suitcase,* he goes yet a step further in allowing the audience to become part author.

PAGE: *Your most recent film,* Tulse Luper's Suitcase, *takes place not only on the cinema screen but on the internet, on CD-ROMs, and on TV. Why did you choose these different media?*

GREENAWAY: They all have different characteristics, but they also overlap. Cinema has a great openness, a giant screen that mesmerizes the audience, and a refined soundsystem. It provides an all encompassing scenario. Television, in contrast, has a serial character. Cinema has mostly failed in doing that. I can still remember how I went to the Saturday matinees as a child. We went to see *Batman* serials and I enjoyed them very much. Television has taken over that job today. CD-ROM, on the other hand, gives the viewer control over the material because it provides an infinite number of choices and combinations. I use these different media possibilities but always in relationship with each other.

PAGE: *How flexible can the user be?*

G: We are familiar with the old discussions about interactivity; does one have much choice at all when the originator selects all the options? But there is that magical moment when quantity of information suddenly becomes qualitative. I'm trying to achieve exactly that. There are 92 suitcases that Tulse Luper has packed in his journey around the world. Among them are some that lead one astray, their story will be narrated in feature films; on the CDs one can unpack each suitcase and apply his own research findings.

PAGE: *Is the use of CD-ROM an attempt to break up narrative chronology?*

G: Already in the literature of the eighteenth century, a whole row of authors had exploded the linearity of their stories. I would like to continue doing that; it's boring ultimately to tell a story from A to Z.

PAGE: *Doesn't your role as author then undergo a change?*

G: I believe my present work offers me the possibility to bring together my previous experiments in cinema and elsewhere. I have conceptualized exhibitions, developed architectural projects, staged operas. The new technologies break down the boundaries between them. In the information age, we have to orient ourselves in a new way; we can with lightfooted ease move from one medium to another while tying them all together. I wish to exploit this enormous potential in my work.

PAGE: *Will writing play a big role in your multimedia project?*

G: Yes, as it did in *Prospero's Books* and *The Pillow Book*. It's precisely on the internet that the majority of the writing is terribly bad and uninteresting. I have always taken pains on an exciting presentation of image and text which I intend to continue in the Tulse Luper project.

PAGE: *The form then is just as important as the story itself?*

G: That is true of all my work. My critics would say that I am much too interested in the form and not enough in the content. Nowadays, everyone knows there is no content without context (form). Language itself is content which confuses and disturbs these artless critics.

PAGE: *Can cinema survive only with the implementation of the new media?*

G: Cinema is already dead because it's a matter of an incurable antiquated technique. All old techniques like, for example, frescoe painting, merged over time with other artforms and survived in that manner. Music was added to it and the result was opera which today is developing further into MTV videos. I don't believe that one has to tear down the cinema screen in order to renew cinema. But new input and new energy is lacking. They are flowing above all into new television technologies. We must, therefore, concentrate on the CD-ROM.

PAGE: *But what happens when each solitary individual just sits in front of his monitor? The cinema experience is also a social phenomenon, isn't it?*

G: That is a delusion. Perhaps, one goes to a film with a lot of other people and also exits with them, but the actual experience is that we sit alone in the dark like islands.

PAGE:  *But we do laugh in common at the cinema.*

G:  Naturally, an audience watching a comedy is quite noisy, but that is already its only commonality. When we look into the future of cinema, three directions appear: an historical sector which attempts to conserve the past; Walt Disney films that always tell the same story; and the cinema that interests me and that will broaden itself with CD-ROMs. Obviously, it's frustrating that one can only view CD-ROMs on a small monitor. My dream is to make CD-ROMs for Omnimax located in large halls with excellent sound. From there one can tie into scores of large libraries and museums. Sitting before a giant screen, one has contact with the whole world. That is really fascinating.

PAGE:  *How at home are you with the internet? Is it part of your everyday?*

G:  It's diminishing again because I was spending too much time in front of a monitor. I was continually connected with the whole world and never got any rest. At the moment, I spend only a few hours weekly on the net, that's just better for me.

# INDEX